One Day
You'll
THANK ME

ALSO BY DAVID McGLYNN

A Door in the Ocean
The End of the Straight and Narrow

One Day You'll THANK ME

Lessons from an Unexpected Fatherhood

DAVID McGLYNN

COUNTERPOINT
Berkeley, California

One Day You'll Thank Me

Library of Congress Cataloging-in-Publication Data
Names: McGlynn, David, 1976– author.
Title: One day you'll thank me : lessons from an unexpected fatherhood /
    David McGlynn.
Description: Berkeley, CA : Counterpoint Press, [2018]
Identifiers: LCCN 2017052590 | ISBN 9781640090392 (alk. paper)
Subjects: LCSH: McGlynn, David, 1976—Family. | Authors, American—
    Biography. | Fatherhood—Anecdotes. | Father and child—Anecdotes. |
    Fatherhood—Humor. | Father and child—Humor.
Classification: LCC HQ756 .M3866 2018 | DDC 306.874/2—dc23
LC record available at https://lccn.loc.gov/2017052590

Jacket designed by Nicole Caputo
Book designed by Jordan Koluch

COUNTERPOINT
2560 Ninth Street, Suite 318
Berkeley, CA 94710
www.counterpointpress.com

Printed in the United States of America
Distributed by Publishers Group West

10 9 8 7 6 5 4 3 2 1

For Pop, Little Self, and Hugs

A father is a man who fails every day.

—MICHAEL CHABON

Contents

One Day You'll THANK ME

Daddy Did It

The night before he left Texas, my dad took my sister and me to dinner at a restaurant with a name I always liked: Daddy Did It Fish House. The name seems ironic now, but it didn't then. I was twelve years old, and I'd been to oodles of restaurants in the year since my parents had separated: Whataburger and Two Pesos and questionably hygienic oyster bars down near the Ship Channel where the half shells were served on beds of slimy green ice. In other words, all the places my mother never wanted to go. She didn't like Daddy Did It, either, because she thought the name was stupid and catfish and hush puppies were redneck foods. Compared to most of the places we went that year, Daddy Did It was the Ritz, with chairs that weren't bolted to the floor and utensils that didn't come wrapped in cellophane.

Dad had rented a spare room in a friend's apartment on Lower Westheimer, near the Galleria, in central Houston. He slept in a sleeping bag on a bare mattress on the floor. Everything he owned was still at our house, including most of his clothes. When we visited, Devin, four years younger than me, tucked in beside him on the mattress and I slept on the couch in the living room. He'd talked for years about getting out of Texas and living closer to the beach. Now

Dad's things were in a moving truck, and tomorrow he and my soon-to-be stepmother were lighting out for Southern California.

At dinner Dad showed us grainy Polaroids of his new apartment and gave Devin and me, as going-away presents, boxes of cards already stamped and addressed to him. I recognized my stepmother's elegant cursive and tried to connect her handwriting and the address on the envelope to my father's name. "All you have to do is write inside it, fold it up, and drop it in the mailbox," Dad said. "We'll be pen pals." The idea seemed such a perverse reduction in status, from parent to pen pal, that he immediately took it back. "You can call me anytime you want," he added. That promise made us all feel a little better. The waitress brought out the food and refilled our water glasses. When our plates were clean, Dad gave us each a handful of pennies to toss in the giant washtub at the front of the restaurant while he settled the bill. Devin closed her eyes and wished upon every coin. I tried to bean the oversized goldfish trolling along the bottom of the barrel. The fish darted from each penny I threw.

The divorce stipulated that my sister and I would spend four weeks a year in California. A week at either Thanksgiving or Christmas, and three weeks in August. I thought of our first trip to see him, for Thanksgiving, as an adventure. Dad had only been gone for three weeks, not long enough for me to miss him. His apartment wasn't much larger than his old one, only two bedrooms, the second one occupied by my stepsister, Stacie. Devin slept on the trundle mattress that slid beneath Stacie's bed while I once again sacked out on the living room couch. I didn't mind; there was comfort in the familiar, even if the couch was rattan and creaked beneath me every time I shifted my weight. The balcony off the kitchen overlooked the swimming pool in the complex's courtyard as well as, if you moved to the left, the parking lot of the supermarket, where each morning at three o'clock a garbage truck emptied the Dumpsters. The dining room wall and the floor behind the love seat towered with moving boxes full of my stepmother's mysterious possessions. Very few things had come from our house in Texas, and this apartment, like the place in the Galleria, felt temporary, as though Dad were on an extended business trip. Before moving, he'd talked up California as the cradle of movie stars and endless summers, of a quintessential Americana, and that first trip he was intent on showcasing all that Los Angeles and Orange County had to offer. In five days' time, in addition to celebrating Thanksgiving, we swam in the ocean, spotted celebrities on Rodeo Drive, toured the *Queen Mary* anchored in the Long Beach Harbor, ate at the oldest McDonald's still in operation in Downey, and spent an entire day at Disneyland. The constant pace and activity only amplified my feeling that California was a place to go on vacation but not a state where people actually lived.

Something had changed when I returned later in August. Dad had unpacked his boxes, married, and settled in to his new job. And it was summer: The sun was bright and warm, and the ocean, forbiddingly cold and gray during our first visit, shimmered like a sheet of blue foil. I swam in the Pacific every day. Sometimes, all day. We ate our meals at home rather than at restaurants, often on the little balcony, and whenever Dad wasn't at work he went without a shirt, as he had when I was little. It occurred to me that his old self, his real self, had been pushed underground for the last few years and had finally begun to reemerge in California, fifteen hundred miles from where I spent most of the year. It dawned on me that he was gone and wouldn't be coming back, and the thought of living apart from him, which I'd already done for so long, became suddenly intolerable. I wept at the idea, and wept harder at the airport when it was time to fly back to Houston. I'd just turned thirteen and could sense the people around me at the gate, watching me bawl. I was embarrassed, but I couldn't make myself stop.

Most boys my age were learning to resent their parents, their dads in particular, and did whatever they could to avoid them. But I was desperate to see mine. I began to hoard small moments of time. Events that would have been mundane under ordinary circumstances—eating dinner, riding in the car, watching TV—became freighted with importance, simply because I recognized how quickly they would pass, and how long it would be before we saw each other again. The end of that first summer trip coincided with the twentieth anniversary of Woodstock, an event MTV commemorated by airing the original three-hour documentary movie of the festival. Dad and I stayed up late two nights in a row to watch it, and when I got back to Houston I used the money I'd made mowing lawns to buy up as much of the music as I could. Not only the big names, like Janis and Jimi, but the smaller acts, like Richie Havens and Country Joe and the Fish and Canned Heat, musicians only the diehards cared about. After school, I lay on my bedroom floor beneath the ceiling fan in the listless September heat, the music spinning in my Discman until I had every song memorized, hoping it would somehow form a tether, like a tin-can telephone, between my father and me.

During our long months apart, Dad and I talked on the real phone, too. We had a standing phone date on Sunday evenings, the official call made from the kitchen phone while my mother did the dishes or swept the floor. Other days I called him from a thousand clandestine locations, mostly from pay phones scattered around my neighborhood. I'd call collect, say the phone's number when the operator asked for my name, and wait for my father to answer. He knew to write the number down, decline the charges, and call me back. Pretty soon I had my regular spots. There was the phone outside the Safeway and the phone in my high school between the gym and the entrance to the auto shop, conveniently hidden behind the Dr Pepper machine. I often skipped class to call him, knowing he'd be in his office.

Distilled to only a sound through a telephone, his voice had the power to evoke the entirety of his presence. His cropped hair and mustache, his shirtless torso stretched out on the couch, his distinctive, slightly musky scent, one I could still detect at the back of his closet years after he'd gone and my stepfather had moved in.

But it was his voice I loved most, his voice through the phone receiver like a late-night disc jockey through a car radio, low and measured and calm. From the time I was thirteen until I moved to California for college, on a swimming scholarship, most of our relationship unfolded this way: over the phone in short, piecemeal conversations that lasted only a few minutes. He made good on his promise to always answer when I called, but since I called him at work, it was only a matter of time before he had to go. The so-called lessons of manhood that television and movies depict as being imparted during campouts and fishing trips and ball games, with hair-mussing and arms around shoulders, were for me largely received at a pay phone. Leaning against that Dr Pepper machine, I told him about my driver's test, my SAT scores, the first girl I kissed. I also confessed mistakes other kids tried to hide, like the time I jabbed a broom handle through the front door of the house and blamed it on the UPS man. The conversations were short, but they weren't idle chatter. My father had left his children and moved three states away, and the question of what it meant to be a parent under these circumstances—the yawning distance between what he'd once expected of himself and the realities he now had to confront—was a central concern. Whenever I recall these conversations, I can hear him grappling toward some understanding of why things had gone the way they had, and the lessons that might be learned from one's decisions, be they mistakes or strokes of luck. At fourteen and fifteen, I couldn't quite discern his regret at having left, or his determination to stay involved in my life, but I could nevertheless sense that he was trying to tell me something. Important things were being conveyed. Lessons in miniature. I hung on his every word.

To grow up longing for a father is to grow up preoccupied with fatherhood itself. Years before I ever wanted kids, let alone believed I was equipped to handle their care and feeding, I spent a good deal of time puzzling over the rights and obligations of the job. Most of my fantasies were either revisions to or embellishments of my own childhood. All the fun stuff like learning how to ski and surf and light a fart would be preserved; I'd just never, ever drive my kid to the airport and put him on a plane back to his mother for eleven months out of the year. When I met my wife, I knew instantly that we were destined for the long haul. I could practically see Katherine's perfect nose and dark eyebrows recast in the faces of babies, children. Her children. Mine.

I let it slip that I sometimes thought this way, and it became a game we played together while we drank margaritas on the front stoop of the house I rented in Salt Lake City or rumbled around the mountains in her Jeep. What our kids would look like. They'd have her good eyesight but my long eyelashes. Girls would get Katherine's feet; boys would inherit my swimmer's shoulders and long arms. Any child of ours would be a good swimmer because, well, *duh*. We'd prioritize contact with nature, fluency in at least one foreign language, and concern for the poor, even as we encouraged the kids themselves toward heights that would ensure they'd never know hunger or disappointment. Katherine and I agreed we'd make great parents. Better than our own parents—a given for most young couples who have no idea what they're talking about, but also better than the other sorry schlubs we spied around town, ferrying slimy offspring in minivans littered with goldfish crumbs and deconstructed juice boxes. *Jesus*, we'd laugh to each other, *how do people live like that?* Surely we'd do better. Of course we would. We might possibly make the best parents ever.

You'd think, with all this dreaming and scheming, I would've been ready for fatherhood when it happened. You'd be wrong.

Katherine and I were in graduate school, in debt, and married for less than a year when we joined the nine percent of hapless idiots who conceive a child on the pill. We were so dumbfounded that it took four drugstore pregnancy tests and a trip to the county health clinic for a blood draw before we came to grips with the fact that we were totally screwed. Two years later, having tapped out a large chunk of my thesis with a baby sleeping on my lap (I'd learned to type extra quietly), I landed a teaching job at a bucolic little college in Appleton, Wisconsin, a hundred miles north of Milwaukee. We were packing boxes to move when Katherine handed me another ominously stained plastic stick. This time we'd beaten the Nuva-Ring. I laid my head on the kitchen counter and turned my face to the sink in case I puked.

Katherine shrugged. "At least you have a job this time."

We left for Wisconsin two weeks after I turned thirty. I had three university degrees but had never had health insurance. Our first baby had been born on Medicaid, due to expire when he turned two, which he would the day after we arrived in Wisconsin. The college offered insurance, but with a monthly premium that took a Paul Bunyan–sized bite out of my take-home pay. Worse, our new plan categorized pregnancies as "preexisting conditions" and subjected buns-in-the-oven to a 280-day waiting period before coverage kicked in. To get around the bureaucratic roadblock, we kept our expanding family a secret until after I'd arrived on campus and filled out all the requisite paperwork with human resources. As soon as our insurance cards arrived in the mail, Katherine called the nearest obstetrician's clinic and asked for the earliest available appointment. Any doctor, male or female, young or old, would do as long as he or she could get us in fast. When the receptionist inquired if she was pregnant, Katherine replied, "Well . . . *maybe*." The receptionist took the hint and found a slot for us the following week.

The doctor was a diminutive Filipino man with the flinty stare of a prizefighter who had, unbeknownst to us, delivered half the babies in town. He pumped my hand when he shook it and scolded us for waiting so long to come see him. When I told him the baby had been conceived on birth control, as had our first, he set his hands on his knees, leaned back in his chair, and rifled out a volley of laughter. "It happens more often than you'd think," he said. He slapped his hand over my shoulder. "Some people are especially receptive to pregnancy. You two must be a good match."

"My boys can swim," I said. I was still freaked, but I'll admit it: I felt a jolt of pride. We had friends who'd struggled for years to get pregnant and had dropped some serious cash in the process. I'd somehow scored on not one but two hall-of-fame goalies. That had to be a record.

The doctor looked up from Katherine's medical chart. "How many children are you planning on having?"

"I don't think we can go through this again," I said. Katherine nodded vigorously. We'd end up like the old woman who lived in a shoe if we stayed on our current path.

"I'd recommend a more permanent measure," he said to me. "Once you're certain you're finished."

"Permanent measure?" I asked.

He made scissors with his index and middle fingers. I cupped myself and winced.

"Oh, please," Katherine said. She settled back on the table and lifted her feet into the stirrups. "He can tie my tubes after I deliver. I'll already be in the hospital, so what the hell."

"Good," I said, wheeling my chair toward the head of the exam table while the doctor lubed his gloves. "This way I can father more."

"Not with me you won't."

"I don't think I could afford it anyway."

Katherine patted my cheek. "Sweetie, *money* would be the least of your problems."

Our sons, Galen and Hayden, were born slightly more than two years apart—Galen in Utah and Hayden in Wisconsin, where we still live. They were hazy ideas for years, then too real all too quickly, and I found myself colliding into parenthood as though it were a car accident. No amount of foresight or precaution, regardless of how many videos you watch or practice tests you take, can quite prepare you for the real thing. You just brace yourself. Which means I am, like so many American fathers, full of good intentions, simultaneously thrilled and scared shitless.

Fatherhood, as I've come to understand it, is an endlessly moving target, especially when it comes to boys. Especially *now*, at this quixotic juncture in America, when the country came fewer than 100,000 votes away from elevating the first woman to the highest office in the land but instead opted for a man who speaks and acts like the golden-haired love child of Gordon Gekko and Rodney Dangerfield. What does it mean to parent boys against such a backdrop? Do the old lessons of manhood, handed down to me via pay phone—and before that handed down to my father at the foot of a high school dropout who rode a tank ashore at Utah Beach and worked his way up from itinerant salesman to vice president of a major hardware company—even still apply? If the answer is no, as I suspect it is, what new lessons ought to replace them? How fast do I have to learn them in order to impart them to my sons?

Men, manliness, and masculinity have been the subjects of major reconsiderations in the years since my boys joined the world. The very word, *masculine*, has taken on such a pejorative aura, conjuring forth images of dick pics circling the Internet and presidents landing on aircraft carriers, that the entire enterprise of helping boys grow into men, which they will inevitably become, seems less certain and more imperiled than ever before. I want to do right by my sons. I want them to grow into strong and courageous young men, confident and successful adults. What parent wants any less? Yet there's a fine line between strength and chauvinism, confidence and arrogance.

I hope I'm doing the right things, but I'm never quite sure.

As a dad, I'm supposed to be the one with the schematic for life's problems. I'm supposed to have the answers. But every time I stumble into what I'm confident is a Big Fatherhood Moment, when circumstances require me to step up and dispense wisdom and time-tested paternal know-how, I can't shake the feeling that I'm still a kid on the lam from class, hiding out beside a pay phone, calling across the miles for someone to make sense of things, to whisper in my ear, *Don't worry, everything's going to be okay.*

Dead Santa

The year Galen started kindergarten, our third in Wisconsin, I learned about St. Nick's Day. Children set their shoes by the fireplace before going to bed on December 5 and awoke the next morning to find their Keds and Converses filled with chocolate coins wrapped in gold foil, along with a small toy or two. A mini-Christmas, weeks before the big day, commemorating the Feast of St. Nicholas, the fourth-century Bishop of Myra, famous across Christendom for his good deeds and secret gifts, as well as the patron of sailors, brewers, and pawnbrokers, all of whom had a serious foothold in Wisconsin.

Our own foothold in Wisconsin was less firm. Even after three years, we still found ourselves alone at times when we ought not to have been. The neighborhood pool, for example, was open only eight weeks in the summer, a ridiculously short season for a guy from Texas and California. I could count on one *finger* the number of indoor pools I'd swum in during the years I lived in California. Yet by mid-August the pool was practically empty, down to the bored and over-tanned lifeguards, a cluster of acned teenagers playing underwater grab ass, and us: Hayden blowing bubbles in the baby pool and Galen alternately working to tear out my hair and break my sternum every time he jumped from the side. Weeks before Labor Day, I noticed a certain autumnal chill in the air, the sky starting to thin and the upper leaves of the maples sliding along the color spectrum from green to red. Soon after, my neighbors coiled away their hoses and returned the storm panes to their windows and wrapped their rhododendrons in burlap. Once football season started, Appleton, thirty minutes south of hallowed Lambeau Field, where the Packers had played most home games since the year Joe McCarthy died, became ground zero of the apocalypse. Traffic lights on cloudless Sunday afternoons changed from green to yellow to red without a single car passing beneath. Any establishment that didn't serve beer in front of a gigantic flat-screen closed down. Walking the boys to the park, the earth's axis visibly tilting away from the sun and the temperatures tumbling with the leaves, I noticed television sets glowing inside every window. We learned that Packers games were a great time to shop for groceries. The checkers stood at the ends of their lanes, their eyes pleading for us to wheel our cart in their direction and afford them a few minutes of human contact.

Children grease the skids of community and even friendship, providing entrée to playgroups and music lessons and the like, but they can also keep you outside the fence of other circles. My colleagues at the college had adult children or none at all. They tolerated though didn't exactly welcome an infant and a toddler crashing their parties, plunging their saliva-slicked fingers into the baskets of chips and nuts. Most of the other families with small children we encountered around town were native, not only to Wisconsin but to the immediate area, their kids bound for the same elementary, middle, and high schools they themselves had attended. They weren't typically in the market for new friends. Still, we tried our best. We went to church suppers and joined book clubs and crisscrossed the state visiting pumpkin festivals and eating fried haddock at the VFW and picking apples at a local orchard where, for an extra fee, a woman in a gingham apron dipped our hand-plucked apples into a vat of steaming homemade caramel.

One morning, in the park with the boys not long after Hayden was born, Katherine struck up a conversation with another mother and ended up getting herself invited to join a church group for mothers of preschoolers. Not a Bible study, the woman explained, simply a chance to get together. The church that hosted it was Lutheran, and it was in our neighborhood. Galen was still a year from starting preschool, but the woman said he was close enough. After an isolated winter, Katherine was desperate to connect with people who understood the precarious comedy of wrangling a toddler into a car seat in subzero weather while eight months pregnant, so she said okay. She enjoyed herself enough to go back the next week.

That June, we were invited to a birthday party on the far side of town for one of their children, in what might be labeled Appleton's suburbs: a mile beyond the highway that encircles the city limits, vinyl-sided houses flanked by sapling maple trees held upright against the Canadian winds by baling wire and wooden stakes. I parked on the street behind a fleet of Toyota Siennas and Dodge Caravans and helped Galen out of his car seat while Katherine unbuckled Hayden. The furniture looked as though it had been purchased as a set: a faux-leather sectional with a matching faux-leather recliner, a coffee table made of the same granite as the countertops, an oversized Roman-numeral clock hanging on the wall opposite the autographed Packers jersey enshrined in a mahogany frame. The kitchen table showcased an array of potato and corn chips, M&M's with peanuts and without, celery and carrot sticks dammed against a reservoir of ranch dressing large enough to swamp the entire crop, and a most impressive three-dimensional Thomas the Tank Engine cake, complete with edible tracks and a railroad crossing fashioned from a lollipop. "Damn," I whispered to Katherine. "That's some cake."

Galen's eyes alighted on the enormous play set on the other side of the sliding glass door, and he pushed his way through the crowd of children. I followed him, leaving Katherine inside with Hayden riding on her hip. The patio, I discovered as I stepped through the door, was occupied by three men in khakis and polyester golf shirts, the kind that never wrinkle or wilt, each emblazoned with the logo of a different sports team. Badgers, Packers, Brewers. They eyed me suspiciously.

I shook hands and introduced myself. I asked which child scaling the side of the play set belonged to whom, nodded as the men pointed and said their children's names, and then forgot them all. One of the men offered me a beer from the cooler. Why not? The guy in the Brewers shirt pulled a bottle from the ice and handed it to me. I studied the label. Fauerbach Lager. "I've never had this before," I said.

"It's from Portage," he said. "Where I grew up."

"Did you know John Muir is from Portage?" I asked.

"Who? John Moore?"

"Muir," I said. "The naturalist. He founded the Sierra Club."

The men glanced at one another.

I should have stopped there and changed the subject to a topic more befitting my audience. I hadn't paid enough attention to the football season to say anything meaningful about the Packers, and though I knew the Brewers were Milwaukee's baseball team, I couldn't name a single player. I continued. "The famous historian, Frederick Jackson Turner, was from Portage, too. Aldo Leopold lived in Baraboo, the next town over. That's really something, if you think about it. Muir, Turner, and Leopold were major players in the early environmental movement, and they're all from the same part of Wisconsin."

"Okay," he said, and crossed the lawn to push his daughter's swing. The other men stared into their bottles. A minute later, Galen tugged on my pant leg and said he needed to use the bathroom. I'd never been so happy to hunt for a toilet in my life.

In the car on the way home, Katherine patted my knee and said, "Thanks for being a good sport. I won't make you do that again."

I looked over at her and then into the rearview mirror. The slice of cake given to Hayden had mostly ended up in his hair, and Galen's knees were stained green and black from the yard. The boys needed baths, and I needed a drink, something not from Portage, something clear and cold and Russian. "Everyone was nice," I said.

"You don't have to say it," she said.

One way or another, we had to make a life. I had a good teaching job, spending my days among young men and women whose bright faces and eager voices I loved. Katherine, too, had landed a gratifying gig as a social worker at the local hospital. We camped on Rock Island, the last of the islands off the northern tip of the thumb-shaped Door County peninsula jutting into Lake Michigan, our tent fifty feet from the shore and the boys in our laps as the twilight gave way to a dazzling firmament of stars. We savored local customs like brandy old-fashioneds and Bloody Marys in liter steins garnished with bacon and pickles and side chasers of beer. When we heard about St. Nick's Day, Katherine and I were charmed.

Most American kids grow up with some awareness that St. Nicholas is synonymous with Santa Claus, but few know the story of how one became the other. I didn't until I looked it up. According to legend, the real St. Nicholas saved three poor maidens in southern Turkey from a life of prostitution by throwing purses filled with gold coins—dowries for their weddings—through the girls' window in the middle of the night. In a slightly apocryphal version, St. Nicholas tossed the purses down the chimney where they landed in the maidens' stockings, hung by the fire to dry. As tales of St. Nick spread throughout medieval Europe, his clothes, his body, and even his name began to change. The Dutch gave him a long beard, a red cape, and called him Sinterklaas. In 1809, Washington Irving, of "Rip Van Winkle" fame and founder of the Saint Nicholas Society of the City of New York, cast him as a portly sailor in a velvet coat and renamed him Santa Claus.

In America, St. Nicholas's Day was long ago absorbed by Christmas, but in Europe—and in Wisconsin, which continued to receive large waves of Dutch, German, and Scandinavian immigrants well into the twentieth century—it remained popular. The bakery at the end of our street made special nut cakes and pastries. The boutiques downtown erected displays of inexpensive, shoe-sized toys. I learned about the tradition from the mother of one of Galen's classmates while standing outside the school. She told me that everyone, including the Hmong children whose parents had emigrated not from Europe but from Laos and Vietnam, celebrated the occasion. If Galen missed it, he'd feel left out. We didn't want that, did we?

Of course not. I thanked her for steering me around what, in the cosmos of kindergarten, would have amounted to a major disaster. Katherine meanwhile had gotten the skinny on St. Nick's from the nurses at work. She felt bad that we hadn't celebrated the day before now. Two-year-old Hayden was at her feet, working the toe of my shoe into his mouth. He had his teeth almost to the laces, a lot farther than I thought he'd get it. "Thankfully," I quipped, "we found out before it was too late."

We didn't have a fireplace, so the boys left their shoes beneath the thermostat.

They bounded down the stairs the next morning and dove for the loot. Katherine had gone all out, intent on making up for lost time. A plate of St. Nick's apple miters sat on the coffee table. The boys' miniature kicks were buried beneath a pile of flannel pajamas, yo-yos, Matchbox cars, packs of stickers, and generous parcels of chocolate coins. Hayden sat cross-legged on the carpet and devoured his entire stash, wrappers and all, until chocolate spittle oozed down his chin. Galen, though, was puzzled. He studied the Christmas tree, festooned with lights and ornaments but empty of presents, unsure of whether to be happy or devastated. "Is this Christmas?" he asked.

"It's St. Nick's Day," Katherine said.

"Does St. Nick work for Santa?" Galen asked. "Or does he work for God?"

For as long as I'd been a dad, I'd had my misgivings about propagating the Santa Claus myth. It wasn't Santa's make-believe status that bothered me, but rather how children were so heartily encouraged to believe in him when they're little only to have the fable, and all the magical thinking Santa made possible, later revealed as a fraud.

I was Galen's age when my mother told me she'd once seen the fat man in the flesh. She'd had the flu, and Santa had crept into her bedroom after dropping off the gifts to wish her a merry Christmas. She told me he'd set his white glove on her fevered brow and said her name. I clung to the story as proof that Santa was real long after I'd begun to suspect he wasn't. The pieces didn't add up. How come, for example, the presents supposedly sledded in from the North Pole smelled like my mother's perfume? Why were the cookies I'd set out the night before now in a Ziploc baggie in the pantry? I finally cornered my mom and demanded the truth, and to her credit she came clean, but the revelation nevertheless felt like a betrayal. When I grilled her about her confab with Santa—how could she have seen him if he wasn't real?—she replied more sheepishly. "Well, David," she said, "I had a fever. I was delirious." The thing I couldn't figure out was why I'd been duped in the first place. Christmas seemed neither more magical nor the gifts more lavish because they'd supposedly come from Santa's workshop. If anything, I'd learned to take for granted how much things cost, as well as the copious amounts of human labor required to acquire and assemble all the gadgets and gizmos Santa left at my house. It was an attitude I'd noticed the boys starting to espouse: If I threatened to take away their toys, they shrugged and said Santa would bring them more. If they lost their gloves at school or day care, their solution was to simply add them to their Christmas lists. A five- and two-year-old shouldn't have to ponder the sacrifices made in service of their happiness and well-being, but all the same it didn't sit well with me that they saw Santa as a cash cow who catered to their every desire. What evidence did they have to the contrary? They were my mother's and my in-laws' only grandchildren. They could ask for the moon and expect to receive it.

I saw my chance to set a few things straight.

"St. Nick *was* Santa," I said. "He was a real person who lived a long time ago. He gave presents to children and helped the poor. He was so famous that everyone in Europe and North Africa and parts of Asia knew about him and continued to tell stories about him long after he died."

"He died?" Galen asked. His eyes widened and his mouth fell open. "Santa died?"

"A long time ago," I said. "More than a thousand years ago. We remember him at Christmas because his story reminds us to love others and to be generous."

Galen gazed at the Christmas tree, the lights shimmering in the ornaments. He looked suddenly wise, as though he'd grasped some fundamental human truth—about, perhaps, the ways fables can be understood as fictions and still tell us something about who we are and how we ought to live. The story of Santa, far more than the person, taught us to do for others before doing for ourselves, anonymously and without fanfare if possible, and to find a quiet and abiding joy in the solemnity and solicitude of a lighted tree during the coldest, darkest time of the year. In Wisconsin, that was no small thing.

I congratulated myself for my honesty and for making the truth plain. I hadn't said Santa wasn't real. On the contrary, I'd told him Santa was as real as he and I, subject to the same cycles of life and death. Galen seemed to take comfort in the knowledge that the laws of biology and physics governing the other eleven months of the year also held true in December. Smiling, newly enlightened, Galen handed me one of his chocolate coins. Bursting with yuletide spirit, I unwrapped it for him.

•

The next week, Galen's teacher called. "We had a little trouble to-day," she said. "We were making holiday ornaments when Galen announced to the class that Santa was dead."

"He said that?" I asked.

"Several children started to cry," she said. "I've already had a few parents call. Christmas is less than two weeks away."

"It's my fault," I said, trying to laugh it off. "I was telling him how St. Nicholas was the *real* Santa Claus."

"Well," she said, her voice elongating into a schoolmarmish tone, "some beliefs are better kept to ourselves."

"It's the truth," I said.

"Different families have different truths." She was growing an-noyed and wasn't trying very hard to hide it. "We try to respect that."

"What is truth?" I asked, rhetorically.

"That's what I'm trying to say."

I held off telling my son's kindergarten teacher that she sounded like Pontius Pilate, and she in turn refrained from further cramming down my throat the message she'd already made exceedingly clear: that rumors of Santa's demise, sprung upon a room full of five-year-olds in mid-December, needed to be dispelled, pronto. The conse-quences were potentially dire. Galen could be branded a pariah, the kid who killed Christmas.

Galen was in the living room, watching TV with his thumb in his mouth and clutching his woobie, a dishwater-gray blanket with a bear's head and paws. We'd been trying to persuade him to give it up since he started school, but so far our efforts had only intensified his attachment. I sat down beside him and fell into his episode of *Go, Diego, Go!*, waiting for the right opportunity to broach the subject. The show, however, ran without commercial breaks, Galen never once moved his eyes from the screen, and the longer I sat beside him, the less I knew what to say. *Hey, kid, remember that conversation we had last week? Turns out I was wrong: There really* is *a fat guy in a velveteen suit who can slow time and squeeze through air ducts. His reindeer can fly, his toys are made by elves, and your Christmas presents don't cost us one red cent.* It sounded not only stupid but cowardly, a bald-faced repeal of the first consequential truth I'd ever told him. Parents already tell so many lies in the course of simply holding things together: that we can protect our children from harm or that we'll always have enough to eat, despite the fact that harm and hunger daily befall children around the world. There were plenty of times I brazenly deceived my sons not to guard their innocence but for my own convenience, because I wanted them to go to bed or stop hounding me at the store. The proliferation of the Santa Claus legend itself resulted from the Saint Nicholas Society of the City of New York's wish to transform Christmas from a drunken, working-class bacchanal into a domesticated family holiday. I mean, think about it: How often is Santa invoked in order to get unruly children to behave?

Now that I'd let the genie out of the bottle, I didn't know how to get it back in.

When the next episode of *Diego* started, I patted Galen's knee and slumped back to the kitchen, foolishly telling myself I wouldn't compromise my principles in order to placate a bunch of sniveling kids. Deep down, though, I knew I was simply at a loss for words.

Maybe, I thought, I could make Katherine talk to him. That way, in a few years when he finally wised up for good, I could claim I'd never been anything but honest. That seemed like a cop-out of a different sort, and Katherine, who in her years as a social worker had on more than one occasion engaged in hand-to-hand combat with belligerent schizophrenics and crazed drug addicts, had little patience for buck-passers.

Peer pressure, in the end, did the work for me. Without further intervention from his parents or his teacher, Galen decided to hedge his bets and declare Santa alive again. Apparently, one of the kids at his craft table had laid out the question of Santa's existence in terms of Pascal's wager. Even if Santa *wasn't* real, it was better to believe just to make sure you got the presents. A few days before school let out for the holidays, Galen brought me his Christmas list, scrawled in marker on a sheet of yellow construction paper, and asked me to burn it. The same school friend had told Galen that Santa would read the smoke. Christmas lists sent by smoke signal were faster and more reliable than using the mail.

"You're sure Santa will get it?" I asked.

"Of course," Galen said. "He sees everything."

I carried the paper to the kitchen sink and dug around the drawer for the lighter. Before I touched the flame to the page, I looked down at my son, hoping to gauge his level of seriousness. When I set fire to the list and watched Galen lean over the sink to study the paper as it blackened, I understood why he wanted to believe. For all the hype that attaches to Santa, for all the overspending that occurs in his name, believing in him is ultimately an act of community during a season when community is paramount. Hoping they've made the nice list helps reassure children they're worthy, despite their failings and misbehaviors, of the love, goodwill, and yes, even the presents that come their way during the holidays, all of which can be overwhelming when you're five. It's not Santa's magic that children cling to and need, but his grace. Sharing in Santa gave Galen the very thing I'd been chasing for the past three years: a foothold in his community. It didn't matter that his community still needed help in the bathroom and consumed more Play-Doh than fried haddock. St. Nick's Day and Santa had given him a way in. And in that way, his foothold was also mine.

On Christmas Eve, after church and after dinner, I ushered the boys upstairs while Katherine finished the dishes. The boys kicked their feet inside their sheets and squealed. Christmas was almost here.

Once we were certain they were out, Katherine and I would begin assembling toys and stuffing stockings for the grand reveal the next morning. We'd be up into the wee hours, and the boys would rouse us from bed by six, if we were lucky. "Santa can't come until you're asleep," I told Galen. If the Santa facade granted me even one extra hour of sleep, it was worth the deception. "Stay in bed."

Galen drew an X across his chest. "I promise."

I leaned down to kiss him. "Merry Christmas," I said.

"Merry Christmas, Dad." I backed out of his room and shut off the light. As I pulled the door closed, I heard him say, "Merry Christmas . . . *Santa*." And then I heard him giggling in the dark.

The Ride of Angry Galen

Snow in Wisconsin falls early and heavy and clings to the ground like a remora with lockjaw. As with everything, I learned this lesson the hard way. During the first big storm our first winter, I pulled back the living room curtains at ten o'clock at night only to discover a panorama of merry shovelers. Not so unlike the caroling Whos around their crooked Christmas tree, my neighbors worked to clear their walks and driveway, clad in parkas and boots and wool caps or furry ushanka hats, calling out to one another, laughing and generally enjoying themselves despite the single-digit temps, the arctic wind, and the ultimate futility of their work. As soon as a patch of asphalt was scraped clean, the snow began to pile up again. Inside my living room, the furnace vents exhaling a steady breath of heated air across the floor and Katherine lying curled on the couch in my college swim team sweatshirt, taking to the streets seemed absurd.

The next morning, I had to put my shoulder into the storm door to move it back far enough to squeeze out. The snow on the driveway was at least a foot deep, and my shoes disappeared inside a white crevasse with every step. I was running late for work, so I threw the car (we'd traded in Katherine's Jeep for a Korean SUV with more room) into four-wheel drive and barreled through the fresh powder. My octogenarian neighbor, Don, who'd been outside when I went to bed last night, stood with his elbow propped on the handle of his shovel. His sidewalks were arrow-straight and snow-free, as though cut with a scalpel rather than a shovel. He shook his head at me. "Bad idea, driving over the snow like that," he said when I rolled down my window. "It'll be there come spring yet."

"I'll clear it later," I said, looking at my watch. My morning class started in thirty minutes. "After work."

"Too late. Your driveway will be last to melt. I guarantee it."

Don and his wife, Joan, had lived on the street for more than fifty years. The teenagers who came over to inflate their ten-foot Packers lawn ornament and clean out the roof gutters were their great-grandchildren. His prognosis was time-tested and ironclad. After a few more passes with the car, the snow would no longer accept the shovel. A slight elevation in temperature allowed the top layer to liquefy and then freeze solid, sheeting our driveway in ice so thick a hockey team could scrimmage on it. Deep into April, when Don and Joan were sipping iced tea in lawn chairs on their driveway, I was still chipping ice away from mine. The next winter, I set my boots and parka by the back door and kept the curtains parted. When the front porch lights began to flicker on, I knew it was time to head out. In the spring, when I saw Joan on her knees in the garden, I knew it was safe to plant. When Don and Joan blew out their spigots in September, I went ahead and blew out mine, too, knowing that we'd drop below freezing soon enough. A good front window is sometimes a better source of information than an almanac.

As Galen's kindergarten year wound down, I noticed the metal racks outside his school were crowded with bicycles. Ours was a school surrounded on all sides by houses, and no student lived more than a mile away: an easy distance to ride, apparently even for pregnant moms towing baby trailers. Classmates of Galen's who'd attached themselves to their mother's thighs with python death grips on the first day of school now, eight short months later, leapt down the stairs, extracted their two-wheelers from the tangled heaps of rubber and metal, and glided down the street.

I told Galen it was time he learned to ride a bike. He'd pedaled with training wheels for the last year, often with one of the plastic stabilizers bent several inches off the ground. Taking them off seemed like a mere formality. "Get ready," I said. "You'll be a big boy soon."

Some lives can be divided into Befores and Afters, and the schism between the two can warp time and memory. I can recall key life moments as far back as three years old—the tropical storm, for example, that turned the Houston sky midnight black and sent my mother and me scurrying for the laundry room in case the pines came through the windows. But when it came to recalling my dad before he and my mother divorced, my memories had largely become concentrated around a handful of flashbulb moments that in their stark prominence felt prophetic. Any moment, no matter how ordinary, can become a rite of passage if you never get the chance to repeat it. Thirty years on, I could conjure in its entirety, as if it were a movie I just watched: the day my dad taught me to ride a bicycle the summer I turned five. I could picture his hand cupped beneath the back of my seat, the gold initials suspended from a belcher chain bouncing against his shirtless neck, his voice in my ear telling me to *pedal, pedal, hold the handlebars straight, keep pedaling.* It was July, and the sultry air rippled above the lawns, the sky cotton-ball white. The bike was a metallic blue Huffy with knobby handgrips. It had been a birthday present, the first one I cared about.

A few years later, I taught my sister to ride her bike on our driveway. I was bored, I wanted someone to ride with, and Devin was the only one available. She was five, as I had been when I learned. I unscrewed her training wheels with a pair of vise-grips and told her she could expect to wipe out. No one wore helmets in 1985, or padding of any sort; learning to ride a bike was a form of aversion therapy: the pain of falling taught us not to fall. I'd scythed the skin off both knees and scraped the paint from the handlebars down to the raw metal. In one spectacular tumble, I'd bent my pedal so badly it had to be welded back into place. Even after four years of daily practice I'd sometimes fall for no good reason, inexplicably toppling to the asphalt as though I'd been hit by a sniper. I accepted that falling was part of the deal.

"When you crash, don't cry," I told her. "I don't want Mom to hear."

For some reason, Devin went along with this. She set her feet on the pedals, and I ran behind her, as my father had run behind me. I had the fleeting sensation that maybe my dad ought to teach her because teaching a kid to ride a bike was something dads did. He and my mom were still two years away from separating and three from divorcing, but the cracks were beginning to show. Dad spent more time on the phone with work and Mom more time cleaning the house when she wasn't working herself. I knew that both money and time had grown scarce, and I honestly believed I was saving my parents the chore of having to teach Devin how to ride. Also, the chance to see my sister injured in a manner for which I could not be blamed was a tremendous draw.

I pushed Devin down the driveway exactly twice. The third time, she batted my hand away. She didn't fall once. I took her quick success as evidence that I was a good teacher.

The first Saturday in May, the oaks fuzzed with early leaves, I led Galen to the driveway and made a big to-do of removing his training wheels. I opened my socket set and asked him to help me find the right bit. He tried every one in the box, starting with the largest and the smallest until he Goldilocksed onto the perfect fit. I showed him how to turn the torque wrench, and felt a little like Roy Hobbs helping Bobby mill the Savoy Special in *The Natural*. This was fatherhood at its finest. Together we carried the training wheels to the back of the garage and stored them away.

"Don't forget his helmet," Katherine called from the window. I didn't know how long she'd been watching us, but her amused smirk suggested it had been a while. When she said *helmet*, she didn't mean *just* a helmet. She meant knee and elbow pads, high-top sneakers, long sleeves and pants. Her first job as a social worker, before we moved to Wisconsin, had been in the emergency room of the big children's hospital in Salt Lake, a job that had given her ringside seats to every conceivable way a child could kill or maim himself. In addition to all the weird shit—kids who obstructed their bowels by swallowing magnets that sealed their intestines shut or mistook bags of laundry detergent pods for candy—she'd seen a lot of bike accidents. Her hospital had given helmets away for free to make sure kids had them. One time she brought home, as a souvenir, a helmet smashed to smithereens, a dent in the cranial dome cavernous enough to hold a bowl of cereal. "Imagine," she'd said, eyes narrowed, "this is your son's head." Galen was nine months old then, only starting to pull himself to his feet.

I buckled Galen's helmet beneath his chin and rapped my knuckles against his elbow pads. He could pedal his bike off the roof of the house and hardly feel it. "Are you ready?"

"Ready," he said.

Katherine came outside to watch, Hayden on her hip.

"Don't let go," Galen said.

"Here we go," I said, and we set off down the sidewalk. We jogged past our house and the neighbor's until we had some speed built up. "Keep pedaling," I called, and let go.

I stopped running and watched him roll beyond my reach. I recalled my sister's Strawberry Shortcake bike, the ribbon my mother had tied around her ponytail flapping in the breeze. Time had folded over on itself; I was here and there at once. "You're doing great," I called.

Galen sensed something had changed. "No!" he screamed, and dove for the grass.

"You almost had it," I said, running up to him. He was on his hands and knees on the neighbor's lawn, afraid to stand up. "Why'd you stop pedaling?"

"You let go."

I hauled him up by his armpits and set the bike back on its wheels. "Let's try again."

Galen wiggled his red helmet and looked me in the eye. "This time, do not let go." He squinted in the sunlight and pointed his finger at my chin. "Do *not*."

"Keep pedaling," I said. "Focus on that."

"Promise," he said.

"If you're going to learn how to ride, I'll have to let go eventually."

"Not today," he said. "Promise."

"Okay, I promise," I said, believing my lie would soon prove itself moot. Once he saw he could do it, he'd forget he'd ever been afraid.

We turned the bike around and prepared to start again. I noticed Don and Joan sitting in their plastic chairs in the driveway, their wrists touching across the narrow gap between them. How many children, in their fifty years of occupancy, had they watched learn to ride a bike, as well as parallel park and throw a spiral and preen in front of the hydrangeas in rhinestone dresses before heading off to prom? Don tipped his ball cap at me. I swelled with parental magnanimity. "Here we go!"

Galen pedaled, and I ran past Katherine and Hayden at the bottom of our driveway, past the house on the other side. Galen picked up speed, and I had to run faster to keep pace. I was holding on with three fingers, then two. He had this. When the bike seat slipped off my index finger, I let it. For a few glorious seconds, Galen kept riding. Don and Joan raised their arms above their heads like football refs watching a ball sail through the uprights. *It's good!* I clapped and called out, "You got it! You're doing it!"

Galen hazarded a quick glance over his shoulder, and when he realized I wasn't there, he let go of the handlebars. He went down like he'd been hit by a rock. He landed on the sidewalk, catching himself with his hands, the one surface we'd neglected to pad. He saw the blood on his palms and began to wail.

Katherine came running over. She set Hayden on the ground and bent to cradle Galen's hands in her own. She kissed his bloody palms. I thought, *Oh, come on*. I wanted to say that falling was a part of learning how to ride. You can't make an omelet without cracking a few eggs. Besides, the spill couldn't have hurt that bad, not with all the cushioning. I flashed on another ER memory, from before we moved to Wisconsin: Katherine was working swing shift, three P.M. to three A.M., and I'd gone up to take her some dinner. I was in the waiting room, a polystyrene clamshell in my lap, when I noticed a little boy sitting in a chair with his arm wrapped in a towel, bawling his ever-loving head off. I assumed the man beside him, bouncing one foot like a heavy-metal drummer, was the boy's father. Katherine had already come out to tell me that a trauma was coming in, so I knew it would be a bit before she could break to eat, and I knew that broken bones, neither life-threatening nor contagious, were triaged as low priorities. The kid had no choice but to sit until the ER cleared. At a certain point, the dad grew impatient with the endless waiting and his kid's inconsolable crying and hissed to the little guy, "Suck it up and be a man." The boy opened the towel, and even from twenty feet away I could see the broken end of his radius protruding like a knob beneath the skin. If I'd had a break like that, I wouldn't have been crying. I'd have been screaming bloody murder. The dad scanned the room. Our eyes met briefly before his flicked back to the basketball game going on the corner television. All I could think was, *You asshole*. Katherine, when I told her about the exchange, just rolled her eyes. She saw such triumphs in parenting all the time. And a great deal worse.

"Let's try again," I said to Galen. "This time I think you'll get it for sure."

Galen draped his arm around his mom's shoulder. Not wanting to be left out, Hayden toddled over and took his place at Katherine's left side. Galen looked up at me. "Don't take this the wrong way, but you're a bad teacher."

I'd met Katherine while I was teaching swimming lessons to kids at the city pool. Parents routinely told me their son or daughter had been afraid of the water before they started in my class. By the end of the session, I had them breathing to the side. Teaching was my profession, my labor of love. If I was *anything*, I was a good teacher.

"I just want to ride my bike," Galen said.

"That's the idea."

"No," he said. "The old way. Put the training wheels back on."

"You can't give up so easily."

"Wheels back on."

"Maybe he's not ready," Katherine said. She slid her hand beneath Hayden's rear and moved to her feet. His orange sneakers levitated off the ground.

"No way," I said, resolved. "Once the training wheels are off, they're off." It had worked for me and for my sister. Surely it would work for my son as well.

"Fine," Galen said. He crossed his arms and frowned. "I won't ride then. Ever." His eyes were glassy, injured. He'd expected more from me.

"Suit yourself," I said. I walked toward the house. Katherine held out a hand for Galen. The bike stayed where it had fallen, on the sidewalk in front of the neighbor's house. From his perch across the street, Don sat shaking his head. An hour later I went back for the bike and wheeled it into the garage.

There it lay, on its side, collecting dust for the next two months, unridden throughout the prime weeks of summer while kids and adults wheeled past our house with towels around their necks or baskets full of tomatoes from the farmer's market. In the mornings, Galen watched through the living room window as I took my own bike out of the garage to ride to my office. "This could be you," I said, leaning on my handlebars. "You want to try riding again?"

"No," he said, parroting his mother. "I'm not ready."

By late August, I'd more or less given up. No amount of coaxing or incentivizing would jar Galen from his stubborn resolve to never, ever ride a bicycle. I began to come to terms with the undeniable reality that my firstborn would be one of those kids. He'd grow overweight and socially awkward, afraid of girls and sunlight, and would spend his free time forum-trolling in the basement. Eventually he'd end up in federal prison for hacking into a government mainframe.

Katherine said to look on the bright side. If all that came to pass, he could probably hook us up with free cable.

A week before Labor Day and the return to school, Galen wheeled his bike from the garage to the driveway. He wore the helmet but not the pads, and instead of riding the bike he flipped it upside down so the handlebars and seat were on the pavement. He cranked the pedals with his hand, singing out, "Ice cream! Ice cream! Who wants some ice cream?"

"You know," I said. "If you learned to ride, we could go get ice cream."

Unimpressed by my offer, he called again, looking past me. "Who else wants some ice cream?"

Katherine waved me inside. "Leave him be," she said. "Maybe if you ignore him, he'll keep playing with it."

Ignoring him, though, was easier said than done. On some level I'd been waiting to teach my kid to ride a bike all my life. Teaching him to ride was a link to my past and an atavistic vision of fatherhood vectored through my life as a son. It wasn't enough for Galen to learn how to ride; I wanted him to learn how to ride from *me*. I wanted to transplant my memory of my dad running behind my bike into Galen, who would therefore learn to ride not only from me but also by proxy from my dad, thereby resulting in an unbroken chain of connectedness that ran from my father through me to my son.

There was a slight chance I was overthinking the whole thing.

I pulled the cap off a beer and moved my chair into the shade. I watched Hayden play with the hose, allowing him to spray my feet and, once I finished the beer, fill my empty bottle and pretend to chug it. Galen stood with his back to the yard, making pretend ice cream as fast as his arms could crank.

Throughout the afternoon, cars arrived at Don and Joan's. Their children and grandchildren and great-grandchildren carried foil-wrapped casserole dishes up the driveway. I could smell their grill and hear their music, the amplifying din of the party as more family continued to arrive. Some of the smaller children rode bicycles, circling the block and turning in loops on the driveway. At one point Galen stopped turning the pedals and stood watching a little girl ride a pink two-wheeler. The girl saw him and waved and for a moment lost control of the bike. The handlebars twisted and her knee plunged toward the pavement before she somehow, miraculously, got her hand on the grip and swooped back to vertical. An inadvertently beautiful close call. Galen stood entranced.

The girl rode up to the garage and turned out of sight. Galen turned over his bike and straddled it. He stood with his feet on the ground and the crossbar between his legs. He waddled in circles with the seat poking against his butt. He moved to the garage wall where he leaned against the clapboard siding and eased onto the seat. He pushed off, pedaled once, and tipped sideways into the grass. I sipped beery hose water and tried to make myself invisible.

Galen got up, refusing to look at me, and walked the bike back to the wall. "Okay, dammit," he said, baring his teeth. "This is it. This is the ride of Angry Galen." He clenched his fist and looked down at it, as if his knuckles were a source of power. He shoved himself away from the garage, teeth clenched tight, and this time managed to make it from the grass to the pavement. He was slow and wobbly, but he didn't fall. I listened for the sound of metal scraping over concrete, but twenty seconds later he came up the neighbor's driveway and emerged around the back of the house. He glided across the grass and back to his starting point where he hopped off the bike, turned around to face the driveway, and remounted.

"This is the ride of Angry Galen," he said again, and shoved off once more.

Angry Galen circled the house more than twenty times that afternoon, enough to wear a trail in the lawn. I went inside for another beer and a towel for Hayden and returned to my Adirondack chair in the shade. It wasn't a bad way to pass a summer afternoon, truth be told: the late sun broken by the maple leaves, Katherine's music coming through the kitchen window, the distant echo of a party across the street, both boys in sight but not needing anything from me. Hayden was absorbed in a box of raisins, Galen in the Newtonian mechanics of balance and motion. Learning to ride a bicycle is one of our first lessons in autodidactism, and perhaps the most enduring. Someone gives us a push at the beginning, but the riding itself is something everyone does alone. We are ultimately our best and only teachers.

Toward dinnertime, our next-door neighbor, whose driveway adjoins ours, wheeled her grill out of her garage. I gathered up my empty bottles and told Galen it was time to put his bike away. "We can ride more tomorrow," I said.

Galen put his foot on the ground and turned to me with a look that said, *Where in the world did you come from?* He'd been so absorbed in his task that he'd disappeared inside of it. The rest of the world, including his dad sitting yards away, had ceased to exist. Bicycling was about more than physics, it was also an imaginative act. You have to see yourself doing it before you actually do it. You have to trust the air more than the hand at your seat. Everything we learn, from riding a bike to resecting a tumor at the base of the cerebellum, we learn this way. The primary difference between the acquisition of this skill and all the others was that, thanks to a sunny afternoon and a few bottles of Spotted Cow ale, I got to see the process from start to finish. All that was left was the grand ta-da.

Galen wheeled his bike back to the garage wall. He leaned his shoulder against the clapboards while he arranged himself on the seat. "Dad," he said. "You want to see something?"

"Go for it," I said. "I'm watching."

I Not Did It

By my mid-thirties, I'd yet to accomplish many of the things expected of a married suburban homeowner. I'd never been backstage at a concert or financed a major appliance or eaten at an Outback Steakhouse. I'd grown up within sight of a regulation golf course but had never played a complete round. Having fallen in love with a social worker while spending the entirety of my twenties pursuing an education in literature, the bulk of my furniture had either been purchased at rummage sales or carried into my marriage from childhood. To this day, Katherine and I sleep in the bed she got in the sixth grade. I did, however, have a really bitchin' couch.

The week I received the job offer in Wisconsin, after six arduous months and fifty-five applications for work, Katherine told me about a store in Holladay, a few miles south of Salt Lake, she wanted me to see. The place turned out to be an überhip Scandinavian furniture store, a gallery of sleek, lacquered lines gleaming beneath track LED spotlights suspended from the ceiling. The salespeople wore black turtlenecks and titanium polygonal eyewear. They curled their lips when they saw me saunter in wearing a hooded sweatshirt with Galen riding piggyback. The saleswoman who approached us, though, knew Katherine. She'd been coming here for years to lust over the things she might one day possess, once the uninsured, carless graduate student she'd agreed to marry had secured gainful employment. Our current couch I'd found, no lie, on the street the morning after I arrived in Utah seven years earlier. The fact that we'd laid our newborn son on such a degenerate piece of garbage had long filled Katherine with shame—which she now intended to rectify.

The saleswoman knew "just the piece" to show us: a soft, pale khaki couch with extra-deep seating and a matching oversized chair. I ran my palm across the fabric and had to resist the urge to lay my cheek against it. If you pulled off the back cushions, the saleswoman pointed out, the seat was the size of a twin bed. More than adequate for an overnight guest. "You know," Katherine added. "For when my mom comes to visit us . . . in Wisconsin."

"Who's in Wisconsin?" the saleswoman asked.

"Us," I said. "In a few months. I got a job there."

"Doing what?"

I'd deliberately not said what the job would be so that she'd be prompted to ask, so that I could say, "I'll be an English professor at a college." I'd worked for the title for close to a decade, but now that I'd attained it, it felt surreal. Sort of like landing on the moon after years of studying it through a telescope.

The saleswoman nodded but appeared otherwise unimpressed. She pulled a strand of flaxen hair away from her turtleneck and said to Katherine, "Wisconsin is a long way from here."

Katherine picked up Galen and canted her hip so he could straddle it. "Yes," she said. "A long way." She hadn't expressed a single qualm about any of the schools where I'd interviewed, not even the tiny college in rural Pennsylvania several hours' drive from a hospital large enough to sustain her career. Nor had she balked at the prospect of leaving her job, her family, her friends, or the mountains where she'd grown up. I owed her something, didn't I? Something big?

The saleslady had artfully flipped the price tag over so I couldn't see it, and stood with the back of her knee against it. "So," I said. "How much did you say this was?"

She smiled first at Katherine and then at me. "That's the good news. It's on sale."

The day we loaded the couch onto the moving truck, I draped it in every old quilt and blanket we had and then made several laps with shrink wrap to ensure our one prized possession would travel without incident out of the Rockies and across the Great Plains. We paid extra to have the couch Scotchgarded and the treatment was warrantied for seven years, but I didn't want to take any chances. The couch was unblemished when I pulled it off the truck in Wisconsin, but within a few seconds I discovered a problem: The thing wouldn't fit through the door. Our front entrance led into a foyer the size of a phone booth where there was a coat closet on one side and an archway leading into the living room on the other. Anything that came through the front door had to make a ninety-degree turn to the left and duck through the arch. Eight-foot couches weren't inclined to duck. I could only manage to get half of it inside the house before we ran into a wall or doorjamb. The back door was even worse: The ceiling followed the slope of the basement stairs toward the nether regions below grade and prevented anything larger than a floor lamp from coming through. The front door was the only option, though after hours of grunting and swearing and cursing the heavens for giving me a wife who'd demand such an expensive and unwieldy piece of furniture, I'd made little progress. I was ready to break the front picture window to get the thing inside. My dad had driven the moving truck across the country with me. Replacing such a large pane of glass would probably cost more than the couch itself, he said. As an alternative, he suggested sawing the couch in half and converting it into a sectional.

"Oh my God, no," Katherine said. "It's coming inside in one piece."

She was four months pregnant with Hayden, so she took the

role of boss while Dad and I served as the muscle. Under her direction, we removed the front and the storm doors, as well as the light fixture in the foyer. We backed the couch straight in, then walked it hand over hand until it stood on its arm inside the entryway. The other arm brushed against the ceiling. "Now turn it," she called. I inched the couch around until the front of the arm faced the living room. I stood behind it while my dad pulled from the bottom. The couch moved, ever so slightly, and I guided the back so it wouldn't gouge the wall. The bottom came off the floor and the top sank in my hands. It was in.

We placed the couch against the wall facing the picture window. After returning the doors and light fixture to their proper housings, I stood in the living room and looked at the couch. Katherine was unpacking dishes in the kitchen, and Galen was in the driveway with my dad. I still couldn't believe we'd managed to stevedore the beast through such a narrow opening, but neither could I believe that I had a house to move into, or that after years of using food stamps to buy milk and baby formula I'd completed my degree and secured a full-time teaching job. My salary was small (English professors, like circus elephants, work for peanuts), but it was enough to keep the lights on, the furnace going, and the cupboard stocked. More than I could say for my life up to that point.

Come February, we'd carry Hayden inside the house and lay our newborn son on a couch we'd bought new, in an actual store. We'd take our first family picture on the couch, invite our new friends to fill it, sleep there when we were too sick or angry to share a bed, sit together and watch our neighbors spill into the street, whooping and banging pots and pans with wooden spoons on the night the Packers won the Super Bowl. I couldn't foresee any of that—we hadn't even decided on Hayden's name—but I could, somehow, imagine all of it. The couch contained the promise of the future, this new life of ours.

For most living rooms, couches are the dominant feature, the geometry undergirding a life. A repository for every hope and frustration, every victory and loss. Katherine had been right to want the couch, and righter still to refuse to give up on it. It was a testament to how far we'd come.

I babied the couch more than I babied the babies. Diaper-changing on the furniture was strictly forbidden, as were shoes, hair products, wet bathing suits, and any food containing sauce. Baby food was a special category that was confined solely to the corner of the kitchen nearest the sink. Most of the time we kept the upholstery covered with a quilt, and we only sometimes removed it when company came over. When Katherine's parents visited, my father-in-law remarked how uncannily the couch resembled the spread on Katherine's bed when she was in high school. "Did you match the upholstery on purpose?"

"Of course," Katherine said. She didn't have the heart to tell him he wasn't among the select few allowed to sit on the actual fabric. "I loved that bedding."

"The classics never go out of style," he said, pleased.

One day, on my way to the kitchen from the mailbox, I noticed several long, squiggly stripes below the left arm. It was a part of the couch no one ever touched but everyone could see when they walked in the room. At first I dismissed them as a trick of the light, a shadow cast through the window in the front door. I breezed past them several times thinking, *Nah*. When I came back for a closer look, I tried brushing the stripes away, as though there were a chance dust clung to upholstery in uneven vertical lines. I knelt on the floor, licked my thumb, and rubbed it on the fabric. That's when I saw it, jutting out from behind the couch's foot. A capless ballpoint pen, as obvious and as horrifying as a bloody knife at the scene of a murder.

"Boys!" I called up the stairwell. "Come down here!"

Galen and Hayden appeared at the bottom of the stairs. Galen was still five, and Hayden had turned three two months ago. He had his thumb in his mouth and his index finger plugging his left nostril. I never understood how he could breathe that way. I pointed at the couch. "Who did it?"

Galen shook his head. "Wasn't me."

Hayden shrugged, stone-faced and silent.

"Those marks didn't get there by magic."

"I didn't," Galen said. "Really."

"You colored on your bedspread," I said. My anger was rising. The couch was hardly our first casualty of parenting, but it was by far the gravest. I waved the pen in Galen's face. "You drew on your bedroom wall, too." He'd also poked holes in the kitchen table with a fork and left a half-dissolved Life Saver on the seat of my car. Galen was a logical guess.

"I did those things," he said. "But not this."

He'd never lied about his previous acts of vandalism. In fact, he'd been proud to take credit. I turned to his little brother. "You?"

"I not did it," Hayden said.

Katherine got down on her hands and knees so she could study the marks up close. She considered them for a long time, running her hand up and down the upholstery, as though the lines contained a secret message she might decode. She sat back on her heels and looked at Hayden. He didn't look away or cry or grin. He was like Amarillo Slim at a poker table. Katherine put her hands on his shoulders. "Tell Mom the truth. Did you draw on the couch?"

Hayden shook his head. "No," he said, and shrugged. His face said, *I'd like to help, but my hands are tied.* "I not did it."

Like Bartleby's "I would prefer not to," the phrase was inscrutable and thus unassailable. And Hayden knew it.

The Scotchgard was still under warranty. I called the store in Utah and described the situation. Three-year-old, ballpoint pen, eye-level khaki fabric as inviting as a blank canvas. The customer service representative spoke with a Utah accent strong enough to induce a moment of longing for the place, and for my life before kids. "We'd be glad to help you with that, David," she said. "Go ahead and bring the couch back in. We'll see what we can do for you."

"That's going to be hard," I said. "I'm in Wisconsin."

"Is the couch there with you?" she asked.

I had the fleeting image of my couch on the run, hiding out in flophouses and on the front porches of fraternities. "Of course," I said. "We're very committed to each other."

"Who?" she asked, puzzled.

"My couch and I. When I moved here, I invited the couch to come along and it said okay. We've been very happy up to this point."

I'd forgotten how easily irony was lost on people in Utah. After a long silence, she said, "I didn't realize you lived out of state. I'm afraid there's not much we can do."

"Nothing?"

"Maybe there's a local business that can clean it for you," she said.

One website suggested spraying the ink with hairspray, which ought to promote dissolution in water. Another site said to try vinegar for the same effect. A third, ominously, said that once pen ink came into contact with upholstery, the dye was cast. Literally. The best option would be to buy a new couch. To stave off despair, I dismissed the third website as fake news promulgated by the furniture industry seeking to dupe middle-class consumers into spending beyond their means. Then I doused the couch's arms with an entire can of Katherine's hairspray. The fabric turned stiff as cardboard, but the ink remained. The vinegar did even less. The expensive fabric cleaner I bought at the hardware store caused the upholstery to fade, which in contrast made the stains appear darker than ever. I scrubbed like an inmate trying to tunnel out of prison with a spoon until my back and knees began to ache.

I decided to switch to kneeling on the seat cushions and bend-ing over the arm to work the stain from the top. Seeing the marks upside down gave me a new perspective on the problem, and revealed what I'd failed to notice. Three of the lines formed a large, unsteady but definitive, H. I could discern among the other squiggles an A and a Y.

I shouted for Hayden.

He came around the corner holding onto his mom's hand. Katherine was there as both peace broker and public defender in the parental justice system.

"It looks like you tried to write your name," I said.

"I not did it," Hayden said.

"I can see an H." I pointed to the couch, the floor around it littered with sponges and rags and spray bottles. "And this here is a Y."

"I not did it."

Katherine looked at me. *What's your move now, Ace?*

Up to that point in my parenting career I'd largely relied on the boys' innate inclination toward truthfulness. Babies and toddlers don't know how to lie; it takes a more sophisticated understanding of storytelling in order to concoct an alternative narrative of events. As the boys grew old enough to account for themselves, I'd made a point of insisting on telling the truth, even when doing so wasn't in their immediate interests. Galen, for example, had long been drawn to small, shiny objects, be they fridge magnets or lug nuts, and for a while he'd become a rather accomplished shoplifter. I'd spent one morning running errands with him, and then the entire afternoon backtracking to every store we'd visited to return the things he'd stolen.

Every time I turned on the news, a politician or a pundit was claiming Barack Obama was a Muslim terrorist or comprehensive health care would lead to a government bureaucrat pulling the plug on grandma's respirator even while she stretched out her bony hand and rasped, "Save me." My uncle Tom filled my inbox daily with conspiracies ranging from how Don McLean's "American Pie" predicted the Satanic-Communist takeover of America to the possibility that eating apricot pits could cure cancer. We lived immersed in lies. If Hayden didn't learn the importance of telling the truth now, when he was three, the lesson would only become harder to learn later. Prying the truth from Galen had required nothing more complicated than persistence. If I didn't stop badgering him to come clean, he'd eventually cave. Hayden, on the other hand, had learned from watching his brother and adapted his techniques accordingly. He'd calculated the potential outcomes of his deed and had rightly concluded that I had next to zero leverage. He wasn't old enough to take on extra chores. The one time I'd tried to get him to take out the trash, a forty-foot walk between the back door and the garage, had ended with me scooping up a forty-foot trail of garbage with a show shovel. Besides a few dimes and nickels rattling around a piggy bank, he didn't have any money. A time-out would require either his mom or me to stand guard and would therefore constitute a punishment for all of us. My dignity, indeed my status as adjudicator of the family system of rewards and punishments, was on the line. I saw no way out except to make the devil's wager. "You won't be in trouble if you tell me the truth," I said, trading away all consequences for the sake of the confession. "I promise I won't be mad."

Hayden, though, had figured out that my evidence was at best circumstantial and wouldn't hold up. I had nothing on him. "I not did it," he said.

For the next week, Katherine and I tried everything to get Hayden to confess. We took turns telling him stories about the bad things we'd done as kids—like the time I forged my mother's signature on a school form and ended up in the principal's office, or the time Katherine carved the word *Nike* into her parents' dresser, complete with the swoosh, when she was seven—and how each time the lie had led to consequences far exceeding the original infraction. We stripped him of dessert until further notice. Then we promised him extra dessert if he'd only do the right thing. At night when I put him to bed, I tried to catch him with his guard down and whispered in his ear, "Dad loves you. Admit you drew on the couch."

"I not did it," he whispered back, his eyes closed.

I told Katherine he'd make a great lawyer.

"Or a spy," she said.

"Kid's got ice water in his veins."

On Saturday afternoon, I was grilling chicken while Hayden and Katherine were making a salad and corn bread. Katherine cracked the eggs but allowed Hayden to separate the shells. He was stirring the batter when she leaned toward him and said, "Are you ready to tell me the truth about the couch?"

The answer was already plain on his face. "After we make the corn bread I tell you," he said.

She spooned the batter into the pan and slid it into the oven.

"Okay," he said. "I did it."

"Why?"

He shrugged and extended his tongue to the batter-coated spatula. Of course, he'd never had a reason, not one he could explain. Kids seem to have a radar for marring the objects we care most about, as if to test whether we love our stuff more than we love them. To which I actually have an answer: yes, sometimes, especially since the couch was the only nice thing we owned. The turn-of-the-century activist and writer Charlotte Perkins Gilman, author of "The Yellow Wallpaper," says that children want to mark even more than they want to eat. The need to scribble on paper and walls and furniture originates in a primal desire to make oneself known. Maybe on some level Hayden understood that. Despite my belief that he was special and deserved the world's praise simply because he was mine, he'd never be recognized simply for being. He'd have to *do* something. Get out there and leave his mark on the world.

Or maybe we were settling into the kind of conventional family life I'd pined for, one in which my son could safely see me as his principal adversary because he had no reason to distrust my love or the permanence of my presence. I was his Darth Vader: the source of his courage and the focus of his rebellion.

I came inside with the plate of steaming chicken. Katherine said, "Hayden has something to tell you."

I set the plate on the counter and wiped my hands on the dish towel. I put on my most magnanimous face. The truth was about to come out. At last! I prepared myself to graciously receive it. "Go ahead," I said.

A strange look came across Hayden's face, as though he foresaw the battles to come, the punishments he wouldn't be able to weasel his way out of. In the long run, the house wins. For now, though, he was holding aces. He thrust his chin forward, and in an eerily adult voice, he said, one more time, "I not did it."

Uno Is the Loneliest Number

Galen's first homework assignment for first grade was to learn his home address and phone number, the full names of everyone in his immediate family, and his parents' occupations. His teacher sent home a note encouraging families to work on the assignment together and to supplement the school-provided worksheet with "expressions of our child's individual creativity." Examples included but were not limited to: a three-dimensional representation of the family made from salt dough or papier-mâché, a food dish from our cultural tradition (enough to share, no nuts please), or a performance with a musical instrument. The school's principal was a trained cellist and played with the local symphony.

"I swear," Katherine said, "the school gives out these assignments to mess with us."

We opted to let Galen express his individual creativity by way of a poster board collage of family photographs. He was permitted to use, under strict supervision and far from his brother's skin, the good kitchen scissors in order to cut the pictures into different shapes and to paste them to the board in a manner reflective of his truest, most creative self. In most of the pictures, our bodies were cut in half or decapitated, our heads floating along the top of the poster board like stars in a really trippy sky while our legs and feet lay heaped in a pile on the dining room table. To my surprise, Galen had a solid grasp of the basic family demographics. He knew our address cold and could even tell us how to get from our house to the school and back again. When asked about our jobs, he confidently proclaimed that Mom was a social worker and Dad was a professor.

"What does that mean?" Katherine asked. "What does a social worker do?"

Galen stopped cutting and looked up, the scissors paused guillotine-like over the glossy image of his brother's neck. "Mom takes care of sick babies and sick mamas."

Hayden's head tumbled into a pile of de-limbed torsos.

As a hospital social worker, Katherine covered pediatrics, maternity, and the neonatal intensive care, where she spent the bulk of her time. Neither a doctor nor a nurse, she wasn't involved in the medical care of the patients; rather, it was her job to ensure the babies who came through the hospital—some born so early it was a miracle they survived—had safe homes to go to once they were discharged. Moms were screened for postpartum depression and substance addiction and signs of domestic abuse. From her night shifts in the ER back in Utah, she'd developed a keen eye for spotting problems often missed in the doctors' offices, and thanks to her interventions numerous women had carried their bundles of joy into residential treatment programs and women's shelters and the homes of relatives rather than back to the husbands and boyfriends who'd sent them to the hospital with black eyes and cracked ribs. It was important, if underpaid, work, and I was proud to be connected to it.

"What about Dad?" Katherine asked. "What does a professor do?"

Galen looked at me, his face utterly blank. To protect my books from unsanctioned cutting, gluing, or Magic Markering, I kept everything work related at my office on campus. Unlike Katherine, I didn't carry a pager clipped to my belt, and rare was the day when

I was called away from the dinner table to attend to an emergency. "Hmm," Galen said. "You read your computer and eat your lunch."

Katherine laughed. "You are usually eating when we come visit."

"I stop working when I know you're coming," I said, more defensive than I ought to have been. "I work until I hear you coming down the hall."

Her face said, *Right*. She turned to Galen. "Dad's a teacher and a writer. He writes books."

"You do?" Galen said. Despite the dearth of adult books around the house, our shelves were nonetheless full of things to read. We had, to name only a few, the complete works of Mo Willems, Russell and Lillian Hoban's *Frances* series, Ian Falconer's *Olivia*, numerous *Frog and Toad*s, and so many Dr. Seuss books that, laid flat, they could tile the floor of Galen's bedroom. Hayden also kept on his shelf a galley of my first book, a collection of stories published when he was one. He liked to tote it around under his arm. I'd be lying if I said that seeing him do that didn't thrill me. Eager to join the discussion, Hayden leapt from the floor and ran to his room to fetch the book. He handed it to Galen.

"Oh, that thing," Galen said. "I forgot about it."

I turned to the acknowledgments page and pointed to his name. "You're in it. Sort of."

He tossed it to the rug. "I like my books better."

My profession carried about as much weight with the boys as it did with my neighbors, most of whom assumed I wiled away the day by smoking a pipe in a tweed jacket with my ankles crossed on my desk. In the boys' minds, being a professor wasn't much different than being a mailman. I went off each day with a large bag of papers slung over my shoulder. But a father's work is often veiled, either by intention or accident. Masculinity and work have long been conjoined, and there's a belief among a certain subset of men, including those from whom I'm descended, that the power of a job is inversely related to the amount of knowledge others have of it. To reveal or even talk too much about work is to risk exposing weakness. Only the vainglorious or deluded see themselves as unequaled in their careers, yet boys often idolize men who stand apart from the competition—the LeBron Jameses and Michael Phelpses and Tom Bradys of the world. If we can't actually be the LeBrons of our industries, we can at least promote the illusion among our kids, take refuge in their adoration. It might be said that growing up is the prolonged process of making peace with the lies we were told as kids, both by and especially *about* our parents. And once our own kids get wise to the con, we can only hope they'll love us anyway.

Compared with the prolific output of the writers who filled the boys' shelves, I must have looked like a minor leaguer at best. Yet after the school assignment was handed in, a curious thing began to happen. The boys wanted me, and only me, to read to them at bedtime, even though Mom was better at doing the voices of the characters. I was the book authority; ergo, the job of nightly reader could be filled by no one else. Instead of two books each before bed, the standard for the last two years, they now demanded three or four. At first I was pleased that they saw their old man as connected to their books, but it soon became evident that the whole thing was a scam. Hayden argued that he should get at least one more book than Galen, since he wasn't yet in school, and that took us up to nine books in total before I could be relieved of duty. I couldn't tell whether their contest was for my attention or a coordinated effort to rope-a-dope me into breaking down and letting them stay up to watch TV.

I set a limit of three books each. They responded by choosing the longest books on the shelves. Instead of *Don't Let the Pigeon Drive the Bus!* or *Barnyard Dance!*, they went right for the Dr. Seuss. Dr. Seuss books look slim from far away, but they often contain upwards of fifty or sixty pages each and can take a solid hour to read. Any attempt to skip pages was grounds for protest. Climbing the stairs at night, knowing that *Hop on Pop* or *Fox in Socks* or *Mr. Brown Can*

Moo! Can You? waited for me at the top filled me with an existential dread only Samuel Beckett could imagine.

At a certain point, I started vetoing all Dr. Seuss books. Then I vetoed any book not by Mo Willems. I could burn through an *Elephant and Piggie* in under a minute if I really got after it. I read like an auctioneer trying to offload a bum steer, slamming shut the cover and exclaiming, "There, that's three books. Now go to sleep."

"But, Dad," Galen said, "that didn't take very long."

"A deal's a deal," I said, pulling shut the door.

Katherine met me in the hallway. Her smirk was half amused and half horrified. "I think you might need a change of pace," she said.

The next night, as we headed up the stairs for another round of ritualized torture, Katherine herded the boys and me into Hayden's bedroom. It was by the far the smallest room in the house, but it was the only room with carpet on the floor. From her pocket she produced a deck of Uno cards. She slid the cards from the box, divided the crisp and squarely stacked pile into roughly equal halves, and proceeded to shuffle the deck with the flourish of a casino dealer. The cards flowed from her thumbs to the carpet and then abruptly changed direction and traveled upward, defying gravity, back into her hands. For a long moment the colored squares appeared suspended in midair, a blurry smear in the fabric of space and time. "How do you know how to do that?" Galen asked.

"Practice." She dealt the cards around the circle our bodies formed on the carpet. It was November, below freezing at night, the tiny window at the back of the room fogged from the condensation of our body heat.

We'd played Uno a few times before, on car trips and in airports. Galen liked it because the rules were self-explanatory and he could win if he paid attention. Hayden liked it, too, because he knew his colors and numbers and even the Reverses and Skips had symbols he had little trouble matching. His problem was that he couldn't hold the cards the way Mom and Dad held them, fanned out in one hand like a peacock's tail. Instead he played standing up beside his bed, his cards laid out on his comforter, his back to us and his diapered butt an inch from my cheek.

"Let's try a practice round," Katherine said, turning over a card from the draw pile.

Within minutes, practice gave over to full-tilt competition. The four of us, but especially the boys and I, disappeared into the game with a ferocious intensity. I couldn't really explain it other than my need to get back at them for all the Dr. Seuss. I think the boys saw the game as one more opportunity to stick it to me. Unlike books, which only had endings, each game of Uno added winners and losers to the mix. Katherine's efforts to diffuse the tension generated by story time had unleashed an even darker force. It was too late to go back to our old tricks. We were hooked. We'd end up playing three games of Uno every night for more than a year.

"Let's see," Hayden said one night. We were on our second game. Hayden plucked a card from his bed and laid it on the discard pile. "Six."

"That's not a six, it's a nine," Galen said. I'd already won the first, and had taken three in a row the night before. Galen was desperate for a win.

"It looks like a six to me," Hayden said.

"It's not!"

"Do you have a nine?" Katherine asked Hayden. "How about a red card?"

"No," Hayden said. "I have a six."

"Okay, go ahead and play it," Katherine said. Hayden stood with his arm around his mom's shoulder in his footed fleece pajamas. He looked innocent, but Galen and I both knew better. His social game was a thinly disguised ploy to sneak a glance at his mom's hand.

"It's not fair!" Galen cried. He threw his cards on the floor and crossed his arms. The cards landed faceup and spread across the carpet. I couldn't help sneaking a look.

"We can go to bed," Katherine said, "if you can't play nicely."

Galen picked up his cards and spent a long minute arranging them. He worked like a florist adding the last stems to an already overstuffed bouquet. I dropped a red six on Hayden's blue to restore order, and the game resumed.

Now that I'd seen Galen's cards, I had him in my sights. I dropped a green seven on him, which I knew he couldn't play, and chased it with a Skip and a Draw Two. The more cards he was forced to draw the more sullen he became. "This isn't fair," he protested. "I have too many cards."

"It's how the game is played," I said. "Uno is often rags to riches. And vice versa."

"What's that mean?"

"It means the other way around. You could go from last to first. Or from first to last."

Galen pursed his lips. "Uno stinks," he said. "Who even invented this stupid game?"

My parents were fans of Uno. They regularly gathered at friends' houses to play on Saturday nights while I lolled about on the carpet with the other kids. This was in the late 1970s, before Devin was born. Like all games, Uno seemed at once arbitrary and universal. I never thought to question its origins. Nor did I understand until many years later that my parents, in 1979, were participants in a national, soon-to-be-global phenomenon deeply rooted in a rivalry (more than one, in fact) between fathers and sons.

In 1970, Merle Robbins, a barber in a small town outside of

Cincinnati, got into an argument with his son, Ray, over the rules of Crazy Eights. Similar to the game it inspired, Crazy Eights involves offloading cards according to number and suit, but uses the aces for Skips, queens for Reverses, jacks for Draw Twos. Eights are wild and are sometimes used as Draws. Some people use kings for Reverses. The rules change depending on where you are and with whom you're playing. Canada and the Netherlands have their own versions, with rules that make even less sense. Merle tried to settle the argument by writing the commands on the back of each card in Magic Marker. Not long after, he bought a deck with blank backing, making the handwritten commands easier to read. In 1971, Merle and his wife, Marie, sold their house and moved into a trailer so they could put up $8,000 of the $10,000 they needed to produce five thousand decks of the game they called "Uno." They liked the name because it sounded like Bingo, sonorous and exuberant when called out. Ray and his wife, Kathy, contributed the remaining $2,000 needed. The first decks were khaki green and looked like something the army might issue to soldiers to pass the time. For a while they were sold exclusively at Merle's Barbershop in Arlington Heights, Ohio. Men played in the shop and next door in Lichty's Tavern while they waited for a chair to open.

Within a year the game had found its way into retail shops across Cincinnati and into Kiwanis Clubs scattered as far away as Florida and Missouri. Then a man named Robert Tezak, a twenty-three-year-old part-time florist, funeral director, and aspiring politician from Joliet, Illinois, got hold of the game. He flew to Ohio to meet the Robbins and offered to buy Uno for $50,000 plus a ten-cent royalty on each deck sold. Bob Tezak took the remaining inventory back to Joliet and founded International Games, Inc., a two-man start-up consisting of Tezak and his brother-in-law Ed Akeman, who ran the business out of the back of the family flower shop. Whenever someone called IGI's phone, Akeman put the caller on hold, pretended to transfer the call to a different department, and disguised his voice. He wanted the company to appear big, an international player, though it took until Sam Walton, founder and CEO of Wal-Mart, personally placed an order for his stores that sales began to take off. By 1980, Uno sold eleven million decks a year. Cards were being printed, and the game was being played, around the clock. In 1984, the year Merle Robbins died, two college students played a game that lasted 132 hours.

Born of a father-son dispute, Uno likely caused thousands more as families sat down to play the game. But it's likely that none were as dark as the clash between Bob Tezak and his son, Mark. With the millions he earned from the game, Bob Tezak acquired a fleet of cars, a riverside mansion in Joliet and another in Arizona, and a private plane. He used his money to get elected coroner of Will County, Illinois, and to fashion himself into a political kingmaker. He overspent on local and state elections, bought an AM radio station, invested in an Indy Car team that took the checkered flag at the Indianapolis 500. Since this was the 1980s, he also took an interest in cocaine, and less pertinent to the epoch, his teenage son's teenage girlfriend. The affair continued even after Mark Tezak and the woman were married and ended only after Bob Tezak set fire to his own bowling alley to destroy records subpoenaed by the IRS. His daughter-in-law became a government witness and Bob tried to have her killed. In 1992, he was sentenced to twelve years in prison, and International Games, Inc. sold Uno to Mattel for forty million dollars. By the time Bob Tezak was released in 2003, his millions were gone, and Uno had grown into a megalithic brand encompassing a panoply of forms, ranging from decks festooned with movie and TV and sports logos; online, mobile, and video games; special versions featuring new cards with new commands, new rules, new gizmos for raining down a torrent of cards upon an unlucky opponent. It's now estimated that more than a billion people have played the game in one form or another. It's second only to Monopoly, which had a forty-year head start.

We only ever played Uno old school, with a single deck, 108 cards, our legs in a bow, sitting on the floor.

As I came down to my final two cards, I paused to consider my options. I was holding a Wild and a yellow four. If I played the yellow, I'd be invincible, my victory guaranteed. If I played the Wild, the color and number could change before my turn was up again and I'd be forced to draw.

Deliberating, I recalled a story Katherine had told at least a hundred times about the trip her family took to a remote cabin in the Colorado mountains, a place with a sublime view and no television or radio. The only entertainment was a shelf of musty paperbacks and a stack of board games. Katherine was twelve, her brothers ten and five. Instead of Monopoly or Risk, they chose Candy Land so that everyone in the family could play. My father-in-law attacked the board ruthlessly, disallowing backward moves, forcing his opponents to remain stuck in the Cherry Pitfalls until they drew the right card. He refused to fudge the rules or look the other way. He won every game until his children were crying and dispirited. It was at that point that Candy Land metamorphosed from a simplistic children's game into a morality tale, the family struggle in miniature. My mother-in-law gave up playing in favor of one of the paperbacks. Katherine anted up and played to win, no matter how futile her chances; one brother set his gingerbread man on the first square and refused to move off it, regardless of the card he drew; the other took the unused game pieces into the corner and choreographed a puppet show in a language only he could understand. Twenty-five years later, Katherine had yet to back down from a fight. She was gentle with the boys, but Annie Duke when she squared off with me. If we got into a mano a mano while playing Uno, she turned into her old man. I loved this about her. She loved her dad, but when she introduced me to him, she warned me not to play games with him. I thought she meant in the figurative sense, to avoid excessive sarcasm and beating around the bush regarding my intentions with his daughter. But, no, she meant it literally: Whether the game was cards, billiards, trivia, or Candy Land, he was a killer and an awful loser. A loss in the wrong game, under the wrong conditions, could cost me his blessing. Katherine must have recognized that on some level I wasn't so different.

There was a moment in every game of Uno when I faced the choice of whether or not to swoop in for the kill. My impulse, like my father-in-law, was to take what was mine. I justified destroying a six- and three-year-old at Uno as early lessons in the School of Hard Knocks. And playing Uno every night showed me a few things about the boys. Galen had, whether by instinct or institutionaliz-ing, a watchmaker's faith in fairness and the orderly harmony made possible by rules. The regs ought to apply absolutely and work in his favor. So long as the parameters of the game were properly observed, he saw no reason why he shouldn't win. Again and again he pro-tested his losses by claiming it was his turn to win.

Hayden, on the other hand, was a guerrilla card player, as he was elsewhere in life. After a barbecue the summer before, I stashed a leftover twelve-pack of Fresca in the basement, on a shelf in the laundry room. Hayden opened the cardboard sleeve from the bot-tom, so I wouldn't see the tear, and squirreled out the cans one by one. It was advanced work for a kid who still wore diapers to bed. Weeks later, I still tracked crawling lines of ants toward half-drained sodas hidden behind the furnace and water heater, stashed between suitcases. When it came to Uno, he had no qualms about drawing extra cards if he felt he could use them or liked the colors, or appeal-ing to his mother's affections in order to play a nine when the game called for a six. Rules? Fuck the rules.

Seated on the floor between my sons, I felt I was the junc-tion between two extremes. To my right sat the belief that success ought to come as a matter of course; to my left sat the idea that rules were meaningless concepts only others ought to obey. What neither of the boys were ready to accept was that losing often imparted the greater lesson. The stubbornness to take your licks and keep playing. To persist even when the outcome seemed certain and to abide by the rules given the chance to cheat. It was an important lesson for boys—and lest I forget, white boys, for whom life's playing field has long tilted in favor—to internalize. I had plenty of misgivings about the word *privilege* (especially when used as a verb), but I had even less patience for white men who believed their race and gender were discriminated against. I wanted the boys to understand that rules, much like the truth, *matter.* Even when the conditions ought to work in your favor, sometimes life was just hard. You played and lost and no one else was to blame. No one, in any case, but yourself.

And yet these were my sons and I was their father. If the world was indeed hard, shouldn't I have been a soft place within it? Where the rules might be bent or suspended so the boys might taste victory every now and then? After all, they were six and three. It felt like a simple question, but I honestly didn't know how to answer.

I played the Wild. I told myself I was giving the kids a break when in reality I wanted to see how far I could press my luck and still come out on top. I called for green hoping to lure one of my opponents into playing a yellow. I held up the one card in my hand. "Uno!" I called.

"I'm getting tired of this game," Galen said. "I always lose."

"No, you don't," I said. "You've won plenty."

"Dad hasn't won yet," Katherine said. "He's still got one more card."

I should have recognized the warning, but I didn't. Once you're holding Uno, you're a marked man. The world has it in for you.

•

I escaped defeat twice as the game moved around. After I threw the
Wild, Hayden played a red eight. By luck I drew a red seven from
the deck and immediately cast it to the pile. I went up to two cards
on the next pass, adding a blue five to my yellow four, and then like
magic Hayden played a blue four. I could have gone either way, but
the yellow four had carried me this far so I dropped the blue. "Uno!"
I called.

The next time around Hayden out of nowhere threw a Reverse.
Having him to my right for so long had been an ace in the hole.
Katherine went big and laid down her Draw Four, which she'd been
holding on to for God knows how long. We had Galen between us,
but it turned out he was packing the same heat. He set his own Draw
Four atop hers. I was almost certain the boys were in cahoots with
their mom, but what could I do? I lowered my head and drew my
eight cards from the pile.

"Boom!" Galen said.

"Boom chaka-laka!" Hayden said. He wiggled his butt in my
face. I could smell the baby powder I'd sprinkled in his diaper when
I got him ready for bed.

"You need an Advil, Professor?" Katherine asked me. "Because
that one had to hurt."

"I'm good," I said. "The game's not over yet." But as I looked
around the circle I saw Katherine and Galen were down to two cards
each. I was holding nine rectangles of worthless junk. All the Wilds
and Draw Twos and Skips lay in the discard pile. I was toast.

On the next pass, Galen called out Uno, and the pass after that
he took the game. His turn after all. He sat back on his hands without saying a word, victoriously unburdened. See why my question
wasn't so easy to answer? Slaying Goliath was so much sweeter when
Goliath actually showed up to the fight.

Hayden scooped the cards off his mattress and dropped them

in the center pile. "Shuffle," he said to his mom. While she cut the deck, Hayden came over to me. His pajamas smelled like Tide, his hair like baby shampoo. He put his arm around my shoulder, leaned close to my ear, and recited the very words I used after each game, as hollow and facetious in his voice as they surely were in mine. "You played a great game," he said.

Heirlooms

In early December, I found a large box on the front porch waiting in the rain. With our nearest family five states away, Christmas typically arrived this way: one box at a time, sometimes two, the gifts prewrapped by the jolly elves of Amazon and Toys "R" Us. But this box was unlike any other. I stopped the car in the driveway and stared at it, the wipers working back and forth. About the size of a mini-fridge, the box looked as though it had been dragged behind the UPS truck after being used to smuggle medical waste between rival third-world countries. The cardboard was so thickly wrapped with packaging tape, not only along the seams but across the lids and side panels, that the rain dipping onto the corner from the porch overhang had little discernible effect on the box's integrity. The rain certainly didn't make the thing any worse. I didn't need to read the shipping label to know who it was from. Only my dad, whose forty-year career selling paper and printing granted him unimpeded access to brand-new, never-before-creased-or-folded boxes of every conceivable shape and size, would go out of his way to send Christmas presents to his grandsons in the ugliest container he could find.

I had to bear-hug the thing in order to lift it and then waddle backward through the front door and the archway into the living room. Once I made it to the kitchen table, I needed a hacksaw to get through all the layers of tape. At last I parted the flaps, dug down through several sheets of crumbled pages of the *Orange County Register*, and extracted from the depths of the cardboard the following items:

1. One radar detector with accompanying cigarette lighter plug, circa 1988;
2. One Bobbi Brown Cosmetics tote bag, free with purchase of select products (not included);
3. One Velcro aloha-print wallet from Hawaii National Bank (empty);
4. One gallon-sized Ziploc baggie of used sunglasses. Most, though not all, had lenses;
5. One Tiger Handheld LCD game version of Disney's *Aladdin* (batteries required);
6. Assorted Laguna Beach High School paraphernalia, including three T-shirts, one hooded sweatshirt (size: adult medium), and two terry cloth visors, all strongly aromatic of the lost-and-found crate from which they'd been salvaged;
7. Two large beach towels, one blue and embroidered with the name "Taylor," and the other, yellow-and-white striped, that looked vaguely familiar. A few hours later I'd remember spotting the towel on the bottom of the ocean more than twenty years earlier while snorkeling through the reef between Crescent Bay and Shaw's Cove in Laguna Beach. I swam down, hauled it up, and carried it home. My stepmom washed it and added it to the shelf in the laundry room;
8. Four scuba masks, the straps yellowed and weakened by years of saltwater and sunlight. I couldn't recall whether

I'd used any of them, but judging by their age and condition, there was a strong chance I had.

I dialed my dad's number in California. "The box made it," I said.

"Good," he replied cheerily. "Lots of good stuff in there, huh?"

I was holding one of the masks, massaging my thumb along the cracks in the rubber strap. "You remember where we live?" I asked. "Not much diving up here. At least not during the winter."

"I thought the boys could play with the masks in the tub," he said.

"They're adult-sized. The boys are six and three."

"Bah," he said. "They'll grow into them. Kids that age, they grow faster than you can believe."

I wrapped the masks and arranged them toward the back of the Christmas tree.

I didn't know what else I'd expected the box to contain. My father wasn't ignorant of fashion or incapable of picking up hints, but he'd sucked at gift-giving all of my life. It was as if the ritual of exchanging presents on holidays defied some internal logic in him. The first Christmas after he and my mother were married, he gave my mom a socket wrench set. For her birthday in March, a shotgun. My mother went into labor with me on their second wedding anniversary, so I got him off the hook, but by Christmas he was back in form. My mother bounced me in her lap while she opened her shiny new chainsaw.

My mom vowed Devin and I would never know such sorrow. She made sure our presents were not only exactly what we wanted but elaborately arranged to maximize the wow factor. As an art major who worked in interior design and later event planning, she had an eye for presentation. I'd bound into the living room to find Skeletor and He-Man swashbuckling on the drawbridge of Castle Grayskull, candy and cassettes spilling from my stocking. The year I asked for a tent in anticipation of a scouting trip, I turned the corner on Christmas morning onto an entire campsite on the living room floor. The tent was outfitted with a sleeping bag, an electric lantern, a folding pocketknife, and an aluminum canteen. The only thing missing was the fire.

Dad sat cross-legged on the floor sipping coffee and taking pictures, as surprised as I was by what had emerged from the wrapping paper. When it was my mom's turn to open her presents, she tried to hide her chagrin: an ironing board cover, a paperweight the shape of a gigantic clothespin, a book titled *How to Speak Southern* purchased at the Atlanta airport on the way home from a business trip. "Much-abliged," she said, grinning through her teeth.

Once Dad moved to California, my mom could no longer shield my sister and me from our father's gifts. My stepmom had never bought presents for a teenaged boy before, so when it came to me, she deferred to my dad. He did most of his "shopping" at work, since his company, in addition to printing business forms and brochures, screened corporate logos on the knickknacks handed out at trade shows. Over the years I collected a cornucopia of ballpoint pens, miniature flashlights, key chain compasses, ceramic mugs that changed colors when filled with hot liquid. Even the remote-controlled Lamborghini, a gift I leapt onto the floor to play with, was papered over with American Express decals.

I moved to California the week after I turned eighteen, six weeks before I was to begin college at the University of California, Irvine, a half hour to the north and east of my dad's house. The summer swimming season had ended, and the college season would commence with the start of classes. I felt I needed to arrive on campus in the best possible shape. I swam in the mornings at the local high school, exercised with stretch cords and hand weights in the backyard, and at night, after my dad and stepmom had gone to bed, ran a six-mile loop through Laguna's eucalyptus-lined streets, into downtown, along the boardwalk at Main Beach, and then up the hills back toward home. In between exercising, I painted my dad's house and I ate. I was always hungry, and my bottomless appetite shocked my stepmother. She could never buy enough groceries. When I returned home for Christmas my freshman year, most of my presents were food. I received a cheese sampler, as well as a sleeve of spaghetti noodles and a jar of marinara sauce. The next year the cheese was accompanied by a three-foot Hickory Farms summer sausage, a full yard of cellophane-sheathed meat. I took the sausage back to school where my roommates used it to mime a series of sexual gestures so obscene that I could not bear to eat it.

The Christmas before I left California for Utah to begin graduate school, I received the usual haul. The cheese sampler had become by that point a tradition, as had the orange in the toe of my stocking. The tree had been mostly cleared out when my dad passed me a narrow rectangular box, the size and shape of a Maglite flashlight, which I thought would be cool to have. The box *thunk*ed against the floor when I set it down. I tore into the paper and extracted a Ziploc baggie filled with spare change, mostly dimes and nickels but some quarters, too. The money was the sum contents of his car's ashtray, a stash I was ordinarily forbidden to touch. I spent it all in a single night at the Laundromat, eating the cheese while my clothes tumbled around in the dryer.

Katherine read about an annual Dickens Christmas festival in Ripon, an hour south of Appleton. I imagined storefront windows twinkling with lights, bonneted women in pagoda sleeves and tatted collars, men in top hats and ascots and pince-nez caroling along the snow-dusted sidewalks. We drove down on a Saturday morning. We arrived too late for breakfast with Santa, in the Ace Hardware, so we opted instead for the parade of historic homes. The woman who sold the tickets saw Galen and Hayden sitting in the back seat and said, "Children aren't allowed."

"No?"

"Too many temptations for busy hands. You and your wife could go one at a time."

"That's okay," I said. "We'll go somewhere else."

We headed to the craft show at a place called Maplecrest Manor, which turned out to be the nursing home across the railroad tracks from the grain cooperative, a squat, dim building so acrid with urine and decay that we didn't make it past the front desk. A mile from the highway, I considered turning toward home, but after driving all the way down here and with a storm moving in, we had to at least see *something*. We decided to check out the nativity exhibit at the Episcopal church. We followed a hand-lettered sign through the narthex and sanctuary to a yellowed flight of stairs leading to a basement room with a ceiling low enough to create a static current between the asbestos tiles and my hair. I'm not sure what, by that point, I expected, but I suppose I descended the stairs hoping to find live animals and human actors dressed up like Mary and Joseph and the Wise Men.

A dozen folding tables had been set up end to end, and the Ripon townspeople had all brought in their personal nativity scenes—the holiday decorations that graced the sofa table from Thanksgiving to New Year's and spent the rest of the year in a soggy cardboard box in the basement. The woman guarding the entrance wore a Christmas tree sweater and beamed with pride at the spread. Eyeing the boys, she reminded us that the nativities were for eyes only, but in the corner they'd find some wooden trains and books. They could have a cookie afterward, if they behaved. "The Dickens festival isn't really good for kids, is it?" I said.

"There was breakfast with Santa," she said. "Did you make it to that?"

"I'm afraid not."

She shrugged, and I paid the small entry fee. My plan was to stroll up and down the aisles, declare this one, this other one, and oh, wait, this one over here, my top three, loudly enough for the woman to hear, and then get the hell out of there. Katherine led the boys to the play area. All the fruitless driving around, I could tell, was staring to wear her out.

"Five minutes," I said.

I walked with my hands behind my back, dipping forward to read the typed three-by-five index cards that captioned each scene. The first one read:

> Bob gave this nativity set to Barb for Christmas in 1967. I think he bought it on sale at Dillon and Vosburg's. Bob doesn't remember where he bought it, but then again, Bob doesn't remember much these days.

How could I not read the next one?

> My brother-in-law used to date a woman from Bolivia, and one year they decided to spend the holiday there. I asked her to bring me back a nativity set. I didn't think she would do it, but she did. My brother-in-law has dated a lot of women over the years, but I've never liked any of them as much as that girl from Bolivia.

Katherine glanced up from the picture book she was reading to the boys and caught me laughing. I waved her over, and together we roamed from nativity to nativity, tilting to examine the sets' constructions, their colors and arrangements, and to read the cards. Five minutes turned into an hour. The longer I read, the more the captions began to feel like a conversation among neighbors, full of inside jokes and allusions lost on outsiders. It was one of the things I loved about Wisconsin, along with its dense trees and striking winter light:

its deeply ingrained sense of community. Galen and Hayden, to my stunned delight, remained occupied by the books and trains, and on our way out the old woman praised our good parenting and told us to make sure we each got a cookie.

Coming up from the church basement, I took Hayden outside while Katherine led Galen to the potty. The snow looming all day had finally started to fall, the first flakes big and wet and the air now ripe with brine, strong enough to remind me of the ocean in winter. Watching the cars move through the snow, the December sky washed-out and flat, I thought of how, on Christmas afternoons when I was a teenager, once all the presents were opened, my dad and stepmom and sisters and I would walk down to the beach before we settled into eating and watching whatever movie was showing on TV. Winter tide could swell high enough to crash over the stairs, leaving them slick with wet sand and depositing sea urchins in the rock depressions near the base of the cliffs. The beach was usually deserted except for the two Labrador retrievers, Beau and Max, who lived in one of the big houses overlooking the sand. Their owner threw tennis balls into the ocean with a long-handled plastic launcher, and the dogs charged right in after them, diving headlong through the shore break, impervious to the cold. If we walked down later in the afternoon, we'd catch the start of dusk, the horizon going orange and purple over the outline of Catalina Island, twenty-two miles across the sea. As the light faded, I'd begin to feel sad. The sun setting meant I'd soon zip my meager gifts inside my suitcase and fly back to Texas. The long countdown to the next time I saw my dad, in August, would begin all over again.

Devin and I spent a lot of Christmases on airplanes, flying on Christmas Eve or Christmas Day because where we spent Christmas morning was a point of contention between our parents. We met other kids winging between one parent and another, all of us pawns in custody cases of varying sorts, and once an old lady told the flight attendant to bring us milk instead of the Cokes we'd asked for, patting my sister's hand, promising to look after us until the flight crew handed us over to our dad. One Christmas Eve when Devin and I were on separate flights, an ice storm shut down the Dallas–Fort Worth airport, where I was supposed to change planes. I pooled in with two brothers and hopped a cab across the city to Love Field, Dallas's smaller airport, and made it out on Southwest Airlines. The next morning, I awoke grateful to simply be in a place on Christmas where I knew the people in the other room. The boxes beneath the tree were gravy.

The thing that bothered me about my dad's god-awful gifts was that I'd never really wanted anything in the first place. I wanted stuff in the way that all teenagers did, I suppose, but when I looked forward to going to California for the holidays, presents were never a part of it. But when it came time to leave, I had nothing to show for it except an odd assortment of junk poached from corporate trade shows. As though my dad's house were a place I'd gone to transact some vague business rather than my second home.

Standing in the snow outside the Episcopal church, the wind-shields in the parking lot starting to glaze with frost and snow, I thought ruefully about how I didn't own a single thing I'd received for Christmas as a kid. Everything had been eaten or dropped into a coin-operated machine or simply thrown out; I certainly didn't have anything worth displaying at a town holiday festival, an object worthy of being called an heirloom. My father's gifts had been tangible symbols that had to stand in his place during the long months we were apart. Because he hadn't spent much time choosing them, I'd worried that he didn't spend much time thinking about me. Or now my boys. His grandsons.

I jostled Hayden into his car seat and started the engine and cranked the heat. I was scraping the fresh top layer of ice from the windshield when Katherine and Galen came out. Katherine saw my face and asked, "Are you okay?"

"Peachy," I said.

She shook her head. "Christmas."

"Exactly."

Our cable subscription included a DVR. Galen was proving himself more adept at the system than either of his parents. He'd figured out how to record his favorite shows and pause on his favorite commercials. Since his birthday in August he'd been fetching me from the kitchen or the basement in order to show me an ad for a Thomas the Tank Engine train table. It was the size and shape of a foosball table, though only a foot off the ground. It wasn't cheap and I'd been on the fence about getting it, but one night the week after the Dickens Festival I left work early and drove out to Toys "R" Us. I came home with the table as well as a hundred-piece train set. I hid the boxes beneath a plastic tarp in the back of the garage and hauled them inside on Christmas Eve after we'd put the boys to bed. The table pieces, when spread out, covered most of the living room floor. Beside the open box were a dozen miniature baggies filled with screws so tiny they looked like chia seeds through the plastic. Thankfully, the set included a tiny screwdriver and a tiny Allen wrench, each the size of a stick of gum. I stayed up until two in the morning fitting the pieces together, jigsawing the tracks into place and arranging the scenery: the fueling station beside the airport; the tunnel through the mountain; Sir Topham Hatt, the station master, waving from the platform beside the depot. It was a staging my mother would have admired.

The boys woke us up about forty-five minutes after I'd fallen asleep, yelling from their beds. I descended the stairs with my temples pressed between my fingers, one eye crusted shut. I brewed coffee and slid the camera battery into the slot. Settled into position, camera at the ready, I blew the wooden train whistle that had come with the set.

"You hear that?" Katherine said from the top of the stairs. "What's that noise?"

"Trains!" Galen hollered. The staircase shook as they thundered down it. For a few minutes it was as glorious as I'd imagined. The boys jumped and screamed and zoomed the trains along the tracks. But with other presents waiting and their stockings overflowing with candy, the table could only hold their attention for so long. They emptied their stockings onto the floor. Bows shot across the living room. The train table turned into a landfill for discarded scraps of wrapping paper.

I waited until every other gift had been opened to slide the scuba masks around from the back of the tree. I hoped the boys would be so saturated with presents they wouldn't have any interest in them. They'd blithely toss them to the pile like the garbage they were. Instead they put them on and stomped around the living room, pretending the masks were space helmets. The jetsam from my father's garage! I couldn't help feeling a little indignant, even if I knew the boys didn't attach the same symbolic importance to their gifts that I once—and, apparently, still—attached to mine.

As I watched the boys moonwalk across the couch, I thought again of the beach below my dad's house, all the languid, low-tide afternoons I spent snorkeling in the reef, in all likelihood in one of the masks the boys were wearing, descending toward the rippled bottom to fetch the towel that was now on my basement shelf. I had a thousand memories like that one: waking up before dawn to go surfing at Trestles, the Old Spaghetti Factory in Newport where Dad liked to eat on Saturday nights, drinking triple sec on his living room floor and listening to the Everly Brothers the night I got dumped by my first college girlfriend. The gigantic box of cast-off junk was perhaps his way of sending those memories back to me.

The boys, of course, had no idea about what I was feeling, nor did I want them to. I wanted Christmas to remain as uncomplicated as possible. The table and trains would wait for them.

Over the years, I grew to love the day after Christmas much more than the day itself. St. Stephen's Day in Europe, Boxing Day in Great Britain, Canada, and Australia, in America it's a non-holiday holiday, a day off wanted simply for its proximity to the biggest day of the year.

The boys were once again awake before six, but this time, instead of going downstairs, they crept one at a time into bed with Katherine and me. Our queen-sized bed was plenty comfortable for the two of us, but a sardine squeeze with four. But once they settled in, they fell back to sleep. I lay beside them, smelling their foul breath and listening to their rhythmic snuffling. Their mother's hair filled up the horizon beyond their heads. Snow whitened the window screens. There was nowhere we were expected to be. No planes to catch. No trains, either. *Give me ten more minutes like this*, I thought, *and I'll never want anything again.*

The Deep End

The scuba masks were still in the toy box when a January blizzard shut down the city. Katherine came home on Friday night with a family-sized take-and-bake pizza, two magnums of wine, and a stack of DVDs. We hunkered down, prepared to laze away the weekend in our sweatpants. Between movies and spells of preemptive snow shoveling (I'd learned my lesson), Galen and I hauled the train table to the center of the living room where, with the help of Lincoln Log girders and Lego support trusses, we extended the Isle of Sodor's railway infrastructure from its hilltop perch down to the rug and through the legs of the couch. A single engine could make the drop without derailing, but any train pulling a payload inevitably resulted in a mass-casualty incident. We lengthened the decline and reduced the pitch angle, and I swear we were on the verge of seeing a five-car carriage cross Dead Man's Gulch, disappear beneath the couch, and reemerge on the other side powered by nothing more than Newton's first law of motion, when Hayden stomped into the living room like Godzilla through Tokyo and laid waste to the metropolis.

"Hayden!" Galen screamed.

Hayden squealed and dashed up the stairs, Galen in hot pursuit. Their feet thundered across the ceiling. A door slammed. Hayden cried out in pain. In our house, vengeance rode hard on the heels of every provocation.

Hayden may have struck first, but the attack didn't occur in a vacuum. A long-simmering tension had been escalating for weeks, rooted in nothing more complicated than prolonged proximity and cold weather. Sitting on the couch, Galen would, apropos of nothing, lick his finger and plunge it into his brother's ear. A few hours later, we'd find Galen's Lightning McQueen underwear, his all-time favorite pair, floating in the crapper. Not yet four, Hayden was developing a keen and sophisticated capacity for ironic revenge.

Even Uno couldn't calm them down. On Saturday night, we played five games rather than our usual three to make sure both boys notched a win, but long after the extended rigmarole of tucking them in and creeping slowly downstairs, Katherine and I could hear the boys jumping on their beds and taunting each other from behind their doors. At first light, while Katherine and I slept, Galen slipped across enemy lines and mounted a surprise attack. I woke up to Hayden screaming and had to pull the boys apart before I'd had my first cup of coffee. A good portent it did not make.

By Sunday afternoon, the snow had thinned out, but the house's internal engine was running into the red zone. The Packers played at three, which meant a window of opportunity for grocery shopping and a trip to the YMCA. "I'll shop," Katherine said, "but only if I can go alone."

In the household division of labor, grocery shopping was the chore I liked the least. I hated spending money as matters of principle, history, and family identity. As a devoted garage-sale patron, my dad routinely came home with brown grocery bags stuffed with three-quarter filled bottles of shampoo and body wash and shaving cream, a year's worth of slightly used shower supplies he'd picked off someone's lawn for a dollar. I'd also known him to buy six-packs of beer, water sealant, cans of WD-40. If someone was willing to sell it, he was willing to buy, provided he could pay out of his coin tray. Certain things, like brooms, he refused to buy altogether. He plucked them from trash cans when his neighbors deemed them too worn to be of further use. I had adopted several of his tactics over the years as a means of survival. The year Katherine was pregnant with Galen, we'd been so broke that we'd squirreled home the leftovers from a funeral, ate up what we could, and returned all the unopened boxes of Triscuits and fridge-packs of soda to the grocery store for enough credit to buy a week's worth of lunch meat and cheese. Seven winters later and gainfully employed, I still had a hard time loading up a cart without my heartbeat two-stepping over the cost.

Katherine and I had struck a deal years earlier: She'd run the gauntlet at Woodman's while I took the boys to the YMCA to swim. For the most part I was happy with the arrangement, but after the pent-up chaos of the weekend, the prospect of managing the boys by myself felt like the short straw. I deserved added concessions.

"Such as?" Katherine asked, her dark eyebrows raised.

"You make dinner."

"Like I wouldn't anyway? Unless I wanted eggs for supper."

"Or spaghetti," I said. I was good at spaghetti.

She opened the freezer and peered inside, a cloud of icy vapor around her head. "I'll make dinner, but you do the dishes."

"Don't forget the kids will come home showered and in their jammies," I said.

"Those are my terms."

I extended my hand. "I accept."

She curled her fingers around my palm. "Anything else?"

Snow was falling again. I'd have to shovel at least one more time before the day was finished. That should count for something. I wiggled my eyebrows. "Maybe later . . . you know."

She leaned in to kiss me goodbye, her car keys jangling in her jacket pocket. She pressed her cheek to mine and whispered in my ear, "For a writer, you suck at sweet talk."

Not so long ago, a snowbound weekend was all the romantic

enticement we needed. The house we rented in Utah had a wood-burning fireplace and a video store and decent Italian restaurant within walking distance, and no matter how much snow came down, Katherine's Jeep could go practically anywhere. So long as the canyon roads stayed open, we could always get into the mountains. When we couldn't afford lift tickets, we could find a trail to snow-shoe. We snowshoed so much I grew to love it at least as much as skiing, if not more. It was quiet for one thing, often transcendentally so, as though we'd stepped across an invisible threshold into an out-door sound booth. The flocked pines and cedars creaked as the snow piled on their boughs, but noises from farther away couldn't pierce the bubble. We'd pack a thermos of hot tea sweetened with milk and sugar and hike until we could no longer hear the highway, and then hike farther until one of us fell over in the snow. The snowfall unlocked the earthy smell of the woods and granite, and everywhere inside our perimeter the mountains rose up, so large and envelop-ing, it felt to me as though we were the only two people on Earth. As I neared the end of my degree and commenced my program of earnest worry about finding a teaching job, Katherine and I agreed, while sipping tea in a snowbank, that if the academic job market came up snake eyes, we'd join the Peace Corps or teach English in Asia, maybe rotate back to the States after a few years to teach at a prep school nestled in an idyllic New England hamlet. To find our way back to the car, we had only to follow our own shoe prints, but it sometimes felt to me that if we kept going forward through the untrampled snow, we'd eventually go up and over the mountains and come down into another world, one where anything was possible.

Before the boys came along, I had a general, if vague, conception of the attention children required. But I'd conceived of children's needs solely in physical terms. Babies had to be fed, changed, and toted from place to place. Kids were more mobile but must be given food and watched after closely, lest they do themselves or others harm. What I did not anticipate was how much the boys would consume my inner life. Not only did I find it difficult *not* to think about them, my mind drifting during the day to how they were faring at nursery care or school, or staring down as they slept and wondering what they might be dreaming about, I also found I could no longer entertain a single one of my old fantasies about reinventing myself. The boys' abilities to imagine the far-flung splendors of the world ironically relied on a stable home, a stable conception of Mom and Dad; they needed us to be the people they thought they knew in order to become the people they were meant to be. Every parent is a lighthouse on the shore of their children's lives. Most of the time I accepted the trade-off.

We scanned our membership card at the front desk of the YMCA and jostled down the corridor toward the pool. Our path took us past the large glassed-in cage known as the "Family Fun Center," containing an expansive climbing set outfitted with narrow tubes, plague-infected netting, and Plexiglas gunners' turrets where trapped children pressed their faces against the plastic and pleaded for help. The crawl-through tubes were way too small for a regulation-sized adult (about half the size of a Wisconsin-sized adult between the months of November and April), so once a kid went in, he or she could either come out the other side or stay there forever. The Family Fun Center, like nearly everything that bore the "family" label, was only actually fun for the smallest members of the clan. The rest of the family suffered. The glass walls made the chamber deafeningly loud, cries from the criminally insane rained down from the upper tubes, and the steady production of soiled diapers perfumed the space. Children weren't allowed to play inside without direct supervision, but given the tight dimensions the Y had allotted for the space, the Family Fun Center lacked a single chair. Parents hugged their knees on blue tumbling mats, heads slumped forward as though awaiting the plunge of a guillotine. One mom lay supine, arms and legs splayed and her head buried beneath her fleece as if the blade had already struck. The lone dad in the room made eye contact. *Help me*, his eyes said. I ushered the boys quickly past the windows, before they asked to go inside.

We hung our jackets and jeans in a locker, and I unfolded the boys' swimming suits from my duffel bag. Hayden grew incensed when he saw which suit I'd packed for him—his green striped trunks instead of his *Finding Nemo* trunks. He'd eagerly stripped out of his clothes but refused to don his swimming attire. "No!" he yelled. "I'm not wearing that one!"

"It's the only suit I have for you."

"I hate it," he said, teeth bared. He bolted, naked, for a toilet stall. The metal latch clicked shut behind him.

Galen looked at me, confused. "What do we do now?"

"We wait," I said. The toilet stall didn't have a back door, and I had all of Hayden's clothes. As far as I could tell, I had the upper hand.

Thirty seconds later, the latch released and Hayden reemerged. I held the green trunks open by the waistband, and he slid one foot inside. From the bottom of the bag I produced Dad's scuba masks. Here, perhaps, they might be of some use. If not, we could always leave them on the bottom of the pool.

Through the showers and out to the pool deck. The boys had long ago declared the shallow water for babies, and they plunged into the deep end before the lifeguard, a pimply adolescent with Martin Scorsese eyebrows, could head them off. "Kids under ten aren't allowed in the deep end," he said.

"These boys can swim," I said. "I taught them myself."

When it came to swimming, I was a complete and unabashed snob. Snobbery is rarely a good quality in any man or woman, and most of the time I made a conscious effort to counteract it. The only person who'd ever called me "doctor," even though I had the degree to warrant the moniker, was my mother, and she did it to tease me.

Students either called me "Mister" or "McGlynn." I preferred the latter, unaccompanied by the former. But around water, my snobbish impulses were allowed free reign. I'd yanked Hayden out of swimming lessons last year after his teacher patently refused to advance him from the Tadpoles group to the Guppies because, in her words, Hayden "spent too much time underwater." As though that weren't the entire point. Under my tutelage, he'd flourished.

"They're good swimmers," I said to the lifeguard.

"They'll have to take the deep-water test," he said. "They have to tread water for a whole minute without touching the side."

The way he said it, it sounded like the first task at Navy Seals training camp. "I think they can handle it," I said.

I stood on the tiled deck beside the guard and kept the time. Hayden failed his first attempt on a technicality: he grew bored treading with his head above water and about halfway through his minute, made a dive for the bottom. The guard insisted his head had to stay up the entire time. I demanded a retest. The second time, he passed.

Jumping into a pool in which the boys were swimming was a little like throwing a bucket of chum into a frenzy of sharks. As soon as my feet broke the surface, they lunged for my hands, my arms, anything they could grab. Hayden followed me below the surface, slithered between my legs, and bit me on the calf. "What did you do that for?" I asked when we came up.

"I want to play Starbucks," he said.

Playing Starbucks consisted of Hayden paddling to the corner of the deep end where he extended his arms backward, one hand anchored on each wall, and leaned his chest and head forward in a manner uncannily similar to a drive-thru barista. "What can I get started for you?" he asked with a smile.

"I guess I'll have a coffee."

"How about a grande nonfat vanilla latte with no whip?"

"Is that what you're making today?"

He nodded.

"That sounds fine," I said.

He turned his back and for a moment appeared very busy at the corner. When he finished, he choo-chooed himself along the coping, the invisible cup in his right hand and carefully held above the waterline. He passed it to me and said, "Here you go, sir."

I took a long sip. "No whip, huh? How often do you and Mom go to Starbucks?"

"I don't know," he said. "But it sure is a lot."

Buzzed on pretend coffee, the boys next wanted to play "elevator" by holding onto my shoulders as I slid down the wall toward the bottom. Despite their many attempts, neither Galen nor Hayden had quite figured out how to propel himself all the way to the floor of the twelve-foot tank. They relied on me to get them there. As a boy, I'd learned to hold my breath exactly this same way, by clutching my father's shoulders as he plunged toward the pump grates at the deep end of our neighborhood pool. I could recall the panic I felt when he dove, a feeling similar to being pulled under, except that I was the one hanging on. I could feel the tension in the boys' grips, their small fingers digging into my skin, as we neared the bottom. Their stubborn refusal to let go. It's a father's job, I suppose, to lead his sons into the deep end, to show them that every abyss eventually has a bottom, to teach them not to fear it.

The boys didn't fear the bottom; they just couldn't touch it. Once their fingers grazed the tiles, they rocketed back to the surface inside a swirl of bubbles, leaving me alone on the bottom. At last I was enclosed in a silence as complete as the one I'd found on the mountain trails in Utah. No place had ever been more tranquil or restorative for me than the water. Not even the mountains. Water was where I went first in times of anxiety or sadness, and no trip away from home was complete without a swim. Oceans, lakes, rivers, pools—at a certain depth it all felt like the same water, a viscous conduit for every bygone dream and harebrained idea, every grand design and foolish hope. Sunday afternoons at the pool were as much about me as they were about trying to wear the crazy out of the boys. At the nadir of the YMCA pool in Appleton, Wisconsin, on a winter Sunday afternoon, I could recover a little of my imaginative life, and a few of the possible alternative futures that had once, a long time ago, seemed so infinite.

But also: watching the boys scurry up the rungs of the metal ladder and disappear from view, it struck me that the present would give way to my real future all too soon. In a few years, the boys would become more interested in spending time with their friends than with Mom and Dad, and a few years after that, they'd move away. Before I knew it, my Sundays would be as quiet as they once were. I'd be free to snowshoe for as long as I wanted, to investigate the realm beyond the trees without anyone whining or tugging at my pant leg or plopping down in the snow and refusing to go one step farther. I could foresee the day when I'd miss the boys clinging to my neck, chomping on my calf.

I called their names, but my words bubbled silently toward the water's mirrored surface.

Right when I started to feel sad, Galen dove in. His eyes were enormous behind the pane of the scuba mask, and his lips were pressed flat like a fish's. He grabbed my hair in his fist and hauled me up, back to the surface. Back to now.

Sleep or Die

Friends told us were lucky because both boys had slept through the night by the tender age of three months old. I could still recall the first night Galen slept without waking from ten P.M. to seven A.M. Katherine and I blinked at each other in the soft morning light as if we'd both emerged from separate comas, certain we'd failed to hear the baby-snatcher breaking the front window and escaping with our twelve-week-old son in his arms. When we went into his room, there he was, lips puckered and palms near his face. Two years later, Hayden squeaked in for the record at eleven weeks. It seemed we had accomplished the impossible. Twice.

Truth was, luck had little to do with it. From the beginning I'd approached the battle for sleep with the deadeye grit of a field commander. With Katherine juggling nights in the emergency room and the second year of her master's degree, and me hammering away at my doctoral thesis while teaching and editing a literary journal, our choices were clear: sleep or die. The day we brought each boy home from the hospital, we set about implementing a rigid schedule: thirty minutes of eating followed by an hour of playtime, generally consisting of the baby watching Katherine or me shower or run the vacuum, terminating in a ninety-minute nap. The cycle repeated every three hours. The goal was to get as much milk down the hatch during the feeding time and then keep the baby awake until it digested, at which point he'd be as desperate for shut-eye as a long-haul trucker. Laying the boys in their cribs, sleep took hold with such force that I could have run a table saw in the nursery. Teaching a baby to eat and sleep this way was a little like stopping for gas every hundred miles on a cross-country road trip, which is to say tedious and maybe a little overkill, but by God, it worked. After about six weeks, the boys' stomachs had expanded to the point that a full belly could carry them half the night. Six weeks later they made it the whole night, and Katherine and I rejoined the cast of *The Young and the Rested*.

I was sure I'd stumbled onto a secret others needed to know about. I tried to convert every baby-toting or pregnant adult I met to our method, though, to my honest-to-God surprise, very few moms were eager to hear a guy philosophize about the virtues of sleep scheduling. My fellow college professors, vanguards of rationality, logic, and scientific methodology turned downright hostile toward any program smacking of rigidity or routine, as though nine consecutive hours of sleep would dampen their child's creativity and future brilliance. I took the hint and yielded the pulpit, preferring instead to judge other zombie-faced parents in silence, gleefully picturing them pacing their hallways at all hours of the night while I floated on waves of bountiful, lustful, uninterrupted sleep.

In hindsight I can see how I was primed for a comeuppance.

Galen would occasionally break his cycle, wake up when he should have been asleep, and cry to be let out. If this tactic worked one time, as it often did, he expected it to work forever. The pediatrician told us it was okay to let him cry himself back to sleep; he'd tire himself out in forty-five minutes to an hour. Galen, though, had the lungs to go much longer. As long as I could get the television loud enough, I could deal with the noise, but Katherine hated hearing her baby cry. One night the crying lasted so long that she drove to the liquor store and came home with a pack of cigarettes and a box of wine. Our elderly Mormon neighbor led her dog into her yard to pee, saw Katherine smoking on the front stoop with a beer stein of Chablis by her foot while Galen's wails echoed through the front door, and called out, "Stay strong, Sister! Don't you dare go in there!" Two hours later, after nearly four hours of near-constant howling, Galen threw in the towel. The next night we were back on schedule.

Hayden was more interested in escape than protest. It was here that our troubles began.

He was two the first time he sprang himself from his crib. When I say "sprang," I mean it literally: He gripped the crib and bounced until he worked up enough height to vault the rail like a cop going over a fence in pursuit of a suspect. His bedroom was directly above the living room, so Katherine and I could hear his crib squeaking as he jumped and the ensuing thud when he landed. To lessen the threat of injury, I laid a spare mattress on the floor beside the crib to break his fall. The crash pad only encouraged him. He went over the rail backward, like a high-jumper, or headfirst with his hands at his sides. Once I caught him standing on the corner rails like a pro wrestler on the turnbuckles of a ring. "Stop!" I yelled, but Hayden shot me a wild-eyed Hulk Hogan look, and jumped.

The worst part wasn't the jump. Had Hayden leapt from his bed to play with the toys in his room, I might have let it slide. The problem was that once he was out of bed, he wanted our undivided attention. Most nights he showed up about sixty seconds after I'd poured a drink and had settled into the couch. It was only then I'd hear the ceiling creak and the dull *clonk* of his weight against the floor. We'd pause the show while one of us led Hayden back upstairs, holding his hand on the staircase because he insisted on walking himself, laying him in his crib with the satiny side of his blankie against his cheek, the way he liked it, before tip-toeing, Elmer-Fudd-hunting-wabbits-style, back downstairs.

Five minutes later, he was back.

By his first year of preschool, I was going up and down the stairs a dozen times a night. A single thirty-minute show stretched to hours. On many nights Katherine and I gave up and went to bed with eight minutes left in the episode because we were too exhausted with parental rage to finish it.

We moved Hayden out of his crib and into a big-boy bed so one of us could lie with him until he fell asleep. He knew that once he drifted off we were going to leave him, and he managed to outlast us. I lost entire evenings to lying in the dark on the edge of a twin bed the size of a locker room bench, my ankles crossed and my hand on the floor to keep me from falling off, bored and irritated as hell, hostage to a four-year-old's stubborn refusal to shut his eyes.

Something had to change.

Hayden's room was on the same floor as the other two bedrooms, but was tucked beneath the eaves of the roof overlooking the front yard. It had originally been used as an attic. Due to the pitch of the ceiling, his door opened outward, into the hallway. My first attempt at keeping him inside involved wedging his door shut with an old pair of Teva sandals, the original square-strapped model favored by hacky sackers and river guides. I'd had the sandals since college, when I briefly fancied myself a student of the footbag, and for whatever reason I'd never thrown them out. I pressed the toe beneath Hayden's door and worked the rubber back and forth to cram it into place. I got the sandals so far in that the heels lifted off the floor. At first it worked perfectly. The knob turned, but the door wouldn't budge. "Is anyone there?" Hayden called through the wood.

"It's bedtime. We'll play tomorrow."

"Don't leave me, Daddy." The knob spun left and right. I heard him panting as he pushed against the door. I backed down the stairs. I kept a pint of Italian gelato hidden in a plastic sack at the back of the freezer where no one else could find it. To the victor go the spoils.

I'm no physicist, but in theory the more Hayden pushed on the door, the more the wedge should have locked into place. I underestimated his hunger for freedom, however. He kept his shoulder pressed to the door until he'd managed to slide the shoes back a mere two inches. It turned out to be all the space he needed.

"I'm here!" he said, when he bounded downstairs. His face was red from pressing against the wood, and drenched in sweat, which I actually think worked as a kind of lube. His eyes fell to the bowl of ice cream in my lap. "Hey!" he said. "Where you'd get that?"

No matter how far I pushed the sandals beneath the door, Hayden found a way to fly the coop. A part of me suspected he was an octopus, with hydrostatic bones that could flatten to get through almost any seam. After a few months he'd worn the carpet beneath his door down to the threads, and the sandal wedge was useless. I spent an hour on YouTube learning how to secure an outward-opening door with rope. I tied a long piece of nylon cord around his doorknob, looped it around the other knobs in the hallway, then ran the whole thing back to the banister rail where I fastened it with a trucker's hitch knot. The cord was so taut it hummed when I plucked it, and the hallway looked like the laser maze in a bank-heist movie. Hayden beat it in less than two minutes. Next, I stacked laundry baskets full of clothes and books in front of the door, and when he knocked those over, I tried a toy chest. Walking through my neighborhood one day I spotted an old wood-and-velvet chair on the street, a sheaf of paper with the word FREE taped to the cushion. I carried it home precisely because it looked like I might be able to brace it against Hayden's door. It worked okay until the night I forgot to move the chair out of the hallway before going to bed. I tripped over it in the middle of the night, hitting my face on the wall and breaking two of the chair's legs. I carried it back to the curb in the morning, and by the time I came home from work, it was gone.

"How do we keep him in there?" I asked Katherine the next night. I'd given the sandals another shot, this time with a second pair beneath the first. It was at best a wad of chewing gum on a leaky pipe, and as we sat together on the couch we could hear Hayden working the doorknob, the unmistakable screech of the brass. We needed something strong to hold him in. A padlock seemed barbaric, but at this point all options were on the table.

"Why won't he go to sleep?" Katherine said. She tipped her head forward and began massaging her temples. "He's four years old. He makes English muffin pizzas and pipe-cleaner animals all day. This can't be so hard." She stood up on the coffee table and yelled at the ceiling, "Go to sleep!"

"No!" Hayden called back.

I sat thinking. No matter what I put in front of the door, Hayden found a way to move it.

He only needed an inch. Less than an inch. If he could get a finger between the door and the jamb, he could weasel his way out. I needed something that spanned the entire hallway and kept the door firmly shut. Like a refrigerator or a bank safe.

"Maybe you could get a piece of wood or something," Katherine proposed. "Like people put in the tracks of their sliding glass doors."

"It's not a bad idea," I said. That was when it hit me: the idea I still number among my most elegant parenting innovations. I had an old shower curtain rod in the basement, leftover from our bathroom renovation. It had rubber feet on both ends, so it wouldn't gouge the door or the baseboard, and an internal spring-loaded screw that allowed the rod to be shortened or extended to almost any size. I found it leaning against the back wall of the storage closet and ran upstairs with it, like Lancelot wielding his lance. I kicked out the sandals and squeezed the bar between Hayden's bedroom door and the baseboard across the hallway. It snugged perfectly into place.

Hayden ran at the door. It didn't budge an inch. "Let me out," he called.

Unable to move the door with his shoulder, Hayden lay on his floor, lifted his feet to the wood, and tried to hip-sled it open. The door inched back ever so slightly, enough for me to see Hayden's determined face, his gritted teeth and eyes narrowed to dagger points, before the rod's spring-loaded action pushed the door shut again. He pushed again, harder and faster. The shower rod began to groan like a box spring in a cheap motel; the door appeared to breathe as it pulsed open and shut. But the bar held. At last the pumping stopped, and I held my breath, waiting for it to start up again. "I'm stuck in here!" Hayden said.

"The only way out is through your dreams, kid."

"It's not fair!"

"You're right, it's not," I said.

Katherine and I were sitting on the couch, enjoying our drinks with the TV turned up loud enough to drown out the porno squeak echoing through the ceiling, when through the front window I caught sight of a woman walking her dog along the sidewalk. While the dog sniffed the grass, the woman turned and stared up at the house. It was then that I noticed several of Hayden's stuffed animals lying on the grass. A pair of green-and-orange underpants cascaded to the ground as gently as an autumn maple leaf.

I muted the TV and heard Hayden's voice above me. "I'm trapped!" he called from his window. He'd pushed out the bottom of his screen. More underwear rained down. "They put the bar in and won't let me out."

I went to the door. "It's okay," I said to the woman. "He has a hard time staying in his room."

"You use a bar to keep him in?" she asked, frowning.

"It's a shower curtain rod, actually," I said.

The woman scowled and pulled her dog, midstream, away from my lawn. I thought to call after her, "We take it out once he falls asleep!" but that sounded like a weird thing to yell to a stranger. And anyway, she was already two houses away. I hurried to gather up the drawers and dolls and carry them back inside.

Katherine had grown concerned. "This is so ridiculous," she said.

"I'm a social worker. This is the kind of thing we tell parents *never* to do. How long is this going to last?"

"Not very long," I said. I reminded her of the period when Galen got out of bedtime by throwing up. He did it at first to get attention, but he soon grew to enjoy taking three baths a night, the fresh sheets every forty-five minutes. After a few weeks, I covered his mattress and floor with towels and told him that he could barf all he wanted but no one was coming to get him. Two nights of sleeping in puke was enough to persuade him. He hadn't thrown up in bed since. In fact, Galen could sleep through almost anything, though thunderstorms and dogs barking and train whistles. Even through his brother's incessant racket.

"Now that Hayden can't get out, I'm sure he'll get the picture pretty fast," I said. "I give it a week, two at the most."

Six years later, the bar remains in use.

It's become a family secret, the fact that we have a child with adult teeth, his own iPod and library card, a ten-year-old who can stay home alone, walk unaccompanied to and from school, and bake a birthday cake with only minimal supervision, but who will not stay in his room at night without the steely encouragement of a repurposed shower curtain rod. Hayden's face grows red with embarrassment whenever the bar is mentioned, and his brother is forbidden from ever speaking about it. We've tried to do away with the thing. We've bargained for extended bedtimes, extra dessert, privileges surpassing a young boy's age and station. We've shaken hands on more deals than a used-car salesman. Once Katherine even drafted a contract and we all signed it. But as soon as the bar comes out, the old pattern returns. Hayden's downstairs ten times a night because he needs a drink of water, a Band-Aid, a cough drop, an ibuprofen; he needs to tell us about his dream, even though he hasn't been upstairs long enough to sleep; he's finished his book and needs another from the shelf in the basement; he needs a dollar for school next the day. Pretty soon we're threatening the bar again. Pretty soon we're using it.

A few years ago, Katherine and I left the boys in the care of a babysitter, one of my students from the college, so we could attend a dinner party. Arriving at the party, I handed my jacket to the host, absentmindedly leaving my phone in the pocket. When I went back for it a few hours later, I found I'd missed five calls, all from the same number. I called the babysitter in a panic, and she answered in tears. I started tugging on my jacket while I worked to calm her down. All I wanted to know: Do we need to rush home or meet you at the hospital?

"It's Hayden!" she blubbered. "He won't respect me."

"What'd he do?"

"I've put him to bed like a million times, but he keeps coming out."

"Oh," I said, relieved. I lowered my voice and told her where she could find the bar, at the back of Hayden's closet, and explained how to secure it into place. I whispered conspiratorially, "It's the only way," and crossed my fingers she wouldn't start Snapchatting pictures of the rod to her friends.

The babysitter agreed to try it, but begrudgingly. "You left me in charge," she said. "He should respect that."

"If it makes you feel any better," I said, "he's no easier for his mom and me."

"It doesn't," she said, and hung up.

Katherine looked up as I settled back into my seat at the table and asked if everything was okay. I must have reassured her too loudly because the host raised his eyebrows and asked, "Trouble at home?"

"Thing Two won't stay in bed," I said.

Thus commenced a round of raucous, wine-fueled storytelling about parental low points. The host had once spanked his now-adult son in front of his mother-in-law, after which Grandma had looked at him warily for years. Another woman's daughter had peed in her dress in front of the church during her baby sister's baptism and had to be carried, screaming and dripping, from the ceremony. Katherine looked at me and mouthed, *Don't you dare*, but of course I did. I told them all about the sandals, the rope and chair, the inspiration for the shower rod, the dog walker Hayden called to for help. I was on my third glass of wine, and I spared no detail.

I'd been yammering for a while when I stopped to take stock of the table. I was glad to see several people laughing, but down at the other end one woman—who had only daughters and at previous gatherings scowled at the boys the way Bichon Frise owners look at German Shepherds—glowered across the empty glasses, tight-lipped and stern, as though every bad thing she'd ever suspected of me had just been proven true. Katherine stared down at her napkin spread across her lap. The ride home wasn't going to be much fun.

The problem, from Katherine's point of view, was that the bar (as we have affectionately come to call it) made us look like bad parents. Impatient at best, cruel at worst. Parents were already so judgmental of one another. In her years as a social worker, especially in pediatrics and maternity, Katherine had seen a lot of women, and more than a few men, shamed by other likely well-intentioned parents for bottle- rather than breastfeeding, for co-sleeping or not co-sleeping, for letting their kids watch TV or play with balloons at a birthday party. For every decision you made as a parent, someone was waiting to tell you it was the absolute worst thing to have done and that you were morally corrupt for having done it.

Katherine didn't believe me, but I hadn't told the story of the shower rod simply to score a cheap laugh. A part of me was actually proud of the bar, not because I had thought of it or because I'd finally solved the riddle of keeping Hayden inside his room, but because of what it symbolized. So much of the talk about kids, whether about school or sports, musical aptitude or kindness toward animals, clustered around the notions of *talent* and *gifts*, as though success in life depended on a magical power descending from heaven. I understand the desire, but I don't buy it. I'll take grit over genius any day, and my son has grit to burn. He's squared off against his mother and me for most of his young life, and he hasn't once backed down. He's as stubborn as a mule, but I'll give it to him: He doesn't tire easily, and he doesn't readily admit defeat. I hope these qualities will make him strong, and that his nightly assaults against the bar are teaching him to fight—against me for now, but one day, I hope, for causes that really matter.

The babysitter waited with her purse in her lap and her backpack by the door. I paid her and drove her back to campus. At home, Katherine was on the couch with a glass of water. She wasn't ready to talk to me yet. The babysitter had, as instructed, installed the bar, and it was still in place. "That you, Dad?" Hayden called down. I heard the bar begin to squeak, its telltale protest. Hayden's refusal to go gentle into that good night. "Let me out," he called.

"I'll be up soon," I said to the ceiling, but what I wanted to say was, *Don't give up, kid. Keep fighting.*

In the Tank

I found Galen in the ready room. The meet's organizers had commandeered a multipurpose room deep in the bowels of the Green Bay YMCA where they'd shoved the exercise mats and therapy balls into a corner and hauled in a dozen wooden benches, now arranged in parallel lines from the front of the room to the back. Each bench contained a heat of the Boys 8&U twenty-five-yard freestyle. The boys sat shoulder to shoulder in their Speedos and caps and goggles, their muscleless bodies small beneath the fluorescent tubes in the ceiling, vying to see who could make the loudest fart noises. Their eyes bulged as they blew against their palms and biceps.

Galen sat stone-faced with his hands in his lap, his eyes hidden behind his goggles. I tried to take a picture, since this was his first meet, but he wouldn't smile. I laid my hand on his shoulder and could feel it trembling. "What's the matter?" I asked.

"What if I don't win?"

A woman standing in the doorway hollered, "First heat, here we go!" The front row of boys stood up and exited single file, all of a sudden solemn and silent, as though marching to certain death on a battlefield. It was a walk I'd taken many times in my life, and it never got easier. The other boys in the room moved forward a bench.

"Swim as fast as you can," I said. "Don't worry about where you finish."

Galen turned to me, his eyes bug-shaped behind his goggles. "Could I have some time alone, please?"

I felt the blood rise in my face. I was surprised, though I shouldn't have been. I never wanted anyone, especially not a parent, to talk to me when I was in the ready room. I shuffled backward. "I'll go wait on the deck," I said. I set my hand on his shoulder again, then quickly jerked it away. "Try to think of a song you like. That used to help me."

He nodded absently, shooing me away. I ambled through the doorway and into the corridor, crowded with volunteers and coaches in team apparel. The doorway to the natatorium at the end of the hallway glowed with pink and yellow light. Crossing the threshold into the pool, a vast, tiled room two-stories tall with windows encircling the upper level and an observation balcony on the far side, I felt myself travel through space and time, from Green Bay, Wisconsin, in 2012 to Houston, Texas, in 1982. Thirty years hence and fifteen-hundred miles north, the scene had hardly changed. The tiled deck was slicked and shiny with pool water; officials paced the lanes in white polos and matching trousers; coaches crowded the edges of the pool, whistling and cheering with their arms in the air. The chlorine was so thick it clung to my skin. I could taste it in the back of my throat, a not entirely unpleasant sensation. I still swam every morning and even raced now and again, but it had been many years since I'd walked the deck at a meet so resonant of my childhood, so full of children in racing suits with their event numbers inked in Magic Marker on their arms, so brimming with confusion and wonder and expectation. After a few obligatory seasons of rec-league soccer, my firstborn son had, of his volition, asked to join the aquatic fellowship to which I, as well as my father and sister, had belonged our entire lives. Dad had held several national age-group records in the early sixties and had been a serious competitor until he went to college; Devin and I had both competed for Division I university teams. Standing in the natatorium, taking it all in, waiting for my son to take his place on the blocks for his first-ever swimming race, as well as in the closest thing we had to a family heritage, I thought I might weep.

My boy can swim!

Right then, as I was lifting my hand to my eye to dam my welling tear, a woman shouted, "You!" She was broad-shouldered and boxy and wore a Green Bay YMCA T-shirt. Her sleeves were rolled into cuffs and the badge pinned across her ample breast said MEET VOLUNTEER. Jarred out of my reverie, it took me a moment to register that she was talking to me.

"Are you a coach?" she demanded, index finger pointed at my face.

My first thought: She needed my help. Someone who knew how to work a stopwatch. I'd coached and taught swimming on and off for twenty years. "Not today," I said, smiling at her. As in, *Lady, I could tell you stories.* "I'm waiting for my son to swim."

"Parents aren't allowed on the pool deck." Her flared nostrils and narrowed eyes conveyed an anger far exceeding my trespass. Nor did I think of myself as an ordinary swimming parent. I'd seen records broken, time barriers shattered. Galen's godfather, my college roommate and oldest friend, had coached in three Olympics.

"This is his first meet," I said. "I want to make sure he knows where to go."

"You need to get off the deck," she said. She pointed to the crowded viewing balcony upstairs where Katherine and Hayden had gone to stake out a spot. The bleachers were crowded, the air close with trapped chlorinated heat and two hundred parents in winter sweaters squeezed miserably close together.

"His race is up in a few minutes," I said. "As soon as he swims, I'll go."

"No," she said. "Absolutely not. Off the deck . . . *Now!*"

I managed to slow-walk my exit long enough to see Galen's heat march from the ready room to the lanes. I lingered in the doorway until I saw him stand up on the blocks. When the starter told the boys to take their marks and he bent over, he disappeared behind the crowd. I waited a few seconds more, hoping to see him dive in, but from where I stood, I couldn't see the water.

It's a cliché of American life: Youth sports, intended to instill character and camaraderie in children, bring out the worst in adults. The stories are abundant and galling and perpetually renewing. A dad in Massachusetts beat a fellow parent to death at a pickup hockey game; a mom in Virginia slapped and knocked to the ground a teenage official at her nine-year-old's soccer game; a Little League coach instructed his ten-year-old pitcher to take aim at an opposing player. My all-time favorite is Wanda Holloway, who tried to hire a hit man to rub out the mother of the girl who defeated her daughter for a spot on the junior high cheerleading squad. The story was big news for a while. I remembered her because the Holloways lived on the south side of Houston, about an hour from where I grew up.

My mother and the other parents on my swimming team speculated that Wanda Holloway was either mentally ill or utterly depraved. Yet on a deeper level, I understood that Mrs. Holloway was connected to and even in some respects produced by the same take-no-prisoners parental fury I'd seen on display at every event from Friday-night football games to peewee soccer to my own swimming meets. My mom had once cheered so hard for my sister during a race that she lost control of her pen and heat sheet and both ended up in the water. I'd also seen parents stab fingers at each other's faces. Once, when the divisional champs were on the line, a trophy contested by a whopping six teams, I watched two grown men, dads of swimmers, fist-fight in the parking lot.

It all sounds a bit absurd, and it is. The English-American novelist and transatlantic sports fan Wilfrid Sheed explains, "When a politician says he hates something viscerally—whether it's John Major on terrorism or Senator Windbag on flag-burning—one doubts his insides are much disturbed: as Dr. Johnson might say, he will eat his dinner tonight. But a sports fan who has seen a sure victory slip away in the bottom of the ninth, or the work of a whole season obliterated by a referee's call in overtime, is disconsolate beyond the power of description, although Sophocles comes close." I admit that I've walked away more calmly from debates about politics and religion than I walked away from the Nurse Ratched who yelled at me. I was so hot with rage that before I could return to Katherine and the boys, I had to step outside into the winter air to cool down.

The YMCA stood at the center of downtown Green Bay, two blocks east of the Fox River, which bisected the city as it flowed into Lake Michigan. Commissioned and built in the twenties, the building still proudly displayed its gabled dormers and pointed rooflines. Close one eye, and it looked a little like the Dakota building in New York where John Lennon and Yoko Ono chatted each other up while sitting on the toilet. The Green Bay Y was a testament to the optimism and prosperity that once streamed through the city—a busy port with access via the Saint Lawrence Seaway to the Atlantic Ocean and the world, and home to several major paper, meatpacking, and manufacturing companies. These days, of course, Green Bay was most famous for its NFL team, which, given the city's size and economy, it ought not to have had.

The parade of football team paraphernalia, from the standard-issue sweatshirts and iconic foam cheeseheads to the bumper stickers and toy flags affixed to car windows, was likely nowhere more ensconced in the local culture than in Wisconsin. Fire hydrants were painted green and gold, and on game days everyone from the supermarket baggers to clergy dressed in jerseys. When Katherine and I were looking at houses, we toured several proudly featuring wall-to-wall Packers carpet and displaying mantles crowded with annual family portraits, taken by professional photographers, in which everyone in the shot, including the infant, Grandma, and the dog, proudly showed off the Big G. But the garb was much more than a display of pride and love for the team; I often read it as performance of loyalty, as if Wisconsinites needed to prove that what they lacked in market size they made up for in zeal. As if they knew an awful truth: If tradition were to buckle to the colder logic of capitalism and the team were to relocate to a more populated city where it could jack up ticket prices, the city of Green Bay, as well as any remnant of the industrial prowess signified by Lambeau Field towering over the squat city skyline, would die.

Our city, Appleton, was only a half hour to the south. It shared Green Bay's area code, congressional district, and local news channels. Visiting NFL teams stayed in Appleton whenever they came to town. The two cities were in many ways twin communities, rooted in the same German-Scandinavian culture, subject to the same weather, struggling against the same economic hardships. After six years in Wisconsin, I'd developed a sentimental affection for the Northwoods, the Great Lakes' jigsawed shoreline, the opalescent summer light. But I also battled a misgiving roiling around in my gut whenever I drove past the empty downtown storefronts and the parade of chain restaurants crowded near the highway.

Standing in the icy mist, my breath steaming around my face, it occurred to me that I was all alone on the street. No cars drove past. No pedestrians strolled along the street. The downtown city center was as deserted on an ordinary Saturday in late January as Christmas morning. It was possible, I thought, to love a place and hope your children will leave it.

If the Packers symbolized Wisconsin's enduring ability to compete in a rapidly changing world, it stood to reason that youth sports likewise symbolized a kid's ability to compete in life. Parents learned, by the same cultural osmosis that taught boys to swear and girls to gossip, to go on the offensive for their children, to make sure the system worked in their favor, that they had the shot we'd dreamed of for them. It was natural for parents to want our kids to stand out, if for no other reason than because we feared they'd be left behind. Such an impulse seemed enhanced by living in a city that itself felt left behind.

I didn't personally know any moms or dads who banked on their children becoming professional athletes, but almost every parent I knew whose kids played sports with any kind of intensity or talent talked about college. Some hoped their son's or daughter's athletic accomplishments would help pay the tuition; others only wanted sports to help them get in. In *The Game of Life*, sociologists James Shulman and William Bowen point out that college admissions have become increasingly competitive in the last several decades, especially as "career advancement in our knowledge-based economy has increased the premium that prospective employers, and consequently applicants, place on attending a school with an impressive reputation." As application numbers climbed, Shulman and Bowen note, admissions offices became more interested in students with distinctive qualifications and specialized talents—like, say, music, or computers, or sports. And as sports culture grew in America, vastly outpacing both music and computers, athletics proved an ever-greater advantage when it came to getting a big envelope in the mail. Despite the perennial claim by a mildly acned but still well-rounded white student that a black or Latino kid "took his spot" at his first-choice school, the chances were much greater that the "spot" went to an athlete. And yet, though athletics might help with admissions, the chances of getting a scholarship remained tiny—by most estimates, only one to two percent.

I was a product of this very system and a member of that statistically exclusive fraternity that paid for my undergraduate education in muscle and sweat. Earning a scholarship did not seem particularly special when I was in high school largely because the opportunity was in no way unique to me. I swam for large club teams in Houston and Orange County, California, large urban metropolitan areas replete with large clubs, and nearly all the swimmers were recruited by some university somewhere. I was neither a star nor the fastest swimmer. But *not* receiving a scholarship offer would have felt like a failure, and when the offer finally came, I remember feeling, more than anything else, a great rush of relief.

In addition to the financial incentive, swimming in college afforded all the benefits one hears about: paid tutors, supplemental study tables, advocacy from the athletics department staff when my schedules conflicted, a haul of emblazoned apparel, and at least a dozen friends with whom I remained close after twenty years. Any one of them would get on a plane if I asked them to, and I'd do the same. Swimming allowed me to earn an undergraduate degree without accruing a nickel's worth of debt, and for that I was grateful. But it wasn't without its costs. For close to a decade, including all of high school and college, I swam four hours a day, six days a week, fifty weeks a year. I didn't study abroad, for a semester away from the pool would have irrevocably disrupted my training; I didn't pursue internships or join clubs or write for the campus newspaper because I didn't have the time. I lived five miles from the beach, and yet went weeks and even months without seeing the ocean. Some days I swam for more hours than I slept, and God only knows how many wild nights and epic misadventures I missed, how many one-in-the-morning pizza runs or jaunts to Vegas or late-night bullshit sessions, how many love affairs I passed up because I had to wake up at five the next morning to swim.

Now Galen was on the cusp of this world, and I couldn't help wondering whether it had all been worth it. Though swimming remained my daily habit and a major component of how I thought about myself, I didn't come to really love the sport until my competitive days were finished. Throughout most of college, in fact, I dreaded the water, the constant fatigue I felt in my bones and joints, the twice-daily grind that lasted forever and granted too little reprieve in between, the long streak of races where I had my ass handed to me by everyone I went up against, my pride in my throat like an apple in the mouth of a luau pig. I used to dream of quitting and envied those who had the courage to tell our coach to his face what we all said behind his back before throwing their goggles on the deck and walking away. My dad even told me I *should* quit if I was so unhappy; we'd sort out the tuition another way. But I couldn't let myself, and I could never quite say why. I was stubborn, I suppose, but more than that I was afraid of what quitting would say about me. I imagined all my coaches, my friends, my parents' neighbors all shaking their heads when they heard I couldn't cut it. The release I felt when I touched the wall at the end of my last race—tellingly, my last race was the mile, the longest and most grueling of the lineup—far surpassed the relief of landing the scholarship in the first place. I hugged my coach for the first and only time, and, still panting and radish-red from scalp to toes, I chugged two beers in the shower before I bothered to rub shampoo through my hair. The late afternoon light over the Pacific, a hundred yards beyond the natatorium, was stunningly bright. I felt like I was seeing it for the first time.

The freestyle had finished and the breaststroke was underway. A line of hairless bodies was frog-stroking down the pool, their mouths breaking the surface with each stroke for a gulp of air. Intent on seeing Galen swim at least one race, I slipped down a back flight of stairs and came through a door at the far end of the pool deck.

I found an empty rectangle of wall beside another dad. He wore an Australian outback hat, a team T-shirt, and a stopwatch around his neck. He wasn't a coach, but he passed for one and no one bothered him (note to self). I asked to see his heat sheet so I could figure out Galen's heat and lane. The folded sheet in his hand was heavily annotated with splits and finish times, for his three daughters as well as the other kids on the team. "You're staying busy," I said.

He shrugged. "What time is your boy going for?"

"It's his first meet," I said. "I just wanted him to get some experience."

"The time he clocks here will set the standard for the season," he said.

I tried to remember a single one of my swimming times from when I was eight and was grateful that I couldn't.

He nodded and looked across the pool. "Looks like he's up."

I could see Galen's blue cap and goggles, his lanky alabaster chest. The starter announced the race, and the boys mounted the metal step and balanced atop the blocks. The starter told the boys to take their marks, waited for them to bend forward and grip the rail, and then sounded the horn before any got the shakes that would inevitably result in a false start. Bend, grip, launch. For a few seconds, as the boys glided underwater, the water was glassy and still and the natatorium was cocooned inside a dome of chlorinated silence. Galen came up first, ahead of the field. His shoulders were down and his hips were low, but he glided like a twig on a string. I couldn't help myself. I cupped my hands around my mouth and yelled his name. "Come on, Galen!" I yelled. "Go!" I waited for the other boys to catch him, but instead he pulled farther ahead, and watching him, I felt a flutter of the old, adrenaline-spiked thrill that racing produces, only now magnified by the incredible and contradictory fact that the swimmer in the water wasn't a teammate but *my son*. The body in the water was the same body I'd held afloat in a basin an hour after his birth. I set my hands on my knees and whooped him all the way to the wall.

He won. No other boy even got close.

"Good swim," the other dad said to me.

"He did all right," I said, grinning. I stopped short of punching the guy in the arm.

Galen climbed out of the water, and the time runner handed him a blue heat winner's ribbon, the same size and thickness as a bookmark, and a fun-sized pack of Famous Amos cookies, because nothing says you're a winner like a pouch full of sugar. The boys in the heats to come would all post faster times, but for the moment he was the victor, alone under the lights. His mom and brother beamed down from the balcony. "Good job!" I said. I held up my hand for him to slap. "Way to go!"

Crocodile Dundee flipped the pages of his heat sheet and said, "You know, that time was a state cut. He just earned an invitation to the big dance." He pursed his lips and nodded, delighted to convey this information.

I'd heard some of the other parents talking about the state championship, a three-day invitational in Milwaukee. A long way to go for a twenty-second race, though I had friends who'd flown across oceans for shorter swims.

"I did?" Galen said, all teeth and golly-gee. Apparently he'd heard about the state champs, too. He peeled off his cap and goggles and handed them to me. "Do I get to go, Dad?"

I could see my future. I wasn't ready, and at the same time I was so tingly with pride I could hardly contain myself. The textbook definition of ambivalent. Galen's excitement flowed like a mighty river. The gravity alone could have carved a hole in my chest.

"Of course," I said. I set my hand on his wet head. "We wouldn't miss it for the world."

Sh*t Kids Say

Katherine and I were in the kitchen on a chilly Saturday afternoon in April when we heard Hayden say it. The word slithered off his tongue.

"Give me the remote control, you *ass*."

Katherine had been chopping onions and leeks on the cutting board, sliding the bits into the pot on the stove. I was peeling potatoes at the sink. The word breezed through the kitchen, and Katherine's knife paused in midair. She canted an ear toward the living room but turned her eyes toward me. Her dark eyebrows disappeared beneath the curtain of her bangs. "Did he say what I think he said?" she asked.

I'd known the echoes of our house to warp sounds as they ricocheted off the hardwood and turned the corner from the other rooms. Some noises, like sitcom laugh tracks and the voice of Special Agent Oso came through vexingly undistorted, while others disappeared into the static waves of the house. The boys' voices were smack in the center of the spectrum, always audible but often confused, and I'd been known to hear things they hadn't actually said. The cauldron of water on the stove didn't help, either.

It sounded like Hayden, but I couldn't be sure.

Hayden saved us the trouble of having to guess. "Give it here, you ass," he said.

Katherine laid her knife on the board and dried her hands on the dish towel before methodically draping it over the edge of the sink. She moved with great deliberation from the sink, past the stove, into the hallway. "Come in here," she called. "Right now."

Hayden moseyed around the corner. He was five years old, his dirty blond hair was overdue for a haircut, and he was naked except for his *Transformers* underpants, which he wore backward, the fly a kind of thong between his plump cheeks. The outfit, or lack of one, was one of the contradictions of child-rearing every parent sooner or later encountered: the refusal to dress for the weather. So long as the mercury hovered below thirty, Hayden wouldn't wear clothes. As soon as hot weather hit, he'd suddenly discover his drawer of sweaters. On the sultriest nights, when I showered before bed to feel the cold water against my skin, I'd find Hayden asleep in a woolen turtleneck and fleece pants, sweating like a wrestler trying to drop weight before a match. And despite our persistent arguments that undies were most comfortable when worn the right way, he insisted on wearing them backward. He cared less about comfort than seeing Optimus Prime flexing his metallurgic muscles across the seat.

Hayden's thumb plugged his mouth, and he was blithely dismissive of his mother's tone and not in the slightest bit worried about the consequences for swearing. In all fairness, I didn't expect the punishment to be great. Let's be honest: Few things are funnier than profanity in the mouths of babes.

Katherine dropped to a knee. "We don't use that word," she said.

"What word?" he asked.

"The bad word you used."

"Which one?"

"You know which one." Katherine had been fighting hard to keep it together, but eye contact and the sweet breath of her baby made it nearly impossible not to laugh. She stood and turned toward the coffee pot.

I tried to play it straight. "See what bad words do?" I asked. "They make Mom cry."

Hayden slid his thumb back inside his mouth. "It doesn't look like she's crying," he said, his lips like a camel's around his wrinkled thumb. Katherine leaned her forehead against the cupboard, her shoulders shaking.

"Say you're sorry," I said.

He extracted his thumb and bared his baby teeth. Braces were a future expense to which I was already resigned. "I'm not sorry," he said. "Galen sucks. He's a big, big ass."

Katherine turned around, cheeks and forehead pomegranate-colored and moist with steam from the stock pot roiling on the stove. "Who taught you those words?" she demanded. I crossed my arms and tried to play the part of silent backup. Mom lays down the law, and Dad brings the muscle. It was a posture I succeeded in holding for only a few seconds before I realized Katherine wasn't waiting for Hayden's answer. She wasn't even looking at him. Her gaze was aimed at me.

I'd loved swear words for as long as I'd been able to talk. Any word deemed inappropriate for public voice felt imbued with magical properties that gave it a special place in the lexicon. But words themselves had long been a source of wonder. I could remember standing in my backyard when I was maybe seven or eight marveling over the word *shovel*. The more I said *shovel* aloud, the more it began to sound strange. Say *shovel* slowly and it sounds like a grunt; yell it and it sounds like an insult. A *dig*. When I discovered a cottonmouth coiled on the back patio, my dad used the long-handled spade to separate the snake's head from its body in a single, searing blow. Well into adulthood, the word and the tool both retained an air of danger and violence.

Swear words I found even more fascinating. They were the scantily clad dancers gyrating in the shadows behind the lead singer, all flesh and titillation and slander, the very things I ought not to have noticed and therefore ogled with my mouth hanging open. They were language candy: nutritionally worthless, an embarrassment when you pulled one out of your lunch box, and yet so sweet on your lips.

As my parents' marriage careened toward its ultimate demise, swearing in my family, especially among my uncles and grandfather, became a kind of Dadaistic performance art, the exhibition of bluster mixed with the spontaneous eruption of rage. My uncles could barely utter whole words without pausing to swear. They were fond of *unbe-fuckin'-lievable*, while my stepdad, once he came on the scene, introduced *guaran-damn-tee* to the batting order. My grandfather, a longtime Disney fan, favored *Mickey fuckin' Mouse*. My mom's divorce lawyer was Mickey fuckin' Mouse; the television was Mickey fuckin' Mouse (or else the fucking boob tube); the placement of the pin on the seventh green was Mickey fuckin' Mouse. My father usually earned a double: Fuckin' Mickey fuckin' Mouse.

By the time Dad moved to California, he'd done his best to make his life new again. My stepmom, a former evangelical missionary, saw the move to California, where she'd grown up, as an opportunity to return to the ministry. Within months of their arrival, she became the children's pastor of a small church in Laguna Beach; a year later, she moved to a much larger congregation in Laguna Hills, a few miles inland. She rarely if ever swore and relied on antiquated words like *cross* and *shoot fire* to see her through the rough patches. She once, in anger, used the word *shit* in a restaurant in Tijuana, where we'd gone for the day. If I needed further proof that the border city was a den of iniquities, that pretty much iced it.

My dad wore a cross beside the gold initials charm on the chain around his neck and prayed with his eyes closed before every meal. He swore much less than before, and rarely in my stepmother's presence. It was different when we were alone. In the ocean or sealed up inside his car on the freeway, language could roam wherever it pleased. We talked about school and swimming, but also about the divorce and the nasty things the family in Texas still said about him. On occasion he'd release a torrent of swear words intended to make me laugh as well as to remind me that despite all the slander from back home, the miles between us and his newfound faith, he was still him. Swear words thus became a language of trust, a kind of Boolean algorithm for intimacy: If I could use without reprisal language that would get me in trouble elsewhere, then I could safely admit to those parts of myself that I felt uncertain about or embarrassed by—which, at thirteen and fourteen and fifteen, included pretty much everything. If Dad swore, then it meant he was telling the truth. If I could handle the conversation's language, in other words, then I could also handle its content.

As a result, I never lied to my father as an adolescent, and I believe he didn't lie to me, either. To this day, there's a part of me that continues to view swear words as litmus tests for truth-telling, even if I also recognize that such a test is vulnerable to false positives.

It was entirely possible, as Katherine assumed, that the boys learned to swear from me. Maybe it was the night I recounted an argument at work, believing the boys were in bed when they were huddled together on the staircase. But no word, obscene or otherwise, springs from a single source; like the flu, they're transmitted by doorknobs and countertops. Chances were greater that an older kid on the playground first passed the words to Galen, who infected his little brother, who spread them around his kindergarten class until his teacher, a few weeks after the episode in the kitchen, called us at home.

"The first time Hayden used the F-word, I tried to laugh it off," the teacher said. "None of the kids knew what it meant anyway. But now the other children are asking me to explain it."

"He used that word in school?" Katherine asked. Her face was once again turning red.

"I'm afraid so," the teacher said.

The week before, Hayden had fallen asleep while riding in the shopping cart. Today his teacher was calling to tell us he said *fuck* in class. It was a contradiction I couldn't reconcile.

"Thanks for letting us know," Katherine said. "We'll take care of it." She pointed at me. *You take care of it.*

Hayden perceived the seriousness of the moment by the look on my face when I appeared in his bedroom door. Or else he'd figured out on his own that saying *fuck* in kindergarten would eventually come back to bite him in his backward-underwear-clad butt. Either way, he didn't resist. I held out my hand, and he took it, sliding from his mattress to the carpet and walking beside me to the bathroom like a condemned man on his way to the gallows. I flipped on the light and sat down on the toilet lid. Hayden cupped his hand over the coping of the pedestal sink. He waited for me to make the first move. The bar of Irish Spring lay on its grated tray on the corner of the bathtub, unused since the morning and dried out by the heat from the furnace. I bounced the bar of soap in my palm. "If you won't stop saying bad words," I said, "I'm going to have to wash out your mouth. Do you think it tastes good?"

He slid his thumb into his mouth and shrugged.

"Taste it," I said. I held the bar close to his mouth.

His chin doubled as his eyes turned to saucers. "You first."

I raised the bar to my nose and gave it a good sniff. It smelled almost minty. How bad could it really taste? I dragged my tongue across the slightly rippled arch. It was much worse than I imagined, bitter and obliterating. I tossed the bar into the tub and dove for the faucet, running the water at full blast.

"Yucky," I said to Hayden, sticking out my tongue. "No good."

I dried my chin on the towel, collected the bar, and held it out to him. "Your turn."

"No way," he said. He turned and bolted for the staircase. I could hear him screaming all the way up the stairs, "No way, no way, no way."

"No more swear words," I called after him. I leaned over the sink to further flush the soap from my taste buds. I squeezed a huge glob of toothpaste onto my brush and worked up a mouth full of minty foam and swabbed my tongue until I about gagged. I caught my reflection in the mirror, the goatee of white on my chin elongating and detaching and splattering against the basin. The absurdity of my condition was a lesson I'd been trying to laugh off instead of learn. Regardless of where Hayden had learned to swear, the swearing needed to stop, and not only from him. I needed to watch my big mouth.

Katherine stood in the kitchen with her arms crossed, leaning against the counter in the corner between the dishwasher and the toaster. The spot, I'd learned over the years, had a number of advantages, including clear views of both the back door and the doorway to the hall and quick access to the block of knives. Katherine looked a little like a boxer in the corner of a ring waiting for the ding of the bell. "I can't believe he said that," she said. "At *school*."

"Well," I said.

"Well, what?" she said. An entire argument took place within those three words.

A teacher calling Mom and Dad was always a cause for alarm. I remembered the times a teacher called my mother (and once, after I forged my mother's signature on a disciplinary report, my dad at his office) and the sheer terror they incited in me. Thirty years later, the teacher calling home still produced a sinking feeling in both Katherine and me, as though we were the ones in trouble. Over the last several years, as Galen moved from kindergarten through first and second grades, teachers had called at least a few times a year to discuss incidents of bad behavior in class. Dead Santa had been only the beginning. In nearly every case, the incidents—running the gamut from minor infractions like talking too much at the craft table to major offenses like throwing wood chips on the playground—had provided a pretext for hinting (always a hint, never a direct hypothesis) that Galen's outbursts and impertinence were signs of ADHD, a diagnosis I resisted tooth and nail. Galen was a young boy, I countered, squirrely and Irish and emotional. I was so much the same way that my eighth-grade English teacher bought me a poster of Taz, the Tasmanian Devil in *Looney Tunes*, because she said it reminded her of me. I'd outgrown it, sort of, and I believed Galen would, too. Youthful, boyish energy was not a disorder.

Disorder was a word I'd gnawed on quite a bit, in anger and in fear. The word contained the stigma it projected, and to be saddled with a disorder meant talk of separate classes and special schools, medications and therapies, a limit to what could be expected of and hoped for him. That was the problem with language: It had the power to both define and confine us. By using ugly words, the boys exposed themselves to having the same ugliness used against them. The days I picked up the boys from school, I watched the other parents and wondered what they'd heard. Would another kindergartner point at Hayden and finger him as the bad apple? As much as I told myself that I didn't give a lick what people thought, the truth was that I wanted to protect the boys from judgment and negative opinion. In my secret fantasies, they'd one day run for office—hell, maybe even president—as crusaders for justice and fairness and universal health care. I wanted to ensure that no amount of opposition research would turn up anything against them. The world would see them as the good people I already knew them to be.

It would be several years before the *Washington Post* released the *Access Hollywood* tapes of Donald Trump bragging to Billy Bush about grabbing women by the pussy (though the conversation itself had, by that time, taken place years earlier). When the recordings did surface, I was struck by Trump's characterization of the lewd language as "locker room banter": the kind of randy, not-fit-for-public talk that takes place among men, especially young men, when they're sequestered from women. The pleasure of locker room banter was in saying the very things one wasn't supposed to say in mixed company. The pleasure was its *badness*. It wasn't so unlike my conversations in the car with my dad.

Trump was hardly the first public figure caught on tape saying awful things, and long before the recordings came to light, I understood that the line between run-of-the-mill, back-of-the-garage swear words and the language of misogyny and homophobia and prejudice was exceedingly thin. Around the time Hayden's teacher called us, I'd seen a sign for sale at the supermarket, in a rack of discounted party decorations left over from the last Super Bowl. The plastic sign had been molded to looked like a riveted steel plate, reminiscent of a MEN WORKING sign. Only this one read, MAN CAVE: NOT MUCH THINKIN', JUST A WHOLE LOT OF DRINKIN'. My first thought had been, *Who in their right mind would hang such a thing in his house?* Now, searching for a way to put the kibosh on the kids' swearing, I thought something else. Masculinity didn't have to be violent to be toxic. It needed only to be thoughtless.

I considered the usual tricks, like a swear jar. The boys didn't have any money, so a swear jar would likely have ended up costing me more than it punished them. For a while, an overheard swear word was an automatic ticket to walking the dog, which made our poor little beagle a pawn in a conflict she had nothing to do with and doomed her to getting hauled around the block by an enraged grade-schooler muttering that his piece-of-shit suck-ass brother was the true criminal while he'd been acting in self-defense. Hayden thankfully swore less at school, but every neighbor on our block likely heard him speak in a manner unbecoming of a kindergartner.

Near the end of May, we were driving to a wedding in Saint Paul, Minnesota. After four hours in the car, I could feel the boys growing amped in the back seat, whispering "sucks" and "balls" under their breath, their language steadily creeping toward the gutter. This time, instead of trying to stop the swearing, I decided to let it out. I turned off the radio. "See that bridge up there?" I said. "That's the state border. You can swear until we're across."

"We can say anything we want?" Galen asked. "Anything at all?"

"Only as long as we're on the bridge," I said. "It stops once we're on the other side. Got it?" In the rearview, the boys nodded and grinned.

The car cleared the trees. Below us was Lake Saint Croix, blue and gleaming and dotted with boats. "Fire at will."

Galen leaned forward and shouted, almost right in my ear. "Fucking asshole!"

I swerved hard toward the suspension cables but managed to pull the car back to center. Galen was slapping his knee, his eyes squeezed tight.

"Does it always have to be *that* word?" Katherine asked, her head against the window.

"Shit nuts," Hayden said.

"Buttohmygoddamn!" Galen howled.

"Sexy!" Hayden said.

"Sexy?" I said. Our eyes met in the mirror.

"You're sexy, Dad." The look on his face said the word wasn't a compliment.

This was how their swearing had been all along: compliments turned into insults, the profane spliced together with the banal. Their cursing was an experiment in the ways language—and the thoughts that preceded words—could be bent and repurposed. Swear words, if nothing else, had volume; say one aloud and someone, somewhere, would take notice. The boys were figuring out which words were polite and which words rose up against the manners that made us too compliant, too willing to do what we're told, too willing to accept the world the way it was rather than how it might or ought to be. Some things in life were obscene enough to warrant protest. And because we were in the car, I also hoped they'd learn the same lesson that I had years before: There was nothing they couldn't say to me. A broken heart, a lost job, a run-in with the police, not to mention all the worse things I tried not to imagine. I wanted to be the one they talked to, no matter what they had to tell me.

A hundred yards before the bridge ran out, Hayden swallowed hard enough to squeak in one more. "Holy crab cakes!" he shouted. He pumped his fist, as though *this* were the phrase he'd been waiting all day to say, the brass ring on the swearing carousel. The fact that "holy crab cakes" wasn't actually a swear word didn't matter. I'd given him a chance to speak.

He and Galen sat back against their booster seats. The river swept along beneath us. Katherine said, "Now that that's done, how about some goddamned music?" The boys squealed, and a few seconds later we crossed into Minnesota, a car full of outlaws.

For Sale by Owner

Katherine's parents, Paul and Laura, came to Wisconsin for Easter. Paul was a high school principal in Salt Lake City, and because the Easter holiday coincided with his spring break, they decided to stay with us for the entire week. The boys were thrilled. As the only grandchildren on Katherine's side, Papa and Nana visited with the expressed intention of granting the boys' every wish and whim. A few years earlier, I'd woken up to find Galen eating a bowl of peanut M&M's with a spoon.

The sing-along movie franchise *High School Musical* had been filmed at Paul's high school, which made my father-in-law, as principal, sort of like the Wizard of Oz. Families on cross-country road trips exited the interstate to visit the school. Driving past the campus, we'd often see groups of girls in East High T-shirts twirling on the wide concrete plaza outside the main entrance. There was something undeniably sweet and *so Utah* about seeing groups of teens and tweens dancing in front of a high school—a place I was more inclined to associate with suffering and despair than the impulse to break out into song.

Since moving to Wisconsin, we'd returned to Utah only a few times, despite the many friends and extended family that still lived there. Our absence owed something to the expense of four round-trip tickets and the staggering amount of freight needed to transport small children. Car seats, car seat bases, strollers, portable cribs, duffel bags stuffed with enough diapers and wipes and Cheerios and books and toys to endure a nuclear winter. The trip from baggage claim to the car alone was a Sisyphean trudge. So Katherine's parents visited four times a year. When I'd first welcomed Paul to our new house, extending my hand across the threshold and saying, "*Mi casa es su casa*," I had no idea he'd take it literally.

Katherine and I had learned that when her parents started hinting about flying out to see us, we needed to provide the smallest possible window of availability. Whatever dates we gave, her dad punched into Orbitz and clicked on the "+/– 3 days" box in the hope of finding a slightly lower fare. Thanks to the crack team of coders at Orbitz, a long weekend of egg-dyeing and brunching became eight days of close quarters with the boys so hopped up on sugar their eyes spun in opposite directions. Ten inches of fresh, wet snow only added to the Donner Party atmosphere.

"I saw that YMCA of yours is sponsoring a 5K run on Father's Day," Paul said a few days into the visit. He sat in the chair by the picture window while Katherine, both boys, and Laura sat cheek by jowl on the couch. I sat on the rug beside the coffee table, crisscross applesauce like a kindergartner. Our refrigerator was chockablock with magnums of chardonnay and six-packs of Mike's Hard Lemonade, the only alcoholic beverage Paul liked, while our one bathroom overflowed with the econo-sized shampoo and conditioner bottles Laura never left home without, her curling iron and hair dryer still plugged into the sockets and teetering over the edge of the pedestal sink, our medicine cabinet spilling out with makeup pouches and hairspray and prescription bottles. Last night I'd gone to brush my teeth and had discovered my father-in-law's still-moist toothbrush lying bristles to bristles against mine.

"Are you thinking about running a 5K?" Katherine asked her dad.

"More than thinking about it," Paul said. "I signed up for it. It'll give me a reason to get in shape."

"So, you're coming back in June?" Katherine asked. I could see the alarm in her face.

"Well, I can't do the run if I'm not here, can I?"

"Don't worry," Laura said. The knitting needles in her hands moved with hummingbird rapidity. She rarely went anywhere without them, including the Life Flight helicopter and airplane when she worked as a transport nurse. She was the only person I knew who could knit a pair of socks at three-thousand feet, drop the needles and yarn into her tote bag in order to intubate a premature infant born to the fifth wife of a polygamist in a rural desert clinic, and then pick up where she left off without so much as a kink in the pattern. "We're still coming back in July," Laura said. "For vacation."

"June *and* July?" Katherine asked.

"The Father's Day run will only be a long weekend," Paul said. "I'll look at flights as soon as we get home." He pressed a fresh bottle of Mike's into the skin beneath his elbow and twisted off the cap.

"Yay!" the boys said, leaping from the couch. "I love it when Nana and Papa are here!"

Nana and Papa beamed. Katherine looked at me, on the cusp of panic. I hugged my knees close to my chest and tried, unsuccessfully, not to rock back and forth.

Lying in bed that night, Katherine said, "We can't go on like this."

"They're your parents," I said. "Short of a suicide pact, I'm not sure what we can do."

She rolled to her side and leaned up on her elbow. The moonlight through the drapes shined in the whites of her eyes. "As tempting as that sounds, I was thinking we should look for a larger house."

"Oh," I said. "That could help, too."

We'd bought our house the summer we moved to Wisconsin, insistent after years of living upstairs from an assortment of drug addicts, small-time criminals, and young Mormon couples on the verge of a nervous breakdown that we'd never rent again. Our house had been built in 1947 with people like us in mind: first-time buyers with expanding families. Two doors down lived a woman in her nineties, Lorraine, who'd been one of the street's original inhabitants. She'd first stepped through her front door before the silver maples canopying the road had even been planted. Don and Joan had arrived in the mid-fifties and were, according to Lorraine, "still kids." Whoever had owned our place in the seventies had converted the attic into bedrooms and added a half bath, doubling the living space to almost 1,500 square feet. Tiny by contemporary standards but palatial compared to the hovels Katherine and I had rented as students. In our seven years of occupancy, we'd done a fair bit of our own work to the place, tearing out the pet-stained carpet and cracked bathroom tile, replacing the siding and windows, and painting every room from the master bedroom to the basement. But as the boys had grown, the house had begun to feel as though we were wearing it around our shoulders. Even when my in-laws weren't in town, the four of us battled for the one shower. I fell down the basement stairs carrying a basket of laundry because the steps were so crowded with jackets and shoes. If more than three people visited, the living room became standing room only.

"It would be nice if we had a room for us and a room where the kids could watch TV," I said. "Like a living room and a den."

"A kitchen with some counter space," Katherine said. She rolled onto her back and wiggled her fingers in the silver light above her nose. "Imagine it."

I'd recently earned tenure at the college and negotiated a small pay raise. Katherine's salary had increased some, too. I imagined a house with two full stories, a foyer with a Persian rug and an antique gilded mirror, a dining room large enough for a dinner party. A proper room for guests.

"With a guest bathroom," Katherine added. "My God."

We started trolling the real estate websites, visiting open houses and setting up appointments with realtors. Clicking around on Zillow, I zoomed in on a street I liked and saw a house listed under the heading, "Make Me Move." It wasn't officially on the market, but it could be if the price was right. The asking price was within our range, so I messaged the owner. He invited us over that night. Katherine and I wandered the rooms with a giddy sense of awe. The house was fifty percent larger than ours, every bedroom had a walk-in closet, the massive kitchen was brand-new, and—cue the church choir— not two but *three* full bathrooms, the third adjoining a guest suite so private I'd never again listen to an overnight guest move his bowels while I sipped my coffee.

Katherine yanked my earlobe. "We are buying this house," she said. "We're buying it tonight."

We went home and made an offer. Twenty-four hours later, the owners accepted. The terms were agreeable. All we had to do was sell our house.

By Monday we'd spoken with a real estate attorney and put our house on the market. Since we'd bought our place with no money down, at the peak of the housing bubble when banks and brokers were handing out mortgages like lollipops, we needed to get the best price we could in order to secure the loan on the new place. We decided to sell by owner to save on the realtor's commissions. In a city the size of ours, good houses went fast and by word of mouth. We totaled up the home's purchase price, added our improvements, and came up with a number the attorney agreed was reasonable. We knew we wouldn't make back all the cash we'd put in and that was okay. Making money wasn't the goal; we only wanted to go forward.

The day the house hit Zillow and various other FSBO sites, we received a call from a potential buyer. She was in her mid-fifties, a nurse like Katherine's mom. She'd been renting since her divorce a few years earlier but was ready to own again. "Is the house still available?" she asked on the phone.

"We just listed it," I said.

"I've had three other offers fall through already," she said. "I liked your pictures. I don't want to lose it."

"Well, come take a look," I said. This could be easier than I thought.

She moved through the rooms with her hands clasped tight to her chest, resisting the impulse to touch the walls. I showed her the windows we'd replaced, the hardwood floors we'd exposed and sanded and refinished. "It's beautiful," she said. "Absolutely gorgeous."

Katherine nudged me with her elbow and mouthed, *Bingo*.

The nurse called us that night. In her voice, I heard the same dreamy enthusiasm for our house as I had for the house we were trying to buy. She wanted to move in as much as I wanted to move out. This was how home buying ought to work—less a business transaction conducted by brokers arguing over cell phones and more of an exchange of stewardship, of care for the places that made life possible. Our house had sheltered us through seven winters, had received us on good days and bad, had provided the floor where Hayden learned to crawl and walk, the driveway where Galen taught himself to ride a bike, the kitchen where we cooked our first Thanksgiving dinner in Wisconsin, when we knew not a soul in town. I wanted the next owner to see the house as more than a place to sleep and eat and store her clothes, but a locus for her life.

The nurse's offer was below our asking price, but it was a solid starting point. We countered in the middle, and she asked for a few days to think it over. No problem, we said. The house had been on the market for five days.

The nurse called on Monday. We were eating dinner in the kitchen. All four of us looked up from our plates when the phone rang. This was it; this was the day we sold our house, the day we started moving on up. Katherine walked away with the phone into the dining room and closed the glass door to separate her conversation from the din and clamor of the house. I could see her from my chair at the kitchen table, her voice muted but her face in plain view. She glanced my way, and I gave her a thumbs-up. She propped her head on her knuckles, and I watched the excitement on her face descend into disappointment. She stood up and opened the door. "No, of course," I heard her say. "You shouldn't rush into it. It's a big decision." She hung up and returned to her place. Her face told me everything I needed to know.

"We'll get other offers," I said. "She was the first one to see it. It's only been a week."

It was early April, the crocuses only now pushing up through the snow crust. The market, we'd been told, heated up during the warmer months. Our offer on the new house didn't expire until the first of July. There was plenty of time.

For the next three months, we welcomed strangers into our bedrooms, invited them to peek inside our closets, inspect our drawers and cupboards. We kept our family pictures boxed up, our refrigerator free of magnets. We shook hands with single mothers and young couples on the cusp of childbearing. I noted the other kids on the street, the big park seven blocks away. More than once we heard a buyer whisper, "This could be the one."

Yet the offers didn't come. In May, we dropped the price and I called everyone who'd come to see the house to let them know. I called several realtors, too, to ask if they had any clients looking for a house like ours. We'd pay a commission, I offered, if they found us a buyer. A few promised to get back to me, but none did. By June, we'd paid for an inspection on the new place, negotiated the work the sellers would do before the deal closed, visited the school the boys would attend, all the while ignoring the fact that not a soul had shown up for our last two open houses. On July first, we had no choice but to let our offer expire. Another family swooped in and bought the house—the house I'd foolishly allowed myself to think of as ours—within two weeks. By the time Katherine's parents returned in July,

I'd yanked the FOR SALE sign out of the yard and tossed it in the back of the garage. I sat on the living room floor and drank vodka on ice while Paul powered through his Mike's and called me a pansy for drinking out of a glass.

In August, we went to Ireland. A writer I know had offered us a month in his family's cottage in County Clare, an old farmhouse on the peninsula between the North Atlantic and the Shannon Estuary. Katherine and I had squirreled away a little money, hoping to spend our tenth anniversary sipping umbrella cocktails on a tropical beach, but when the chance to go to Ireland came up, we jumped at it. I hadn't been out of the country since the year I started graduate school. The boys had never been. Last spring, I'd been certain that all our buying and selling would have concluded long before we made the trip. Now going felt like a retreat from our failures. I welcomed the chance to escape.

The cottage was more than a century old and tiny, a single main room that doubled as the kitchen and two small bedrooms at the back, the second added only after our friend had inherited the place from his elderly cousins ten years earlier. The cousins, a brother and sister, had shared the original back bedroom their entire lives. The brother died in his late seventies, the sister in her nineties, both in the same room where they'd been born. The black-and-white photographs on the wall showed the original structure, the thatch roof and soot-blackened hearth over which the family had cooked and heated water for tea. Modern improvements added running water, electricity, and a phone, and the second bedroom expanded the house to not even seven hundred square feet, less than half the size of our house in Wisconsin.

The back garden separated a horse barn and a donkey pen, both of which were occupied. The donkeys grazed along the side windows, eyeballing us while we dressed or read, frequently commencing a low, guttural braying that crescendoed into a full-throated *hee-haw*. We laughed every time we heard it, and we heard it a lot.

I worked at the kitchen table in the mornings while Katherine and the boys lazed in bed and fed apples to the friendly beasts in the manger and yard. In the afternoons, after the rain let up, we swam at the beach and picked through the ruined abbeys and played cards in the pubs. One windy day, I drove an hour north to the port town of Doolin where we boarded a ferry bound for Inisheer in the Aran Islands, a dozen or so miles off the western coast. The boat looked broad and steady in the harbor, but once it motored beyond the barrier island and into the open sea, it began to pitch and roll like a roller coaster. Within minutes the pleasure cruise turned into a spew-fest. The family in the row ahead of mine bent forward in unison and vomited into the plastic bags the crew handed out. The man directly behind me turned a pale yellow-white, and I sat in terror while I waited for him to puke down the back of my neck. Finally, he crawled to the head on his hands and knees, where he remained for the rest of the crossing. The little girl beside me clutched her father's neck and wailed for forty-five minutes, "Make it stop! Make it stop!"

I turned back to check on the kids, seated a few rows behind me, and saw that they had their hands in the air and their mouths wide open. They weren't sick; they were having the time of their lives. And that's when it hit me: The house I'd spent so much time yearning for wasn't necessary. I didn't even want it anymore. There were possessions far more enduring than a house or the stuff they contain.

That afternoon, over pints in Tigh Ned, Katherine and I agreed to stay in our little house, our first and only house, to put away our lust for larger rooms and extra space and to instead indulge our lust for the world. We couldn't wait until the boys were grown and we had more money; we needed to travel now, while the kids were young, so that they'd come to see adventure—the opportunity to experience different landscapes, different skies, different cultures and customs—as lifelong values rather than brief diversions reserved for the newly graduated or the retired. Our house may be small, but our lives—with some careful budgeting and a little gumption—could be big.

First, though, we had to make it back across Galway Bay before the high winds stranded us on the island overnight. We waited in the harbor for an hour before the ferry captain decided to give the crossing a shot. Irish language and culture had survived in the Aran Islands better than anywhere else in the country thanks in part to this arduous crossing. Rather than ride inside the cabin, choking on black clouds of diesel exhaust and flanked by hordes of pukers, I suggested we try the upper deck, where at least we'd have fresh air. The ferry motored away from the tranquil little harbor, the stone fences snaking up the hill toward the castle on the island's highpoint, hit the open water, and began to heave so violently that the captain shouted over the loudspeaker that passengers were to remain seated at all times. Lean over the rail to feed the fish and you could end up sleeping with them.

Katherine rode with her head between her hands, gazing intently at her shoes. When the boat finally chugged into the harbor and tied up beside the dock, she shoved Hayden out of the way, sprinted down the gangplank, and made for the ladies. The boys threw rocks at the whitecaps while we waited for her. I looked back at the islands on the horizon: Inisheer with Inishmaan behind it, the larger Inishmore in the distant background. After that, the next land was Canada. Bronze Age settlers and medieval monks had for centuries made this wicked crossing in rowboats. Some believed St. Brendan sailed a leather-skinned currach to the shores of North America, five hundred years before the Vikings and nearly a thousand before Columbus. I was standing on the glimmering edge of the spectacular world. There was no place in it I didn't want to see.

Ordinary Time

After four weeks of sitting in the garage, our bicycle tires had gone soft. I pressed my thumb against the treads and could feel the mushy inner tube flaccid against the wheel rim. I swung my leg over the crossbar and rolled a few feet down the driveway. It felt like riding through a shallow layer of sand.

It was the Saturday before Labor Day, the sun striking, hot, and delicious after our weeks of Irish rain and fog. The boys and I were desperate to make the most of what remained of summer. School started on Tuesday.

I tore apart the garage looking for the pump, but it was nowhere to be found. Whenever I returned from a trip, especially a long one, I got the eerie feeling that strange things had happened in the house while we were gone: an empty mug on the counter, a magazine fanned open on the coffee table. Could I have possibly missed these things on our way out the door, or did we have a ghost? Now the bike pump had grown legs and walked away.

The tires had a little pressure, and if we took it easy we could make it to the service station at the edge of our neighborhood. "Once we get some air, we'll pick up the pace," I said to the boys. They held their bikes by the seats. Their helmet straps dangled loose beside their ears. "Ride slowly until then, okay?"

They buckled the chin straps. "Okay."

Galen straddled his mountain bike. We'd bought it a little big so he could grow into it, and now, three weeks after turning nine, he had. His twiggy legs appeared to lengthen with every turn of the pedals. Hayden was six and still stuck riding the hand-me-down Murray his brother had discarded two years earlier. His was the kind of bike found in Toys "R" Us instead of a bike store. It had come in a big four-color box, complete with training wheels, plastic streamers sprouting from the handlebars, and a sticker book. Scraped and bent and dotted with rust, the wheels were no longer true, and Hayden's knees bumped against the handlebars. I'd put off buying him a new one because it had taken him until July to crack the mystery of riding on two wheels; a month from now, when the weather turned, I'd hang the bikes from the hooks in the garage. Right now, turning circles in the driveway, Hayden looked like a bear in a circus.

The service station bays were empty, the wrecker out of service in the parking lot. Two gray-haired, big-gutted men in striped gray shirts watched us from behind the smeared office window. I waved as I uncoiled the compressor hose, but instead of waving back the old guys looked at each other and laughed. I knelt on the pavement and pressed the nozzle into action. I didn't have a pressure gauge, so I kept the air going until the tires turned hard. I'd filled bicycle tires this way for years.

We glided away from the station, leaving the codgers in our dust, our bikes suddenly zippy over the pavement. We glided down the tree-lined streets toward the park and past it, one block after another, weaving back and forth between the curbs, putting distance between ourselves and home. If all of summer was to be compressed into today, I didn't want to miss even a second of it. After a month in Ireland's pullulating greenery, its dense ferns and mosses and lichens, the grasses lining the highway so long they brushed against the windshield as we drove past, I felt intensely aware of the rest of the color spectrum, all the glories and heartaches of the impending autumn: leaves crackling orange as though about to burst into flame, the sapphire inflatable pool draining into the street. Winter in Wisconsin comes like an atonement, swift and severe. We'd see snow on the ground by Halloween, burying every lawn until April.

We were more than two miles from home when I heard what sounded like a gunshot. The bang was so loud it nearly knocked me from my bike. I skidded to a stop and began scanning the lawns for a body. Instead I found Hayden sinking into pools of quaggy rubber. His tires had blown out.

Though not yet schooled in the physics of tire inflation and air pressure, Hayden understood the basics of cause and effect. I'd inflated his bike tires at the service station; a few minutes later, his tires had exploded. Ergo: it was all my fault. His face bore the telltale look of betrayal—the pouty bottom lip, the eyes darting between my face and his ruined wheels. He intended to make sure I knew that *he* knew who was to blame for blowing up his bike. I told Galen to ride home and tell his mom what had happened, then slung the Murray over my shoulder and began the long, penitent walk home. I offered Hayden my hand as we crossed the busy street, but he refused.

That afternoon, in a stroke of luck, I found a kid's mountain bike on Craigslist for only thirty bucks. Essentially another hand-me-down, except that this one had shiftable gears and hand brakes and, of supreme importance to a six-year-old, a kickstand. I lifted the bike from the hatchback and held it aloft for a moment so Hayden could revel in its secondhand splendor. I set it on the driveway with a ceremonial flourish. *Welcome to the big time, kid.* I'm sure I said something about the importance of wearing his helmet and staying on the sidewalk, but Hayden wasn't listening. He settled himself onto the seat and pushed off, a little wobbly at first but not wobbly enough to put his foot down. A few cranks and he had it. He raced toward the bottom of the driveway, turned the corner, and raced down the block. I didn't know if I was forgiven yet, but it felt close.

The attraction between a boy and his bike, to echo William Maxwell, can be taken for granted. Early the next morning, I felt a moist hand touch my cheek. When I opened my eyes, the light through the window was gray, and I could see only the shadow of a kid standing above me. The clock on the nightstand said 5:47. "Dad," Hayden whispered. "I want to ride my bike."

"It's not even six yet."

He leaned closer, his breath hot and ghastly. "Can I ride at six?"

"Let me sleep," I said, rolling over. "You can ride later."

"Later when?"

"After church," I said, begrudgingly starting to wake up. I reached for my glasses.

"Ugh. *Church*." He bared his baby teeth. "Why do we even have to go to church?"

I blinked in the wan half-light. I didn't have an answer. I wasn't, to be honest, particularly eager to go myself, even though I'd been a churchgoer, regularly if not continuously, for most of my life.

I was Catholic, baptized and catechized, until I was twelve, when my parents divorced. Religion had never been a point of contention between my mother and father, but when their marriage began to falter, it had no power to hold them together. In fact, some might say it hastened and intensified their disunion, since my dad met my stepmother during that time. He converted to her evangelicalism while my mother, whose Catholic foothold had been tenuous at best, became nothing. Yet eight months after the divorce was finalized and barely three months after my dad himself had remarried, a Methodist minister joined my mom and stepdad in matrimony. We attended the minister's church for years afterward, most often when my stepdad's son and daughter flew into town from Dallas. My mom hoped the six of us lined up in the pew in our blazers and hot-rolled hair would cut the image for all to see of an intact family unblemished by divorce.

When I visited my father and stepmom, the audience was far clearer. The money people dropped in the offertory baskets paid my stepmother's salary. My dad, Devin, Stacie, and I sat in the front pew alongside the other pastoral families; after the service, we kids lingered on the plaza between the sanctuary and the fellowship hall while my father and stepmother kibitzed with the deacons and congregants. The summer I turned fifteen, my stepmother presented me with a Bible, my name embossed in gold foil on the cover, and my dad took me to a jewelry store to pick out a silver cross to wear around my neck, similar to the gold cross he wore around his own.

I resisted their pious overtures at first, but a few weeks into my sophomore year of high school, my closest friend, his brother, and their father were killed in a home invasion. Decades later, the crime remains unsolved.

In the immediate aftermath of the murders, my father and stepmother's effusive and demonstrative faith came to feel like a life raft in a tempest. I reached for it and clung to it, and the next June, sitting beside a bonfire at Crescent Bay Beach, I used the words my stepmom had taught me and, as the ritual goes, asked Jesus into my heart. Almost immediately, I was driven into a world that revolved entirely around *going to church*. No longer confined to an hour-long Sunday morning gathering, some sort of church activity became the touchstone of every day of the week. Bible studies met on Monday and Thursday evenings, fellowship was on Tuesdays, Dad and my stepmom attended Bible Study Fellowship, part of a national organization larger than our one church, on Wednesdays. Even Saturday-morning surf sessions began with a prayer on the beach, our boards staked upright in the sand, and ended with a scripture devotional over eggs at Denny's. I was so young, my initiation so swift and powerful, that several years would pass before I'd think to question it.

My dad and stepmom's church wasn't Pentecostal in the contemporary sense of the term. Services didn't involve spasmodic shaking or the casting out of demons or invoking the Holy Spirit in the language of angels, but it did skirt the fringes of that ecstatic realm. More importantly, the *idea* of Pentecost—that after Christ's ascension the Spirit of God descended to earth to abide in the Apostles, and that the Holy Spirit dwells in the heart of every true believer—was paramount. The enduring, ineradicable presence of the Holy Spirit was *the* message. Those mysteriously flaming words I uttered on the beach didn't merely reenact the moment of Pentecost; they directly brought forth God's spirit, as if unlocking the vault encasing the soul. Evangelicals are more restrained than Pentecostals, but not by much. For years I stood among the faithful, in some cases, thousands at a time, men and women singing with their eyes clamped shut and their hands in the air as if to gather in the spirit as it rained down from the rafters. I could never overcome my own self-consciousness enough to sing or pray this way, to allow myself to enter into their euphoria, so I almost never tried.

I'd been quietly edging away from the evangelicals long before I met Katherine, but it was only after we were together that I found the courage to face the exile that came with leaving the faith: the lost friendships, the pleading e-mails from people I hadn't spoken to in years, the sadness in my stepmother's eyes. Once all that was behind me, I realized I could do more than declare myself no longer an evangelical; I could give up the entire hocus-pocus of religion altogether. I could proclaim, like Nietzsche, that God was dead, or like Marx, that he'd never been. But in my most private moments, I still believed in a grand intelligence at the center of the universe, an enduring conviction that my friend's murder would not remain forever unaccounted for, and an abiding conviction that I was part of something larger than myself. Whatever change had occurred in me that summer night on the beach when I was fifteen had been real, even if I no longer trusted the vocabulary used to describe it. The bathwater had been drained, but at the bottom of the tub remained the baby, pink and nascent and demanding to be held.

To believe in God is to believe in a story about God. Regardless of the faith or even the lack of one, belief is an assent to an account, whether mythological or empirical, of how we got here, how we should live, and where we might go next. Belief in a god who espouses only one's individual tastes and values is belief in a small story, no larger than oneself. I continued to drag the boys to church on Sundays because I believed in the big story, the hoary and conflicted one—powerful enough to reorient Western civilization's accounting of time and the unfortunate driving justification behind centuries of war and oppression, a litany of atrocities too numerous to count, but also, contradictorily, a story of mercy and charity and hope. It would have been dishonest for me to claim only the good parts of Christianity without also acknowledging the bad. Or to try to escape the pitfalls of the faith that, for better and worse, had defined my understanding of the divine, by taking up with another story, a different faith.

Katherine and I were married and the boys were baptized in Episcopalian parishes. When they grew old enough for Sunday school, we moved across the river to Congregationalists, far to the left of the evangelicals yet less liturgically formal than the Episcopalians. We weren't as involved as I'd been during my teens, but we were still involved. I took a turn reading the scriptures during the service, and we helped teach Sunday school. Galen sang in the youth choir and performed in the spring pageant. We baked lasagnas for potlucks and ladled soup to the homeless who slept in the fellowship hall during the coldest months of the year.

Yet for all the hours I spent inside churches, I couldn't recall a single Sunday, as a Catholic, an evangelical, or a mainline liberal Protestant, when I actually looked forward to it. Once uncomfortable among the jubilations of the evangelicals, I now found myself restless, struggling to concentrate, staring at my watch. Part of the problem was that church rarely offered much in the way of solemn reflection; a Sunday service was most often the conclusion to a morning of screaming for the boys to hurry up in the shower, a cup of coffee swigged at the kitchen sink as we were running out the door, a *Super Mario Kart* race across town to make it inside before the bells started ringing. By the time we squeezed ourselves into the pews, I was harried and exhausted, and I spent the service waiting for it to end.

Even before the boys came along, church rarely, if ever, yielded the sense of wonder or joy that is the hallmark of a spiritual experience, what theologian Rudolph Otto termed "the numinous" and Christians associate with the presence of the Holy Spirit. Most of my communions with the divine occurred away from church buildings, often away from buildings altogether: swimming in the ocean or hiking the fern trail around Rock Island State Park. Or my favorite: the late-night, profanity-infused walk Katherine and the boys and I took through central Galway after we missed our bus and had to two-foot it back to our hostel. It even happened once or twice while driving in the car. But never in church. Going to church was an obligation, that which I did not because I wanted to but because I felt I should, which predictably led to feeling, well, bored. When I looked over at the boys beside me that Sunday morning, drawing in the bulletin or fiddling with the buttons on my wristwatch, I saw they were bored, too. We were all biding our time.

In the liturgical calendar, the Easter Season spans the fifty days between Easter Sunday and the Day of Pentecost. After Pentecost comes Ordinary Time, which occurs in two cycles: from May to the start of Advent in December, and again from Christmas to the beginning of Lent. Thirty-three weeks of the year happen during Ordinary Time—a stretch similar in its divisions and appropriations to the academic calendar. My life, like every parent's, was bound to the school calendar; it so happened that my job was bound to it as well.

Over time I came to think of the summer, the time between school years, as another kind of Easter Season, a period of resurrection and wonder when striving gives way to being, when the flora and fauna burst forth and the lakes glimmer and the sun floats in the sky deep into the night. Such were the weeks when we rejoiced and were glad. Katherine weeded the garden in a tank top, and the boys moved through the back door without shoes or shirts. This Easter ended not with Pentecost but with Labor Day, after which we returned to school, the boys to their classes and I to mine, the recommencement of homework and sports and the color-coded schedule hanging on the refrigerator. All the obligations of Ordinary Time.

The temptation to skip church was sometimes so great that on many Sundays I could barely resist it. On many occasions, I didn't, and opted instead for a second cup of coffee, an old movie, a long phone conversation with an old friend. If I could only give up believing, I often thought, I could quit churchgoing altogether and reclaim my Sundays for myself. We could be like one of those families in a TV commercial that hangs out all morning in a big white raft of a bed, the sheets and blankets pristine despite the coffee mugs on the nightstands and the dog curled up at the foot of the mattress. We'd yawn toward brunch around eleven, maybe take a leisurely stroll through an apple orchard while holding hands. But despite the nasty mess we'd make of that bed, my faith no longer belonged to me alone. As I watched the boys exit the sanctuary for Sunday school, I could only hope their time there, despite its inconveniences and discomforts and boredoms, would one day prove meaningful, even if they chose to believe in something altogether different. Even nothing at all.

Hayden jumped out of the car before I pulled into the garage. "Careful!" Katherine shouted, but he was already on his bike, without his helmet, still in his khakis and brogans. "Come inside and change your clothes," I said.

"In a minute," he shouted over his shoulder.

"I don't want you to ruin your pants."

"I won't," he said, though the warning itself distracted him and he nearly fell over. He had to put his foot down to avoid eating the pavement.

I let him ride while I made lunch. I set his sandwich on the table, opened the back door, and called for him to come in. "Hand it to me when I ride by," he said.

"How about you come inside to eat, and then we'll all go for a ride together?"

Usually a finicky eater, given to horsing around the kitchen during meals, Hayden sat down to his plate like a bomb expert before a ticking fuse. The sandwich disappeared in less than a minute, and his chips and apple were dispatched shortly thereafter. Five minutes after stepping inside the house, his plate was in the sink, he'd changed into his shorts, and he was standing on the driveway hollering, "Come on! Come on!"

"If we could harness this hurry-up," Katherine said, tying her hair back into a ponytail, "school mornings would be much easier."

"It's a new year," I said.

We rode past the post office and performing arts center, the appliance repair shop, our local congressional office until we reached the path that followed the river. The maples and oaks forking over the path were more golden than the day before and the leaves beneath our tires sounded like paper crinkling. The path crossed the railroad tracks and passed beneath our church, which sat atop a bluff, the sanctuary windows visible above the tree line. Silhouettes moved inside, a postservice meeting of some sort. I felt relieved to be on our side of the glass. I looked away from the church, toward the river, avocado green and passing beneath the trusses of a rusted railroad bridge, the college buildings across the water along the opposite bank. I glanced over at Hayden as he leaned forward on his bike and watched the change move across his face. He took in his surroundings with an awareness I'm still working to name. *Numinous* is too academic; *Pentecost* is the word I want to use—that holy, rapturous sense of wonder—but the word's baggage makes it difficult to wield. Whatever name it goes by, Hayden seemed to glimpse, however briefly, his place among the hidden structures of the universe, and when he looked back at me I felt we shared an understanding, perhaps even the Big Understanding I've been grappling toward all my life. I wanted to tell him, *That's God you're feeling*, or at least the feeling I've always connected to God's echo moving through me. But I didn't want to name it for him. I wanted him to feel it first, to name it for himself.

The trail dropped fast and sharp through the trees, a hairpin turn at the bottom that followed the river's bend. Lose control at the wrong time and you'll end up in the drink. I could smell the algae blooming in the river, the leaves turning to broth. Galen bombed the hill like an old pro, followed by Hayden, his elbows out and his head crouched low over the handlebars, hollering the whole way down. Hayden zipped around the bend and out of sight. I listened for a crash, a splash, metal scraping over concrete. When I didn't hear anything, I started after them, confident I'd find them on the other side.

Please Forgive
My Spotless Home

As predicted, the moment school started we were back to running at full throttle. Work was crazy with students e-mailing me excuses and pleas for extensions and Katherine's patients, whose needs approached actual pathos, saving their worst crises for nights and weekends, as if they somehow knew that social workers, like cell phone plans, worked for free after hours. Add in choir and swimming and Galen begging on bended knee to *please, please, pretty please* take a karate class after a martial artist at a school assembly broke real wood boards with his forehead and, well, we were busy. September nights turned cold and smoky, fireplaces across town all of a sudden crackling and blazing. Katherine and I referred to the previous summer as "Ireland," which was our way of saying that the entire season, not just the month we spent there, felt like a lush but distant country.

We did our best to keep up during the week and then used the weekends to make up the difference. Galen had crossed the five-foot mark and now stood a mere three inches below his mom. Hayden appeared shorter only by comparison. In that year's school photo, he looked like Big Bird among the Muppets. Groceries intended to last all week disappeared quickly, and the wrappers and boxes and stems ended up inside the couch cushions or chucked behind the television.

By Friday, the fridge and cupboards were picked clean. Our dinner choices were either cans of baked beans heaped atop bowls of rice or else leftover "Crock-Pot shit," which consisted of a slab of meat excavated from the back of the freezer and thrown into the slow cooker on Thursday morning as Katherine ran out the door for work. When I came downstairs on Saturday mornings, the house looked like the grounds at Woodstock the day the music died.

Okay, not quite that bad. But bad enough that cleaning the house was the top of the weekend to-do list. Katherine took the bathrooms and kitchen, and I took the beds and floors. On Sunday afternoon, after mopping the kitchen and hallway and running the vacuum over the rugs, I was working the wand attachment into the corner of the basement stairs where the finest mites liked to hide. The dirt crackled as it whirled up the tube and I took no small delight in watching the cyclone of dust and debris spin inside the transparent canister. The boys never grew tired of bragging that our vacuum really sucked.

I could hear the boys above me, through the plaster and wood that separated the basement ceiling from the living room floor. They were jumping between the sofa and the coffee table, built from a massive hunk of reclaimed wood and standing on iron legs sturdy enough to jack up a car. Their noises, though, were a dangerous mixture of laughing and grunting that portended someone—Hayden, usually—getting hurt. I shut off the vacuum. Then, the sound of a kid landing on the floor. Hayden started to cry while Galen kept right on cackling. "Galen!" I screamed at the ceiling.

It was after three, and I was scrambling to finish cleaning while Katherine was at the grocery store. The boys had commenced their tirade of evil only minutes after she left, clomping in dirty sneakers across the kitchen floor and then proceeding to shower graham cracker crumbs over the living room rugs.

Galen appeared at the landing, five steps above me. His unlaced high-tops made his feet look enormous, a reminder of how much he'd grown in the last year and, I thought, confirmation that he ought to know how to behave.

"What do I have to do to get you to settle down?" I asked. My voice was high, a little whiny.

"I'm bored," he said. "There's nothing to do."

"Go outside."

"There's no one to play with," he said.

"Play with your brother."

"My brother's an asswipe."

"Hey!" I jabbed the vacuum attachment in the air. "Language."

The sky above our neighbor's roof was the same lapis blue as the shirt he was wearing, and the sunlight through the window in the back door turned his ginger hair the color of a new penny. He looked back at me. "Do *you* want to come outside with me?"

For some reason, one I can neither explain nor justify, his request only further inflamed my ire. I went from steaming red to white hot. "I'm working!" I growled. "What do you think I've been doing while you and your brother have been tearing the house apart? I'm trying to get the floors clean before Mom gets home. You two are making a mess faster than I can clean it up!"

Galen's eyes narrowed, and his chin balled up beneath his bottom lip. He turned to look out the window behind him. "Sometimes I hate weekends," he said. "All we do is chores."

"Go ride your bike," I said, waving my hand. "Let me finish."

He left through the back door, and I returned to vacuuming, muttering to myself the list of tasks still to accomplish: unloading the car once Katherine returned, moving the food from their sacks to the refrigerator and cupboards, packing the boys' lunches, ironing a shirt for work tomorrow, getting started on dinner. I looked up again in time to see Galen's red bike helmet, like a carnival balloon against the backdrop of the sky, glide past the window. I moved another step down and pushed the wand into the corner of the stairs.

For as long as we'd been together, save the few months between moving to Wisconsin and Hayden's birth, Katherine had worked full-time. She worked full-time throughout college in order to pay her own way (and graduated a year early, I'll add proudly). She managed the lifeguards at the county pool when we met but soon after left it for the hospital, first as a clerk in the emergency room and then as a paid social worker once she'd finished her degree. She'd worked in hospitals ever since, and hospitals, as most people know, never shut down. That meant she worked a lot of irregular hours at inconvenient times (like, say, when she ought to be sleeping), and trouble could crash through the door at any time.

My schedule, though plenty busy, had more flexibility. I couldn't recall a single death resulting from a skipped faculty meeting. We didn't have the cash for a house cleaner or a private chef, so unless we wanted to stew in our own filth and order pizza seven nights a week, someone had to clean and someone had to buy and prepare the food. I wasn't much of a cook, but I could clean better than Alice from *The Brady Bunch*. I was a maestro with a vacuum cleaner and even more of one when it came to making beds. I could make a bed so square and tight that were a drill sergeant to inspect our rooms, he'd raise his hand in crisp salute.

It would be inaccurate, however, to say that my cleanliness was purely the product of my desire to be a good husband. My mom was fairly obsessive when it came to keeping a clean house, and as an adult I'd inherited a number of the same anal-retentive habits. My mom made the bed when she stayed in a hotel. I was in third grade when she stood in the driveway in her bathrobe, the school bus idling in front of our house, while I refolded my hospital corners until they were tight enough to pass inspection. By high school, the conditioning had become Pavlovian: I straightened and tucked the sheets the moment my feet hit the floor, even if it was five in the morning and I was headed to swimming practice. To this day, lying down in a pile of rumpled blankets makes me feel sick for no other reason than because, as a kid, fever and vomiting were the only allowable excuses for not making the bed in the morning. And only then because I was still sleeping in it.

In our house in Texas—a house that, it's worth mentioning, backed onto a muddy bayou that filled with snakes and mice and bugs every time it rained—my mom decorated our front sitting room entirely in white. White twill sofas, white cabinets, a white coffee table, white lamps spilling white light through white shades. Even the carpet was white. To make sure it stayed clean, she forbade anyone from ever setting foot inside it, including our golden retriever. The dog used to lie on the tile floor in the foyer with his chin nested on the living room carpet, and he knew to move his head when he heard Mom coming down the hall. We were granted access on two days each year—Easter Sunday and Christmas morning. The splendor and solemnity of those two holidays seemed compounded by the thrill of crossing that forbidden threshold into a room devoid of color. When some years later my mom and stepdad decided to sell the house, they gave the sofas to my stepbrother. They still looked brand-new.

For much of my growing up, my mom, like Katherine, worked all day and then spent all afternoon and evening shuttling between swimming and ballet and soccer, juggling dinner with homework and making sure our clothes were clean. I remember her switching out loads of laundry from the washer and dryer directly across from my room at eleven o'clock at night. Children are by nature blind to their parents' sacrifices; I took my mother's good efforts and hard work for granted as surely as the boys took for granted the things Katherine and I did for them. Ironically, though, it wasn't our lack of gratitude, or even her job, but rather the cleanliness of our house itself that often seemed the source of my mom's greatest stress. Occasionally one of us would tell her to let a few things go, to give herself (and us) a break; that a pile of dishes left in the sink overnight or a footprint in the vacuum tracks wasn't the end of the world. But a disorderly house was for her emblematic of an inner state of disorder, while a clean house meant she had everything under control, even when she didn't.

During the divorce, the house stayed as pristine as a museum. At the time, I took her compulsive cleaning as an unwillingness to accept the sordid state of her life, the fact that she and Dad had bottomed out. She didn't like me hanging around other kids from divorced homes, as though a broken marriage were some kind of virus she needed to quarantine. I thought her too concerned with the optics of respectability, and I accused her, sometimes venomously, of being shallow and materialistic. Years later, I could finally see her differently: When I recalled her Windexing the bathroom mirror with one hand while applying her makeup with the other, I saw her wishing she could undo her mistakes, hers and my dad's, and return them both to a former unblemished state. I also saw her finding the courage to move forward in the wake of what she couldn't repair. When the dust of the divorce finally settled, both my parents were deeply in debt and the mortgage was underwater, but no matter how bad things got, my mother never once called in sick for work or spent the day in bed with the curtains drawn.

The night after I yelled at Galen, I woke up at two in the morning racked with guilt of a different sort. Though the boys and I had been home together for two days, we'd spent most of the time in different rooms. An entire weekend had slipped by, and we'd barely looked each other in the eye . . . until the moment I'd spurned Galen's invitation to join him outside. Our exchange on the staircase was the closest we'd come to a conversation all weekend, and I'd screamed at him. I pictured Galen's contorted face at the top of the stairs, his big feet, his oversized adult front teeth docked into place, the basement stairs descending to a room we used only for laundry and storage. I saw the irony with a clarity only insomnia could provide: My urgency to clean the space where we stored the artifacts from our past had cost me time with the boys in the present. I lay awake for the rest of the night, foreseeing the day when the mention of my name would cause my sons to remember not our days together at the beach or the pool or even Ireland but a plum-faced man brandishing a vacuum wand.

When my alarm rang out at five, I slipped downstairs to brush my teeth and gather up my clothes before heading to the pool to swim. I stopped in the driveway and stared up at the house. The sun wouldn't be up for two more hours; because of an event that night on campus, the boys would be in bed when I returned home. The weekend, my next best chance to make good on my promise to be a better father, felt like a long way off.

Then, as if I'd summoned him, Galen's light turned on and his head appeared in the glass. I watched his hands work the locks on the sash, heard the shush of the pane sliding up. He pressed his nose to the screen. "Hey, Dad," he said.

"Did I wake you up?"

"No. I was already awake."

"Me, too," I said. I looked away, into the yard. Brown leaves wreathed the trunk of the maple; winter would be here soon. I looked back up to Galen, his silhouette backlit by the bulb in his ceiling. I could see only the outline of his face, like a priest behind a confessional screen. "I'm sorry we didn't get much time together this weekend," I said. "I'm sorry I yell so much."

"We don't have as much time to do our chores during the week," he said. "We have to do them on the weekend. Sometimes you're too busy to play." I could hear my own flimsy rationalizing in his voice, the litany of reasons my mother used to give to explain why she was upset, the truer sadness she needed to hide. I could imagine Galen one day using these same words to shoo away his own child. We were the links in an unending chain of chores and householding, our meager and ephemeral time away from school and work too often devoted to work of another kind. It felt wrong, standing there in the dark. But—I could hear it in his voice—he was also forgiving me.

Tasks

The old guys, Bob and Joe, were talking about ice fishing and the Packers, the only topics worthy of discussion in January besides the weather. I was shaving in the YMCA shower after swimming and Bob and Joe were carrying on beneath the spray directly across from mine. According to Bob, a brand-spanking-new Aaron Rodgers Edition Ford F-150, the pickup endorsed by Green Bay's star quarterback, had gone through the ice somewhere up north; Bob was convinced this meant the Packers' playoff chances against the 49ers that weekend were doomed. He was in his nineties, as skinny as a broomstick, and had only one nipple. The other one had been shot off during World War II. He'd started swimming during rehab, and seventy-some years later he was still at it, four days a week.

"This is our year," Joe said, refusing to heed the prophecy. "We were ten and six heading into the 2010 postseason and went all the way that year. And that was before Eddie Lacy." Twenty years Bob's junior, Joe was built like a gun safe: maybe five-feet tall and equally wide. His drumstick calves were inked with tattooed portraits of every dog he'd ever owned, his back and shoulders with every trophy-worthy buck he'd ever shot. If you asked (or if you didn't), he could tell you where and when each buck had been "bagged" and how much venison it had yielded. He had a lump beneath the skin in his abdomen the size of a bar of soap. He caught me staring at it and told me it was his pain pump. Instead of him taking a fistful of pills every day, the pump delivered his medications automatically. He crossed the wet tiles between his shower and mine until we stood beneath my one stream of water. "Feel it," he said.

"I can see it pretty well," I said.

"Go on, touch it. It won't bite."

I slowly extended my index finger. A firm island among the pillows of wet flesh, the pump was oblong and hard, neither of which did anything to abate the creepiness factor.

Joe seized my wrist. "Don't be such a baby," he said. He pulled my arm close, and my palm had nowhere to go except over the loaf in his stomach. "Can you feel it in there?"

"I sure can," I said.

"Modern medicine," he said.

In the weeks since the pain pump went in, I hadn't once seen him in a sour mood.

Safely back on his side of the shower room, Joe said to Bob, "Ever since I got Lacy's jersey, we've been winning. I wear it every game now, and we haven't lost yet."

"I've been watching the Packers since before you were born," Bob said. He shook his head. "Jersey or no, trust me. A truck like that going through the ice is a bad sign."

I shut off the water and padded to my locker. I towel-dried my hair and began to dress when my duffel bag began to ring. It was 7:15 on a Tuesday morning, temps were in the twenties with snow expected later in the day, and Katherine and the boys had been asleep when I left the house. My phone ringing now was odd. I fished inside my bag to retrieve it but missed the call before I could answer. It turned out I'd missed seven other calls in the last hour, all from home.

The phone rang again before I could call back. "Are you there?" Katherine said. "Can you hear me?"

"What's going on?"

Her breathing was short and shallow; I could hear the clench in her jaw. "My stomach," she said. "I think my appendix might have ruptured."

My first appalling thought was: *That's no big deal. The appendix doesn't really do anything.* Except, of course, get infected and burst and kill us in the predawn dark.

"I'm coming," I said.

I played the messages I'd missed as I weaved through traffic. The first was from Katherine, her voice calm and informative, like she was calling to remind me not to forget my lunch. "You remember that pain I felt last night?" she said. "I think it's getting worse."

The others were from Hayden: "Dad, Mom doesn't feel good. Can you come home?"

"Dad, are you done swimming yet? Mom's sick."

"Dad, Mom threw up in the bathroom."

"Dad, Mom threw up again, and now she can't get up. Should I call 911?"

Katherine lay naked on the bathroom floor, her knees curled to her chin and her forehead pressed to the tiles. Hayden had covered her with a towel. He sat on the toilet lid with his thumb in his mouth, keeping her company. There was vomit everywhere.

"It hit me as I was getting in the shower," she said. "I haven't been able to move."

"I wanted to call an ambulance, but Mom wouldn't let me," Hayden said.

"I don't need an ambulance," Katherine said. "Help me get dressed. We'll take the boys to school and then you can drop me off at the hospital."

"I'm not going to drop you off," I said. "Give me a break."

"You have class today."

"I'll cancel," I said. "And it's not until noon. Maybe you'll feel better by then."

She lifted her face and managed a weak smile. "Wouldn't that be nice?"

I'd been gone for barely two hours, but the house looked like the boys had thrown a weeklong toga party. They'd tried to make breakfast for themselves, and the kitchen counters were plastered with crumbs and maple syrup. Dog food was scattered across the linoleum. Dirty clothes, socks turned inside out, and twisted cartoon underwear lay in heaps in the living room. With Mom out of commission, the entire enterprise of eating and dressing had descended into absolute bedlam.

I hustled the boys into the back of the car and guided Katherine to the passenger seat. She pulled the lever to lean the seat back as close to horizontal as she could get it. Her head was almost in Hayden's lap. She clutched her stomach. "Holy God," she whispered. "Jesus."

The boys rode in silence for the seven blocks to the school, but when I pulled alongside the curb, Hayden asked, "Is she going to be okay?"

Of course she would be. She was in pain, but it wasn't like she was dying. Right? Then the day Hayden was born came rushing back—a winter day not unlike this one, the sky flat and gray with snow moving in, the hospital hardly two blocks from where we were parked. The pregnancy had been complicated, with multiple trips to the doctor and expensive testing to rule out a genetic disorder that, had the results come back positive, would have meant a death sentence for Hayden. We'd spent our first Wisconsin New Year's Eve in the hospital trying to stop a bout of bleeding that threatened to send Katherine into labor eight weeks early. Katherine and Hayden had come through it all, and the doctor insisted that the baby was big and healthy and that he didn't anticipate any problems during the delivery. I drove to the hospital nervous but not overly so. Everything would be fine; the doctor had said so. Hayden came through okay, but within an hour of his birth he began to get sick and his chest turned purple. After a long night pricking his heel to draw and test his blood, an oxygen cannula pronged into his nostrils, he was rushed by ambulance to a neonatal intensive care unit a half hour south, a slender tube inserted down his trachea to feed air directly into his lungs. Even when the neonatologist told us dying wasn't likely, he did so in a subdued voice and reiterated that he wasn't only concerned about Hayden's lungs but also about his heart. I remembered the doctor telling us it was important to approach the situation one step at a time.

"The doctor will give her medicine," I told Hayden. "That will help her feel better." I waved him out the door. Part goodbye, part scram. Galen had hopped out of the car before I came to a complete stop, and now Hayden, backpack straps over both shoulders, followed his brother like a paratrooper from an airplane. I considered, for a moment, turning back to reassure them. Katherine's face tightened, and she called out in agony, louder now that the boys were out of the car, and I took the next corner fast enough to feel the tires slide on the icy road.

Most parents know that the moment your child is born, a switch flips and you become instantly aware of every lurking danger. You become a connoisseur of dread, pondering the chemicals beneath the kitchen sink, the weight of the television on its stand, the malicious intentions of every cockeyed stranger. And that's not even including the car, the deadliest of all.

I'd long loved Katherine's stories from the hospital, but the fascination really cranked up after Hayden was born. Katherine during this time vacillated between vexingly calm and, even more vexingly, calmly distraught. The cacophonies of the hospital—the buzzes and beeps and overhead pages prompting nurses and doctors alike to take off down the corridor at full sprint—didn't faze her in the slightest, but during the moments when we sat together beside Hayden's Isolette she'd slip into a dark cave, her hidden warehouse of years' worth of gore and freak accidents. Kids run over by their own parents in the driveway; kids who pushed too hard on window screens and tumbled from upper-story windows; kids with strange bruises revealed through a series of tests to be malignant. All rare, yet she'd seen each and every one.

As luck would have it, barely a week after Hayden came home from the hospital with a clean bill of health, Katherine was hired as the social worker for maternity, pediatrics, and neonatal intensive care at the local Catholic hospital. Her hospital was different from the one where Hayden was treated, but the scenery in the NICU was the same: Plexiglas boxes crowded with wires and accordion tubing and surrounded by space-age equipment and frightened parents doing their best to keep their hearts in one piece. The stories she told about work drew me in more than ever, the way a car accident on the side of the highway exerts an irresistible magnetism once you have been in an accident yourself. I loved them because they reminded me that our experiences weren't unique (sooner or later, everyone gets *something*), but also that Katherine—pretty and petite and taciturn in most public settings—was strong in a crisis. For going on ten years, she'd jumped into the worst emergencies and found a way to help. She made sure the grieving or the merely scared weren't left alone. She'd carried in her own arms the babies who could not be saved.

Such was the problem I now faced as I sat beside her in the emergency room: my own utter uselessness. There was nothing for me to do. Every time I left the little room where Katherine had been parked, the nurses eyed me warily and seemed a breath shy of ordering me to go away. Nor could I provide much in the way of comfort. Katherine had been given a steady drip of Dilaudid and lay dozing and grinning like the Cheshire Cat.

If I'd inherited any particularly masculine trait from my fore-bears, it was the need to identify and solve problems and, more importantly, not wait for someone to solve them on my behalf. If I heard a strange noise coming from my car, I'd pop the hood to stare down at the engine, even though I didn't know the first thing about auto repair. I hovered over plumbers, electricians, appliance repairmen, ostensibly because I wanted to make sure they were doing good work but in actuality because I was too embarrassed to read or watch TV while another man worked on my house. My impatience, along with my occasional Irish temper, were my worst qualities. They conjoined me at the hip to a masculinity I otherwise kept at arm's length: the loudmouth chest-pounder who always needed to be in charge.

Even worse: I tended to believe the world was better under my direct control. On a cross-country road trip with friends, I drove all night even after we'd agreed to switch off every few hours because I couldn't stomach the feeling of trying to sleep in the back seat while someone else took the wheel. Another reason I loved Katherine's hospital stories was that they allowed me to vicariously master the things that most scared me: my family in peril, sick or injured or gone forever. I wasn't much different from Bob and Joe and their voodoo shower logic about the Packers. We all want control, a say in the outcome, especially when we can't have it.

The morning passed, then lunch. The shift changed, and at last, seven hours after Katherine hobbled through the ER doors, the tests revealed that her appendix was okay and that the pain she felt was caused by an ovarian cyst. The gynecologist who came down to consult explained that the cyst was in the process of rupturing but hadn't yet. Katherine was young, but she'd had several endometrial issues in the last few years. The best course of action would a hysterectomy, especially given the history of ovarian cancer that ran in her family. A hysterectomy would put her out of commission for several weeks;

it was a surgery she'd want to schedule. In the meantime, he'd drain the cyst and remove it. Barring a major emergency on the delivery floor, he'd do the procedure that night.

"Should I call someone to pick up the boys?" I asked after the doctor left.

"You should get them," Katherine said softly. "They'll be calmer seeing you."

"Should we come back?"

"Go home for a while. Keep things normal."

"I don't want to leave you here."

"I'm fine here," she said. "I'm here every day. Besides, your fidgeting is driving me nuts."

"You've been asleep. How'd you know what I was doing?"

"I've been doped up, not dead." She weakly raised her arm and lowered it back to the sheets. "I could feel you squirming around in my dreams. Except when you were riding on the back of a unicorn and your hair was white."

A foot of snow had come down. While digging out the tires and scraping the windshield, it occurred to me that Katherine had sent me to fetch the boys in order to give me the thing I most desired: a job to do, a series of tasks to complete. I couldn't contribute to the surgery in any meaningful way, but I could set the house right and keep the boys calm, which would help her because the thought of the boys upset was worse for her than the prospect of going under the knife. At least, that's what I told myself as I made my way through the unplowed streets across town. A doctor cutting into the organ that had produced her children, with the intent to remove the core of her biological womanhood a few weeks down the road, was less frightening for her than two kids crying for their mom.

A good portion of Katherine's job involved lessening the fear factor of bad news. She was the one to explain to parents that the tube in their newborn's chest was a good thing and would help their baby heal, or at least not die while they went to the cafeteria for lunch. One of her calming techniques involved assigning little tasks to the most panicked person in the room—to go get coffee or food, to make sure the Kleenexes were close at hand. None of the things Katherine told parents in the course of her job were lies, but they did serve utilitarian purposes. The doctors and nurses couldn't do their jobs if a mom or dad was freaking out at the bedside. Even the tiniest premature infants, Katherine maintained, had the uncanny ability to absorb their parents' emotions, especially fear. Staying calm was in everyone's best interest.

Parking against the curb outside the boys' school, I wondered if I'd been so handled. I sat with the radio off and the heater running, my breath fogging the windshield while I waited for the dismissal bell to ring.

My favorite thing about school pickup was watching the kids come out. Their colored parkas burst forth against the pall of the ugly sky. The smallest kids ran with their arms outstretched, reuniting with their parents as though they'd been in a submarine for months. It cheered me a little to see it, though the joy was quickly eclipsed by a fresh wave of guilt for having left Katherine behind.

I pulled out of line and eased along the row of waiting cars, searching for the boys among the throngs of kids. A car near the front of the line pulled away, and I nosed in before the minivan behind could pull forward. The woman driving that van, a small blonde I'd seen on warmer days pushing a baby in a stroller, laid on her horn and jabbed her middle finger into the windshield. The moms standing together on the sidewalk whipped around and glared. I waved and shrugged. One advantage of being a dad in a land ruled by moms is you're not expected to know shit about kids and their routines. On a day like this, low expectations came in handy.

The boys stood together in their hats and parkas. They sprinted for the car when they saw me, threw open both side doors, and demanded to know whether Mom was okay. "She's going to have surgery soon," I said. *Surgery* was a word Katherine, in the process of recapping a workday, used often; I figured the boys knew what it meant. "When the doctor calls, we'll go back and see her."

"When will that be?" Hayden wanted to know.

"I don't know yet. A few hours. Hop in, you're letting out all the heat."

Hayden stood leaning over the front seat. Galen peered in from the back. Hayden sensed the moment was propitious. "Can I ride up front?" he asked.

"Just hop in," I said.

He made a big show of sliding the seat forward and of pulling the seatbelt across his shoulders. Galen slumped against the back door with his arms crossed. "Doing okay?" I asked.

"Yeah," he shrugged. "I'm fine."

At home I set about accomplishing the list of tasks I'd assigned myself. Job number one: clean up the puke in the bathroom, dried and hardened after sitting all day beneath the furnace vent. I scrubbed the tiles on my hands and knees, my nose and mouth masked by my shirt, then moved on to the breakfast disaster in the kitchen. I carried the mound of soiled rags to the laundry room and started a load. I'd told the boys to keep the TV down so I could hear the phone when it rang, and to my surprise they not only obliged, they sat together without fighting. I couldn't recall the last time they'd been within touching distance without one trying to assault the other. It felt oddly absent, their brawling, as if a preemptive somberness had settled over the house. I called the hospital. The nurse told me Katherine had gone down to the spa. The surgery should get underway before too much longer.

"The spa?" I didn't understand.

"SPA means surgical procedure area," she said. "Pre-op. It sounds better as an acronym."

"Can she get a facial while she's down there?"

The nurse didn't laugh. "I'll have the doctor call you."

When I turned around, Hayden was standing in the hallway outside the kitchen, beneath the red light of the smoke detector. His eyes narrowed. "Where is Mom?" he asked. His face said he wasn't inclined to believe anything I said.

"She's at the hospital."

"No. Where is she right now?"

"She's getting ready for surgery."

"What is surgery?" Hayden asked.

How do you explain the failures of the body and our remedies for dealing with them to a person who didn't yet know what all the body parts were or what function they performed? Especially to a six-year-old boy about his mother's body? Under ordinary circumstances, at both home and work, such questions were Mom's domain.

"She has a pouch of fluid inside her body that's not supposed to be there," I said. "That's what made her sick this morning. The doctor is going to cut it out."

"The doctor uses a knife?" His eyes grew wide.

"It's a special kind of knife. A doctor's knife. It's very clean and very sharp."

"You mean," Hayden said, eyes narrowing again, "the doctor is going to stab Mom and cut out her organs?"

"Not quite like that," I said. I could imagine Katherine rolling her eyes. *I gave you one job.* The kid had a point, though: The sterility of the hospital, the doctors and nurses in their white coats and blue scrubs, their arcane vocabularies, the big locked doors between the units, all worked to sanitize the fact that surgery involved blades piercing flesh. The boys had been taught that all sharp objects, from kitchen scissors to popsicle sticks, were dangerous. The instruments of harm, the makings of mortality.

"I don't like this one bit," Hayden said.

"Me neither."

Hours went by, and the phone didn't ring. I packed lunches for the next day, fed the boys dinner, stood in the bathroom while they brushed their teeth. I didn't have the heart to barricade Hayden in his room with the shower rod. I promised to leave it out and to come wake him up when the doctor called as long as he promised to get some sleep while he could. We shook on the deal, and I tucked the blankets around his chin, kissed his forehead, and backed out of the room, desperate for an hour of trashy television. I lay on the couch and pointed the remote at the TV, and then Hayden was standing over me. "I can't sleep," he said.

"It's been less than five minutes," I said. "You should try a little harder."

"I know myself," he said. "It's not going to happen."

"Okay," I said, sitting up. "Have a seat." A few minutes later, Galen came downstairs and sat with us. I think we watched *Nova*, but mostly we watched the phone.

Our pot refused to boil until after nine thirty. The boys had by that point sunk lower on the couch, their eyelids drooping, but at the sound of the phone they sprang back to attention. The surgeon apologized for the delay; he'd been called to a delivery right before he took Katherine in, and that had set him back an hour. He'd been able to resect the cyst and take a better look at the situation. The hysterectomy needed to happen sooner rather than later. The next six months, at the latest. She was in good shape for now, though. "When can she come home?" I asked.

"I wanted her to stay, but she's insisting she leave tonight."

"Is that a good idea?" The boys' faces were grim. If Mom didn't come home, no one would sleep.

"It's a toss-up," the doctor said. "There's no medical reason for her to stay, other than to rest. She can rest at home, but she has to actually rest. She says her boys are waiting for her."

"She keeps us all calm," I said too hastily, our happiness suddenly a fragile and fleeting thing.

"I've worked with her for years," the doctor said. "I get it."

He said the nurse would need half an hour to prepare her discharge papers. I willed myself to wait a full forty-five before bundling the boys into their coats and boots and herding them to the car. I hoped that by the time we arrived at the hospital Katherine would be seated on the edge of the bed, back in her jeans and shoes, ready to walk out. Instead we found her still lying in bed, still in her gown, her hair a mess around her face. The boys moved carefully inside, attuned to the peculiarities of the room that must seem commonplace, even cliché, to most adults. The sliding curtain between the door and bed, the outlets and oxygen canister on the wall, the television suspended from the ceiling. Hayden fingered the cannulas taped to the back of Mom's hand and fiddled with the controls that moved her mattress up and down. After a cursory glance around, during which he barely looked Katherine in the eye, Galen asked to see my phone. He slumped into a chair in the corner, pulled up Bejeweled, and stared vacantly at the screen.

The nurse folded back the blankets, helped Katherine to stand, and guided her into the bathroom. Hayden watched the nurse's hand at her back cinching closed the gown to keep her backside covered. When the bathroom door clicked into place, he dropped his eyes to the rumpled sheets, the square disposable pads laid over the linens. They were full of blood.

He went not to me, but to his brother. "Galen," he whispered. "*Look*." Galen came over, and together they studied the bright stain.

"It's from the surgery," I said. I tried to think of another word for *discharge* but came up blank. "It's nothing to worry about."

Hayden whispered again, "The doctor stabbed her with a knife."

Galen had pretended throughout the day that the ordeal was nothing to concern himself with; Mom was fine and he was nine and he didn't need any comforting. Hayden had been the one to prod and question while Galen had remained aloof. But a bed full of blood was too visceral to ignore. Returning to his video game in the chair, he began to fidget and scratch at his arms. "Dad," he said. "I'm hot." He began pulling off his jacket and hat. "It's so hot in here."

"We're leaving in one minute," I said. "Soon as Mom's ready."

He mimed a cup at his mouth. "I need something to drink."

"There's a fountain down the hall," I said. "You can get a drink on our way out."

He laid his head on the arm of the chair. "Water," he moaned. "I need water."

It was past eleven when the nurse unfolded the wheelchair and helped Katherine settle into it. The boys were four hours past their usual bedtime, I'd been awake since four thirty that morning, and Katherine, though no longer in immediate danger, was still in pain. We were all exhausted.

"I can walk," Katherine said. "You don't have to take me all the way down."

"You know better than that," the nurse said.

Hayden insisted on walking with his hand on the arm of the wheelchair. I carried Katherine's purse and discharge papers. Galen followed behind, his hands in his pockets, staring at the floor. We rode the elevator to the ground floor and moved our way through the long tunnel of corridors, half-lit and deserted except for a stray nurse carrying a massive travel mug. We rolled past a waiting room full of people sleeping with their mouths open and their arms crossed. I could recall the nights I'd slept in a waiting room while Hayden was in the NICU, the initial shock settling into a dull weight that could knock me out even while I sat upright in a chair. I reached out to touch Hayden's head. He was six and big, his lungs free of fluid or illness. We'd gotten off so easy.

We'd gotten off easy tonight, too. Maybe it was good for the boys to see their mother as both delicate and resilient. Maybe it was good for them to understand that people get sick and, if they're lucky, they get better, and that while I spent my days noodling with words, Mom spent hers here, helping people going through crises far worse than ours because she believed her efforts were worthwhile, people deserved care, and compassion was one of life's greatest and rarest virtues. Thomas Aquinas said he'd rather experience compassion than understand the meaning of it, which meant, I think, that compassion wasn't an attitude that could be theorized. No amount of talking could instill it in the boys. Compassion was rooted in empathy, and empathy was born of experience. Though none of that made the lesson any less difficult to learn—for them or for me.

We turned the corner toward the ER, where I'd parked the car. Galen's shoe caught on the carpet and he fell, first to his knees and then to his face. He covered his head with his hands and wept. "I can't go any farther," he said.

Katherine lifted her eyes to the nurse. "Poor guy's wiped out. It's way past his bedtime."

"We're almost to the car," I said.

"I can't make it," Galen said. "Just leave me here."

"We leave no man behind," I said. I hoisted him by the armpits. "Come on."

I pulled the car beneath the overhang beside the ER, and the nurse wheeled Katherine outside. I helped her into the front seat and the boys into the back. "Thank God," Galen said, as he clicked his belt into place. He leaned his head against the rest and fell asleep. Hayden's eyes were closed before we crossed the river.

The snow had finished, the clouds had moved out, and the sky above the traffic lights, now blinking red and yellow, was full of stars. I paused before each intersection, as reticent as the day I'd driven Hayden home from the hospital after nine days in the NICU, all my energy focused on ferrying my family to safety, keeping us from harm, even if for only this night. My hands, when I finally let go of the steering wheel in the driveway, were slick with sweat. I left the engine running so the car would stay warm while I unlocked the door and guided Katherine into the house. I went back for the boys one at a time, first Hayden and then Galen, unbuckling their seatbelts, hauling them onto my shoulder, and carrying them inside. Galen's long legs dangled nearly to the ground. He was heavy in my arms, and climbing the stairs I could feel every ounce of his limp weight in my back, but I'd found another task I could accomplish and I didn't stop until I'd laid him, sleeping, in his bed.

The Fourth B

Given our one full bathroom, privacy had never been in ample supply, especially after we swapped out the shower curtain for a glass sliding door. No one in the family expected to shower without someone flossing at the sink while another peed in the general, if not always specific, direction of the toilet. Hayden, more than the rest of us, had never honored any requests for time alone in the bathroom and had accordingly never expected any in return. He had zero qualms about pooping in full view of the family.

Following Katherine's surgery, Hayden took a renewed interest in human biology. His bladder, uncannily, seemed to reach capacity whenever his mom was showering, thus providing him an opportunity to inspect her body, in particular the parts of it subjected to the surgeon's knife. Now that he knew what the word *surgery* meant, he used it daily. Did girls have *surgery* to remove their balls? The way he and Galen had *surgery* to remove the skin around the tips of their penises? And if the *surgery* that had sewn his lip back together after he split it at the pool had left behind a squiggly scar in his skin, how come he couldn't, no matter how hard he looked, find one anywhere on Mom?

"The scar's on the inside," Katherine said. She wrapped her bath towel beneath her armpits and tucked in the flap.

"Inside . . . where?" Hayden asked.

For the next twenty minutes Katherine tried, to my great amusement, to explain how a doctor might access an ovary (another word Hayden now knew) without flaying open her entire stomach and pulling out her viscera like a chain of sausages. It wasn't the word *vagina* that gave Katherine trouble so much as the words that preceded it. Such phrases as "reaching inside" or "the doctor stuck his hand in" caused Hayden's mouth to fall open and his eyeballs to roll around in their sockets. When he cocked his head to the side and earnestly inquired, "You mean, sort of like a puppet?" I laughed so hard that the conversation could not in good faith continue.

"Laugh it up," Katherine said. "I'll defer any further questions to you, Professor."

"Bring 'em on," I said. Though, of course, I had no idea what I was saying.

A few nights later, I pulled up Google on our iPad and found, among the boys' twenty-seven still-open tabs for video game cheats, skateboard tricks, and public farting, the phrase "big butts." It seemed logical: Watch enough videos of people breaking wind in Times Square before a crowd of gaping tourists and one would begin to wonder about the source of such hilarity. But when I clicked on the tab, I got a little nervous. The images were a lot more sexual than I expected, even with the SafeSearch turned on. A collage of derrieres, nearly all of them female, bent over car hoods and countertops and beach towels, and clad in striped bikinis or lace thongs or nothing at all. I opened the search history, and my worries grew sharper still. A few spots down were the words "big breasts," "babies being born," and—the perennial favorite of preadolescent boys the world over and a sure indicator of Galen's involvement—"naked ladies." The truly hard-core stuff had been filtered out, but there was still plenty of tanned and oiled flesh, pouty lips, and protuberant nipples. More than enough to titillate a nine- and seven-year-old until their heads exploded.

I switched over to FaceTime and called my dad. His face appeared on the screen after only two rings, calm, sagacious, his hair and mustache completely white. He nodded as I recapped what I'd found, and when I finished, he said, "I expected something like this sooner or later."

The more I thought about it, so had I. When I was the boys' age, the Internet wasn't really a thing. I didn't have an e-mail account, let alone stumble upon the net's vast reliquaries of smut, until college. But I could remember sneaking down the hallway after my parents had gone to bed to watch the late-night skin flicks on HBO and Showtime, my mouth chalky and my pulse galloping as I sat cross-legged before the television in the dark. Or the first time a friend's older brother slid his hand between his mattress and box spring and produced a *Playboy*. Curiosity about sex—and not simply curiosity in the abstract, but the urge to study it up close—is an integral part of childhood. It's as fundamental as playing with matches or turning sticks into swords.

So, on the one hand, I wanted to shrug off their Google searches as normal and let the matter drop. I certainly didn't want to overreact. As long as the parental controls remained on, they probably wouldn't be able to see anything too explicit, and once they'd satisfied their curiosity, they would likely move on to other things. Wouldn't they? But the controls on our one iPad were nothing more than a single locked gate in a thousand-mile fence. When would the boys ever *not* be curious about sex? I thought of the line by the comedian Ron White: "Once you've seen one woman naked, you pretty much want to see the rest of 'em naked." I knew I had to say something.

But say what? And say it how? Was there ever an easy way to talk with your kids about sex? Does any well-adjusted adult look back on the conversation he or she had with their parents and think, *I'm so glad they brought that up*? The next day, during a break in my afternoon class, I polled my students about how their parents had broached the topic. The class was an advanced nonfiction writing seminar populated by juniors and seniors who'd spent the last two terms writing about their personal lives, including steamy romps in the hay reported in such graphic detail that an anthology of class essays could be mistaken for a special edition of *Penthouse Letters*. (My favorite was the guy who'd likened sex with his girlfriend, also a member of the class, to two fish slapping on a table; the young woman seemed not the slightest bit bothered by the description, which led me to wonder if it was more accurate than I'd first thought.) Yet when I asked how their parents had talked to them about sex, they all put their hands over their faces. *Oh my God, so awkward!* One guy said his dad had initiated the conversation while they were in the drive-thru at Wendy's; another recalled his architect father drawing diagrams on a napkin at a restaurant. A woman in the class said her parents had left the matter entirely to her Catholic school health teacher, a potbellied gym coach who'd passed out maxi pads while pacing the classroom in his nylon wind pants.

I thought about the parent-child sex talks I'd been a party to and couldn't come up with anything more ideal. My mother had explained the plumbing basics when I was about ten, but in a voice so hushed I couldn't recall her teeth even coming apart. After my parents separated, the entire topic of sex became a gigantic iceberg bearing down on our once unsinkable family, and from then on not another word was said on the subject. My parents' new marriages to other people didn't make things any simpler. Their bedrooms were no longer places a kid could breeze through freely and without permission. My sister, stepbrother, stepsisters, and I, whether in Texas or California, became scrupulous door-knockers. When my stepmom grew concerned about my burgeoning sexual consciousness, as evidenced by my interest in MTV and *Rolling Stone* magazine, she invited me to sit down on the living room couch and read, aloud, Paul's first epistle to the Thessalonians, chapter four, verses three through five: "For this is the will of God, your sanctification: that you should abstain from sexual immorality; that each of you should know how to possess his own vessel in sanctification and honor, not in passion of lust . . ." I stumbled a bit on the phrase "sexual immorality" and ended up pronouncing it as "sexual *immortality*." My dad laughed and said, "We'll probably need a different book for that."

What dad (or mom) doesn't imagine that, when the time comes, he'll either be cool and casual or else direct and factual, either way a corrective to the floundering conversations we ourselves had to endure as kids? But while we're busy trying to be cool, our kids will remember the drive-thru, the paper napkin we scrawled upon, the ironically misspoken word. It led me to wonder whether The Talk was even necessary in the first place. Did it actually impart any practical knowledge, or did it just drive parents and kids farther apart? The funny thing about straight men is that for all the ribald locker room talk common among adolescents, most adult men in long-term relationships go mute when the topic of sex comes up. The moment sex becomes a regular part of life, it becomes a closely guarded secret. Two of the guys I swam with, both in their late fifties, had recounted their colonoscopies in full detail, including the magazines they read while their bowels were emptying and the lunch they ate after the procedure finished (baked beans on toast, which I'll now *never* eat). But I couldn't tell you when they last made whoopee with the missus. For all I knew it was when their youngest children, now in their late twenties, were conceived.

Yet The Talk still seemed important, and moreover seemed important *now*. Soon enough the boys wouldn't want to talk with me about sex at all, and whatever chance I had to teach them about the most important and dangerous thing they'd ever do with their bodies would be gone. And if polling data were any indication, whatever I said to them they'd one day laugh about with their friends. The Talk was the one conversation they were guaranteed to remember forever. The margin for error was small.

•

Later that week, I saw my chance. Katherine was working late and had left me in charge of dinner. I made spaghetti and set the table for three. Hayden sat on my right and Galen on my left. I waited until their mouths were full before I said, "Boys, we need to talk about something."

Their eyebrows shot up, expecting trouble.

"We've been looking at naked pictures on the iPad," I said. The decision to use *we* was calculated. We were in this together. I was no connoisseur of Internet porn, but it wasn't like I'd never wandered down that road before. First take the plank out of your own eye.

Their faces turned as red as the sauce in their bowls. "I promise I'll never touch the iPad again," Galen said.

"No one's in trouble," I said. "I just want to talk about it."

"I know about sex," Hayden said, pleased to take part in the conversation. "Sex is about your privates."

"What about them?"

"The three B's. Butts, balls, and boobs."

"Girls don't have balls, genius," Galen said, looking up.

"Not anymore," Hayden shot back.

"Well, they never did," I said. "That's sort of what makes girls different from boys. One of the things, anyway. Do you know what girls have instead?"

"I really don't want to talk about this," Galen said.

"I know," Hayden said. He raised his hand, the way he was taught to do in school. "Where the doctor stuck his hand during Mom's surgery. The bagina."

"The fourth B," Galen said.

"Pretty close," I said. "But here's the real question. Do you know how sex works?" They both blinked across the table, confused. Their Google searches had not, it seemed, led them to any images or videos of couples actually in flagrante delicto. Nevertheless, my heart was pounding. This was the moment of truth. "Does your penis ever get"—I struggled for the right word: *erect* was too technical, *hard* too dirty—"stiff? Do you ever feel your penis get stiff?"

"Uh . . . yeah!" Hayden said. "I didn't know it was supposed to do that!"

"When that happens, a man puts his penis inside a woman's vagina. Some stuff comes out that goes inside the woman's body. Seeds for a baby."

"Pee?" Hayden asked, staring down at his lap.

"Not pee," I said. "Something different."

Galen put down his fork. "Does it feel good?"

"No," Hayden interjected. "Not for the woman. The baby's head is too big. She yells and screams and says she hates everyone's guts."

"That's more likely the case when the baby is coming out," I said. "Making the baby feels nice."

"Did you do that with Mom?" Galen asked.

"How do you think you got here?"

"Really?" Galen scrunched his eyebrows together and pursed his lips.

"Really," I said.

There was a lot more I needed to say. I'd sort of implied that an erection alone was reason enough for sex, and I hadn't even scratched the surface of the reasons people have sex other than to make a baby. Or why some men prefer sex with other men and women with women. I'd talked only about how sex worked and not at all about why it mattered—what it meant to be ready for it, how I'd known their mother was different from all the other girls. I'd been trying to find a reason for why the boys should steer clear of the NSFW pics on the Internet. The problem wasn't that the images were inappropriate in some abstract sense, or that I feared the boys becoming sex fiends, or even because porn arguably exploited and objectified the women it depicted, but that even soft-core, bent-over-the-hood-of-the-Camaro porn portrayed sex as merely biological: faceless and dehumanized, all fluid and flesh and devoid of the richness and mystery that made sex sex. The fire of human existence.

I looked back at the boys. I could tell my window had closed. Hayden squirmed in his chair, and Galen stared down at his bowl. "Can I finish dinner now?" he asked.

I picked up my fork. "Good idea."

I had the boys in their pj's when Katherine came home. They'd brushed their teeth and washed their faces without putting up a fuss. I'd have called it a miracle except for my worries that the talk had opened a gulf between us and none of us knew what to say next.

Katherine leaned down to kiss Hayden good night. He looked up from his pillow and asked, "Are you and Dad going to go have sex now?"

"What?" She turned and blinked at me.

"You know, when Dad puts his penis in your bagina."

"I guess this is a good time to tell you what we talked about at dinner," I said.

"I see." Her face said: *Better you than me.*

"Your penis has to get stiff for it to work," Hayden said. "Like this!" He threw back his covers to reveal a baseball stuffed down the front of his navy blue briefs. He looked like he had elephantitis of the balls.

"Oh my," Katherine said.

There was some measure of relief in the knowledge that he didn't have all the technical details figured out yet. Contrary to my earlier worries, The Talk wasn't a single conversation; it was the culmination of a lot of conversations, some funny and some serious and likely more than one disaster. I could handle a few disasters so long as the discussion remained an open topic for us to take up another time. Nine-tenths of parenting was the willingness to keep trying if the first time didn't go the way you'd planned. A lot like sex, if you think about it. My students, good souls though they were, couldn't see what I was finally starting to figure out. All those awkward conversations in the drive-thru and health class had in common one thing: an adult who cared enough to brave the giggles and the squeals in order to talk about something important. The older the boys grew, the more important those conversations would become.

Hayden pulled the baseball from his underwear and set it on the shelf beside his bed. "That's one big ball," I said. He erupted with laughter. Tonight's joke would turn serious soon enough. I'd be there to help him figure it out.

The D Word

The police cruiser slowed to a stop in front of our house, the lights flashing but the sirens quiet. I could see my neighbor, an old dude with stringy gray hair, sitting in the back seat. The officer shut off the lights and got out and opened the back door. My neighbor's chin was bleeding, and he was holding his elbow cupped in his palm. Another police vehicle pulled up, a minivan this time, and from the back hatch the second officer removed my neighbor's mountain bike. The front wheel was so badly bent the officer had to stand the bike vertically on its back tire to roll it up the driveway.

Hayden was in the yard when the cops arrived. I went outside and stood with him. The leaves were turning, a sudden burst of fire from the upper branches of the oaks and maples. Joan sat in her plastic chair across the street, her swollen ankles crossed and her eyes on the house next door. Together the three of us watched the officer guide our neighbor to his front door. The old guy either had a hard time with the key or the door didn't want to give. When it finally opened, a gust of stale cigarette smoke wafted out, so pungent and powerful I could smell it across the street. It had been years since the house was aired. Joan raised her index finger to her upper lip to hide the smell.

The second officer leaned the bike against the garage, looked into the backyard, and then crossed the street to talk to us. He kept one hand on the radio receiver clipped to his collar, the other on his belt. He asked me if I knew the man they'd brought home.

"Sure," I said. "He's our neighbor." Truth was, I didn't know him well at all. We'd lived across from each other for eight years but had never had a conversation that extended beyond "Good morning" or "How 'bout this snow?" I knew from Don and Joan next door to him that he'd lived there for more than thirty years, along with an old woman who may have been his wife, and an even older guy who was, apparently, the house's owner and who'd died a year ago. They'd been there for so long that no one knew the precise nature of the arrangement, nor did anyone know who owned the house now. I didn't even know their names. Neither the neighbor nor his wife drove a car. They biked everywhere, even in winter, mostly quick trips to the gas station from which they returned with a plastic sack slung around the handlebars filled with a little food, a pack of cigarettes, and beer.

"What happened?" I asked the officer.

"He wrecked his bike near the Walgreens," he said. "The store called an ambulance, but he refused medical treatment. He didn't even want us to help him home. He seemed"—the officer glanced down at Hayden, standing quietly, taking in his every word and gesture—"intoxicated. There's a huge pile of empties behind the house."

"They've always kept to themselves," I said.

The first officer came through the front door, closing it softly behind him, as if he'd put our neighbor to bed and didn't want to disturb him. He crossed the yard to speak with Joan, then came over to join his partner talking to us. "Man," he said. "That place is in rough shape."

"Is he okay?" I asked.

"He'll live," the officer said. "His wife was passed out naked on the couch." He closed his eyes and shook his head.

"Someone comes over to check on them every few days," I said. "Could be a social worker, but I'm honestly not sure. My wife's a social worker, but she doesn't know the person who comes." I looked at the house, its door shut and the curtains drawn. "They're very private."

I nodded at Joan. "She can probably tell you more."

"Not a lot," the first officer said.

Their radios squawked, and they reached to silence them. "If anything else happens," the first officer said, turning toward his cruiser, "give us a call."

Hayden had remained quiet during the confab with the police, but back inside he was all questions. Had our neighbor been arrested? Why did he have to ride in the back if he hadn't been arrested? What did *intoxicated* mean? Was it a bad word like *shit* and *fuck*? I tried to give it to him straight, to explain what it means to be an alcoholic without devolving into euphemism or metaphor or baby talk. "They drink so much alcohol it makes them sick," I said. "They've done it for so long they can't stop." I paused to read his face for signs of confusion, but he was stone-faced. "Too much alcohol is poison," I said.

Hayden pursed his lips. "You and Mom drink it." A statement, not a question.

Well, yes. We kept a wine rack above the microwave, as well as several bottles of liquor. Katherine liked a glass of cabernet while she was cooking, a short tumbler of bourbon late at night. I drank whatever we had in the house, though mostly I drank vodka. We'd always been this way.

My parents drank. Their parents drank. I couldn't conjure a single family memory that *didn't* include booze: margaritas whirring in a blender, beer on the beach, wine with dinner, martinis in long-stemmed conical glasses. My grandmother served crème de menthe on St. Patrick's Day and Cape Cods garnished with lime on Christmas because, she said, the colors of the drinks matched the seasons. My mother and father, now approaching their third decade of divorce, both kept bottles of vodka nested among the ice cubes in the freezer, which they drank the same way, cold and plain, a habit I'd inherited. In Wisconsin, alcohol was a staple of everyday life, sold not only in liquor stores and supermarkets but also at pharmacies and gas stations and the concession stands of Galen's basketball games. Last year, I'd been invited, on the presumption that English professors must be good spellers, to participate in a charity spelling bee to benefit a local literacy foundation. The bee was held at a downtown hotel and featured a full bar. The contestants—local attorneys and librarians and shopkeepers—sauntered to the microphone with gin and tonics and Seven and Sevens cupped in their hands. (My team included an underage student and the dean of the faculty, my boss, so we mutually agreed to abstain and emerged holding the trophy.) After nearly a decade in Utah, the country's most stone-cold sober state, Wisconsin's laissez-faire attitude about booze had come as something of a shock, then even more quickly, a delight. Nearly everywhere we went, unless the Packers were losing, people were in a festive mood.

"Yes, Mom and Dad drink," I told Hayden. "But we try not to drink too much. We don't want to get sick."

Hayden thought about this for a moment. I wondered if he was remembering the night from the previous summer and hoped he was not. "Have you ever been . . ." He seemed embarrassed to say it. "Have you ever been the D word?"

Like many American families, mine numbered among its ranks several uncles and cousins and one or two matriarchs who, it was said, couldn't hold their liquor until it was later revealed they could hold too much. Katherine's family roster contained a similar cast of characters, not in epidemic abundance, but nevertheless as a persistent presence, like the crowd of sooty-faced tramps filling in the backdrop of a Dickens story. I'd never been overly cautious with alcohol, but I'd tried to remain mindful of its perils, especially since a certain dependency swirled through my genetic code and Katherine's, and so doubly through our sons'. Mindful, that is, except for those times when I wasn't.

Katherine's best drunk story is a tale we still tell at parties. Two summers earlier, we'd gone to dinner at a friend's house, a fellow professor from the college. It was June and warm, the sun close to the solstice, and our friend lived in our neighborhood, so Katherine and I decided to ride our bikes. The food hadn't yet gone into the oven when we arrived, and our host told us it would probably take an hour to cook. We drank wine while we waited, a full bottle, then another with dinner, and then we carried a freshly opened third into the living room to enjoy with dessert. The chicken on Katherine's plate, in spite of its long baking time, had come out undercooked, gelatinous in the middle and bloody around the bones. She cut it into bites and spread them discreetly around her plate. It may have saved her from salmonella, but it also meant that her wine splashed down into an empty stomach. To her credit, she kept up with the conversation. She didn't slur a word or miss a step as we headed to the yard to collect our bikes. She hugged our host, thanked her for a lovely evening. We were three houses away when she let her bike drift close to mine and said in a voice so deadpan it's hard not to mock: "This is how it's going to go. We're going to ride by the junior high track. When we get to the long jump, I'm going to stop and puke my guts out. Got it?"

I couldn't tell whether or not she was serious. "You're drunk?" I asked.

"Ride straight and keep your mouth shut," she said.

The long jump had been chosen, I soon learned, because it was in the dead center of the field and was accessible by an asphalt path. Far from houses or the road, no one would see her there. Katherine pedaled heroically, game-faced and tight-lipped, and when we reached the sandy pit at the end of the jump, she very calmly used her foot to lower the kickstand before she staggered away into the dark. I heard her heaving in the shadows. "It's a good thing track season is over," she said, wiping her mouth when she came back to me. She looked back at the sandpit, the hellscape from whence she'd come. "Damn."

By the time we made it home, she was fully sick. Twice she rubbed her tire against the curb and rolled into the grass, and after that I had to hold onto her handlebars to keep her from toppling over. The kids were asleep by then, so when they found her lying in bed the next morning, the lie was easy. She blamed the food.

Anytime we passed by the long jump, crossing through the park in the center of our neighborhood, we stopped and paid homage to the site.

It's a funny story because the consequences were minor. Katherine barfed in a pile of sand, swallowed fistfuls of ibuprofen between plates of eggs and hash browns for twenty-four hours, and neither the boys nor my colleague knew anything about it. My own low point, in contrast, was less comical. It happened the summer before.

I'd taken the boys to a backyard party while Katherine was out of town, firmly reminding them in the car on the way over to remember to say *please* and *thank you* and to address the adults as *Mr.* and *Ms.* The yard was fenceless and crowded with kids; the boys roamed between one house and the next, playing basketball on the driveway and riding scooters along the sidewalk. Temperatures were in the nineties well into the evening, the beer disappeared quickly, and by the time the air began to cool and the stars appeared through the trees the only things left to drink were juice boxes and vodka. I'd already had my fill when the boys went inside the house with the other kids to watch a movie. I could see their heads lined up on the couch through the window facing the backyard, their silhouettes glowing in the blue aura of the screen. I poured another, and then because I was talking and couldn't imagine anywhere else I wanted to be, I poured one more. I had the car keys in my pocket the entire time.

When it came time to leave, I could barely walk. I somehow

ushered the boys to the car and got them buckled into the back seat. I didn't have far to go, only nine blocks, all inside the neighborhood. *I can make it*, I thought. I circled the car and opened the driver's side door. A friend came down the driveway and took the keys out of my hand. He drove us home. I giggled in the passenger seat while my friend drove, frowning. The boys sensed something wasn't right, Dad riding shotgun in his own car, but neither of them said a word.

The next morning, I messaged my friend to apologize. He invited me to take a walk so we could talk in person. I went and apologized some more, but he wasn't over it. He said I'd been reckless and had come close to putting my sons in danger. I assured him I wasn't cavalier about my kids' safety; what had happened was a mistake. Though, of course, I had been cavalier and the mistake was no one's fault but my own. The fact that I found myself standing beneath a streetlamp defending my commitment to responsible parenting shamed me further. We shook hands at the corner, and I apologized one more time. He said he forgave me, but our friendship effectively ended there, on that corner. We hadn't talked much since, a few stray texts for a time and then nothing at all. Now when we see each other, we act like we were never friends.

To the boys, I made no apology, offered no explanation. I hoped they were too young to understand or remember. I suspected I was wrong on both fronts.

Our neighbor fell off his bike again. His wife collapsed inside the house and called 911. She wouldn't answer the door, and the firemen thought they might have to break it down until the social worker showed up with a key. For several weeks, fire trucks and ambulances came howling down our street nearly every day. The pile of cans in the yard grew mountainous and spilled from the backyard into the driveway. The neighbor and his wife were taken away in ambulances and brought home in police cars and taxis, plastic hospital bracelets around their wrists. Their house was put up for sale. An eviction notice appeared on the door.

The boys watched the tragicomedy play out with a mixture of fascination and fear. For a while it consumed more attention than television. We'd be sitting down to watch a movie when we'd hear the sirens in the distance, growing louder until the lights were flashing in our windows and paramedics were running toward the house, tackle boxes in hand. The boys began to anticipate the nightly arrival of the cops. They wondered what time the firemen would arrive, whether they'd bring the ladder truck or the smaller rig, if Officer Peters would let them sit in the back of the squad car and play with his handcuffs, as he had the week before. The boys knew that any sarcasm about the plight of the poor and dispossessed would bring forth from their social worker mother a fury not seen on Earth since God encouraged Noah to study up on shipbuilding. Instead, they teased each other.

"I put a-hol in your cereal," Hayden told his brother. "Good luck riding your bike today."

"It's not called a-hol," Galen said. "It's not a swear."

"You're an a-hol," Hayden said.

"Boys," I said. "Enough."

"The thing I keep wondering about," Galen said, turning to me, "is if alcohol makes you sick, why drink it at all?"

The boys' questions had turned more serious in the last year or so, as Santa had given way to sex and God (and how often God had sex, and with whom, and why people screamed out God's name during sex). And now booze. It wasn't that the questions were hard to answer, but rather that the answers themselves were inadequate. All the open, frank conversations Katherine and I had with the boys, our insistence that they could ask us anything and we'd respond honestly, didn't amount to diddly if our actions contradicted our words. Words too easily crumbled into abstraction and became meaningless.

It seemed like the oldest parenting cliché in the world. Katherine and I still jokingly recited to each other the old antidrug PSA from the eighties in which an angry dad bursts into his son's room with a cigar box full of twisted plastic baggies. The dad wants to know who taught the kid to use drugs. After a few stammering excuses, the kid bursts out, "You, all right? I learned from watching you!" The dad's face turns grim and an ominous, we're-all-gonna-die voice-over comes on to say, "Parents who use drugs have children who use drugs." But as clichés went, it was durable. Our boys *were* watching us. I could still see their faces in the back of the car that night as my friend drove us home, their mouths small and tight but their eyes open and searching, assembling their own understanding of what was happening. I'd never tried to explain that night because ultimately there wasn't much to say. They already knew the truth. They'd seen it for themselves.

Which was why I did my best to tell the truth now, in the least varnished terms I could think of. "Alcohol is a depressant," I said. "It slows you down. If you've had a long day of work, it can help you feel calmer, and that's nice. People talk and laugh more, too, because they don't feel as uptight. But if you drink too much, it can make you throw up. Or worse."

"Worse, like how?" Galen asked. "Like . . ." and for a beat I thought he was going to ask me about that night, what might have befallen us had I tried to drive. My stomach unclenched a little when he pointed out the front window. "Like them?"

"Yes," I said. "Like them."

By Halloween, "they" were gone and their house sat empty. I couldn't imagine anyone buying the place, but an estate-sale company arrived early one Saturday morning and set up a tent and folding table in the front yard. They hammered signs into the grass. Minivans and pickup trucks filled the curbs on both sides of the street. Customers lined up on the walkway leading to the front door. The neighbors' sad, misshapen bicycles were wheeled to the front yard and sold immediately, even the one with the bent wheel. I crossed the street with the boys and got in line. When the front door opened, everyone in the yard coughed and covered their noses, but they filed in anyway. At the threshold, a lady in a yellow T-shirt stopped me. "Children aren't allowed inside."

"They're with me," I said. "We live across the street."

She leaned in and lowered her voice. "There's porn inside. It's *everywhere.*"

"Oh," I said. I told the boys to go back to our yard. "I'll be right out."

"Look out for a-hol!" Hayden called. "Don't get drunk in there."

"You are so stupid," Galen said to him.

I'd looked upon this house every day for the last eight years, but this was my first trip past the edge of the yard. I felt like a scuba diver plunging over the side of a boat. I held my nose to block the smell.

The interior was shabby and old, but less horrifying than I'd expected. No voodoo dolls hanging on the walls, no candle-lit pentagrams drawn on the floor. Nothing but an old house, similar in size and layout to my own, with small rooms full of old people's knickknacks: porcelain figurines and rusted tools, wrinkled paperback books, shoes and clothes, dozens of VCRs and DVD players, one stacked on top of another, crate after crate of videos. One crate was filled entirely with animated children's movies. The promised porn was all from the seventies, featuring hairy models on the covers and titles like *He & She*, *Misty Beethoven*, and *Nylon Party*.

The videos didn't seem especially illicit. If anything, they seemed sad. It was clear the neighbors had done little else over the last three decades besides get loaded, smoke cigarettes, and watch videos. It was a sad way to live, holed up inside this hot little house with the drapes pulled shut, too drunk to notice the life going on outside, the families moving in and having children, the seasons changing—a whole life spent this way only to have it end with a bunch of senior citizens grubbing through your stuff with their butts in the air, haggling over your coffee spoons. I could see my own house through the living room windows, the boys on the lawn with their mom. How good I had it, how much I had to lose. It was enough to tempt me to race home, empty my cupboards and freezer of every drop of alcohol, and swear never to drink again.

If adhering to an abstentious code would allow me to ward off trouble before it arrived, to guarantee that the boys would never have a problem with booze, I'd gladly do it. But I wasn't the only one the boys were watching. They were becoming, more quickly than I'd anticipated, citizens of the world, and I could feel the magnitude of my influence starting to diminish. Only a little, perhaps, but definitively. I'd once been the center of their universe; now I was only a star in their galaxy. Swearing a Puritan's oath would only propel them farther from me by giving them one more thing to reject. The more difficult truth was that the boys wouldn't know how they'd respond to alcohol until they tried it. They'd probably have to barf a time or two before they understood their limits. It unsettled me, knowing that such hard lessons lay in the future—God forbid in junior high, I hoped not in high school, but one day, eventually. In the center of that rank, smoke-filled living room, I closed my eyes and prayed that when the lessons came, neither of the boys would have his car keys in his pocket.

Sea Glass

I didn't tell the boys about the trip until the week before we left. I chose what I was sure was the perfect moment to spring the news. They'd come in from shoveling the driveway, their wool hats were crusted with snow, and their cheeks were throbbing red. It was mid-December, pitch-dark by five o'clock. "A week from now, you know where you'll be?" I asked as they slumped off their coats. I waited for them to step into the kitchen before I gave the answer. "On a beach in Puerto Rico!"

After a month of relentless Googling, I'd scored cheap plane tickets to the Caribbean and found a condo on the beach for a hundred bucks a night. Our kitchen linoleum was starting to peel, our upstairs toilet would run all night if you didn't flush it the right way, and last spring's thaw had flooded our basement, but I hadn't forgotten the promise Katherine and I had made in Ireland a year and a half earlier. We'd sat together on the couch after the boys had gone to bed, totaling up Katherine's holiday bonus and the money we saved at the credit union, and had figured out that if we totally blew off Christmas, all the gifts and cards as well as the peppermint bark we delivered to the neighbors and the ham we ate on Christmas Eve and the bottle of scotch we opened on Christmas afternoon—if in other words we screwed over everyone we knew and loved—we could make it work. For the last few weeks I'd dreamed about lying on a towel in the sun, a book tented on my chest and a beer next to me in the sand. Christmas that year would be sunny and blue instead of our usual white.

I expected the boys to jump and cheer when they heard the news, but in my excitement I'd made what turned out to be a crucial mistake. I led with what had been for Katherine and me a major selling point: We wouldn't bother with presents or decorations or overly complicated cooking. All we were going to do was hang out and swim.

"No presents?" Galen asked. "Not even stockings?"

"The present is the beach," I said. "What more could you want?"

"You mean like a jar of sand?" Hayden asked. Snowmelt puddled around his feet. "How am I supposed to show that to my friends?"

"Your friends will be super jealous," I said. Belatedly, I realized that most seven-year-olds would mortgage their souls in order to get their hands on whatever toy was currently being hawked during commercial breaks. "At least their parents will be jealous," I added.

"Like I care about that," Hayden said.

"You'll miss the last few days of school. Does that sweeten the deal?"

Galen's face twisted even tighter. His lips wrinkled like an elderly smoker's. "Our holiday party is on the last day," he said. "We're doing a gift exchange."

When I was Galen's age, the holiday gift exchanges at school had been invariably lame. Most kids pilfered their parents' desk drawers for something to give away, even while we hoped to be the recipient of a gift from the kid whose mother was ignorant of the five-dollar price limit. In second grade, I received a paint pen, a single marker tied haphazardly with uncurled ribbon. The next year, my prize was a sleeve of golf balls. Of all parties, it seemed like a good one to miss. But Galen's eyes were welling. He turned away so I couldn't see.

"Maybe we can get a few souvenirs when we're there," I offered.

Galen wiped his eyes with the back of his hand. "Can I get something for Max?"

Max's was the first family we met when we moved to Wisconsin. Galen had known him longer than he'd known his own brother. We'd shopped for Max in every city we'd ever visited. We'd combed five-and-dimes along the west coast of Michigan and scoured the Canal Street kiosks in New York in search of tchotchkes worthy of Max's bedroom. We'd wasted a considerable amount of time in Ireland twirling racks of key chains and shot glasses and family crests, including a half hour in a store on Galway's Shop Street that specialized in deep genealogical research. I didn't realize that the place wasn't just another run-of-the-mill keepsake depot until the ruddy-cheeked man behind the counter cheerily offered to find, frame, and ship back to the States Max's family crest for €450. The thought had crossed my mind, more than once in fact, that we ought to bring Max along on our next trip simply in the interest of saving time.

I loved Max like a nephew and I loved Galen's devotion to his pal, but a small part of me worried about it, too, if only because friendships in Galen's world had lately become complicated. What had once been hordes of sweet, moon-faced boys and squeaky-voiced, pig-tailed girls had morphed into warring tribes of preadolescents with hormonal glands rapidly starting to throttle. The boys, I'd noticed, no longer wore T-shirts silkscreened with race cars and Disney characters, as they had two years earlier; they all now donned sports apparel—in our case, the Packers, Badgers, and Brewers—as though they were uniforms. Whenever I witnessed the parade of fandom at the boys' school, I thought of the men at the birthday party we'd attended a year or so after we'd arrived in Wisconsin, the icy stares I'd received when I stepped through the sliding glass door in my non-emblazoned polo.

Galen had pined desperately for the attire, and Katherine had bought him a few shirts at the start of the school year. He'd dig them out of the laundry basket and wear them dirty rather than go to school in unmarked clothes. And to my even greater dismay, Galen had lately begun to show signs of my own propensity for obsession. He now had a difficult time with certain fabrics and shoes. Shopping with him took hours and usually ended with one, if not both, if not all four of us, screaming in the car. He also rejected paper that wasn't perfectly crisp, pencils and pens that didn't feel right in his hand, and every night before bed I retucked his bedsheets to make certain they were square and tight. Within minutes of switching off his light, I'd hear him moving around his room, pulling the mattress away from the wall, unmaking and remaking his bed all over again, growing increasingly agitated the entire time. None of us could ever get it quite right.

Galen had become in the last year especially sensitive to playground teasing, his skin as thin as an overripe peach. The vehemence of his reactions in turn made him an easy target and thus also easily excluded. He'd been left off the invite list for several birthday parties, and his self-esteem had taken a hit. Only later did I fully comprehend why he'd been so upset about missing the holiday gift exchange. It was the one social function he could not be excluded from.

Max, though, was loyal, as steadfast an ally in the fog of childhood as any I could imagine. But I knew neither he nor Galen were immune from the social forces acting upon their peer group. Case in point: I could feel the boys' interest in girls ramping up, especially when Galen and Max were together. They spoke in code, using pronouns instead of specific names. No dates, from what I could gather, had yet been arranged but it wouldn't be long. Desire could provoke jealousies that could topple even the sturdiest friendships. I believed Galen would in due time make an attentive boyfriend, provided he didn't blow it first by getting too clingy. It wouldn't take much for him to be branded the nice guy who tried too hard. In some ways, it was already happening.

Galen came home from school with a list of gift requests. The girls with whom he shared his table in homeroom wanted bracelets or necklaces. They didn't want earrings because they weren't allowed to get their ears pierced until junior high. A boy whose name I'd never heard before asked for a tropical bird, like a macaw or a cockatoo. Max was into pirates and had been teaching himself to speak buccaneer. When he was last at our house and I asked him if he wanted something to drink, he answered with "Splice the main brace, matey," which I took to mean yes. He put in for a bag of pearls, preferably black, but only if they weren't cursed.

"I'm not sure a bag of pearls fits within the budget," I told Galen.

"I'm not going to buy them," he said, rolling his eyes. "I'm going to find them on the beach."

"You'll probably have better luck with sea glass," I said. He crinkled his nose, and I led him to the box I kept on the shelf in my closet. In it, I kept the hunk of sea glass I'd found on the beach in California during my first visit to my father's house after he left Texas. The glass was the size of a walnut and as green as a lime. I'd dug it out of the wet sand, rinsed it in the tide, and carried it in my palm the entire flight back to Houston. It had survived because the box that contained it had sliding parquet panels the kids hadn't figured out how to work. Whenever I opened the box and handled the contents—a dime-store ring I'd take from my father's closet before he moved; a stack of wallet-sized pictures of junior high classmates, many with mustaches drawn in ballpoint ink; a silver chain that had belonged to my friend who'd died—I was so flooded with nostalgia I couldn't bear to part with any of it.

Galen rolled the sea glass in his hand and held it to the lamp. The glass was smoky and opaque; the sand infused inside the glass sparkled beneath the yellow orb of the desk lamp. "These are on the beach?" he asked.

"They're everywhere," I said. "You'll just have to look."

While Katherine lounged on the sand and Hayden and I swam, Galen combed the Puerto Rican beaches for sea glass. He moved along the shoreline bent over with his hands behind his back, while farther down the beach senior citizens in sunbonnets and wraparound sunglasses swept the sand with metal detectors. Galen returned to our encampment with pockets full of sand dollars and horse conchs, Scotch bonnets and egg cockles, but little in the way of bona fide sea glass. Most of the pieces he collected were shards of broken bottles, the detritus of someone else's party. "These are too sharp to keep," I said.

"You said I'd find sea glass on the beach," he said.

"This isn't *sea* glass," I said, holding up a jagged hunk of long-neck. "It's just glass. Put them in the garbage so people don't cut their feet."

He piled the shells by my chair and continued his restless search. To tell him to give it up would have only frustrated him, so I put my head back and closed my eyes and napped in the sun. When I stirred twenty minutes later, he was half a mile down the beach, still hunched over. Among the items he worked out of the sand was a fake pearl bracelet, an elastic band strung with hollow plastic beads. He added it to his stash, but Hayden, either in a fit of jealousy or retribution for some distant wrong forgotten by everyone but him, stretched the elastic until it snapped and the pearls scattered into the sand.

We returned to our condo at the end of each day with a bag full of relics, which Galen methodically arranged on the kitchen table according to size and color. His clothes lay in a salty heap on the floor, but the shells he catalogued and displayed as though they were destined for a museum. He insisted they not be disturbed under any circumstances. Rather than clear them away to use the table for meals, we sat on the floor with our plates balanced on our knees.

The day before Christmas Eve, we drove to the eastern port town of Farjado and boarded the ferry to Vieques, an island once used by the Navy for target practice and since turned into a wildlife refuge. Ninety minutes from the Puerto Rican mainland, Vieques was the westernmost island in the Spanish Virgin Islands and less than forty miles from Saint Thomas in the U.S. Virgin Islands. Because of its long occupation by the military and subsequent protection by the Department of the Interior, the beaches on Vieques were rumored to be among the least spoiled and most scenic in the entire Caribbean.

The waiting room at the ferry terminal was divided into locals and tourists, one roped off from the other. Island residents had priority on the boat and got to board before the visitors. When we were allowed on, we followed the other gringos in their Tommy Bahama shirts and sport sandals through the parked cars and luggage hold to the upper deck. The looky-loos crowded against the windows and covered themselves with their beach towels beneath the air-conditioning vent. I noticed that not a single local sat among us. When the boat puttered out of the harbor, I realized why the folks in the know preferred the windowless lower deck. The pitch and roll was nothing compared to the ferry to the Aran Islands, but it was severe enough to send the people standing at the windows scrambling for their seats. I thought about the narrow staircase we'd climbed to reach our perch and the time it would take to disembark once we reached the other shore. I ushered Katherine and the boys downstairs, abandoning the comfort of our four-in-a-row faux-leather captain's chairs for a spot closer to the exit. The lower deck, though, was so crowded that people sat on the floor beside the toilet. Rather than slink back upstairs in defeat, I insisted we claim a spot on the floor of the luggage hold, *even closer* to the way out than the lower deck. In the hold we were joined by mounds of wrapped Christmas presents, a crated rottweiler snarling behind his wire door, and a seasick Viequean local sitting with her head between her knees and swearing in broken English that she was never, ever going home again.

"You know we paid for seats," Katherine said. "They're included in the price."

"If we stay here, we'll be the first ones off at the dock," I said. "More time on the beach."

"Sometimes I think you have a screw loose," she said. The ferry undulated beneath us. The hold reeked of diesel fumes. "Other times, I know it."

I approached the first taxi driver standing at harbor gate, a bald man in a soiled chambray shirt who walked with a limp. When I tried to bargain the fare down a few bucks, he nodded at the boys and said, "How many kids?"

"Only two," I said, confident he was about to give me a break.

"I have six," he said. "And they're hungry."

He led us through the gate and down a long line of Econoline vans. Most were newer, with metallic paint glinting in the sun and the air conditioner keeping the interior cool. At the end of the line sat our driver's van. It had a gigantic spiderweb crack in the windshield and an interior that looked like it had been through a war. The driver limped back to the terminal to collect another group of tourists, who were by that point jaunting gaily away from the ferry, having made the crossing in a seat with a view of the ocean. Katherine shot me a look that hardly needed to be explained.

"What the hell happened in here?" she said. Yellow foam mushroomed through the torn seat vinyl and lay in clumps on the floor. "Did a dog get trapped?"

"Have to be a big dog," Hayden said. "Like a wolf. This van's all wolfed up."

"Good one!" Galen said. The school gift exchange was that day, very likely going on at that very moment. It seemed as far from Galen's mind as we were from Wisconsin.

We crossed the island with the windows down, the air sweet with mango and mamey, up through a cloud forest and down to the southern coast where the sun glimmered over the turquoise water. The driver let us out in the little town of Esperanza and told us we could walk to the beach from there. He seemed eager to be rid of us, to return to the harbor for more passengers. He stopped the van in a dirt turnout and said the beach was at the end, past the campground, couldn't miss it. "The farther you walk, the better," he said.

"It's nice?" I said. "That way?"

He let out a small, gravelly laugh. "Don't worry, amigo. *Es perfecta.*"

Karma, of course, loves to ladle out comeuppance. In my haste to be first off the ferry, we ended up nearly last. By the time we found our way through the trees and campground and came onto Sun Bay Beach, the sand was already thick with ferry passengers who had arrived via the main beach road. The other beachgoers sat on narrow hotel towels with their socks stuffed inside their sneakers, pale feet sizzling beneath the sun. Others sat with their backs to the ocean in an effort to block the whipping onshore winds. They appeared to be merely waiting for time to pass before they could go back. I noticed that the waves looked calmer at the far end of the bay, at least another mile, if not more, and after everything, the ferry and the wolfed-up van, the bushwhacking hike through the jungle, I insisted we keep going.

"Jesus Christ, Dad," Hayden whined, dragging his feet in the sand. "Just pick a spot. It doesn't have to be perfect."

But Hayden, unlike his brother and me, was not an obsessive. He couldn't understand that perfection was the entire point. I'd spent months dreaming of this week—a week at the beach in the middle of winter. I'd barely slept the nights leading up to our departure, buzzed with excitement but also with angst that something along the way would go awry. Our flight would get canceled or a postseason hurricane would blow in or I'd forget to lock the car door and our luggage would get stolen. It's a father's job to attend to the details, to plan ahead for every catastrophe, to make sure I always had one more trick up my sleeve. To see the journey through.

At the end of the bay, far from the madding crowd, we landed on the beach I'd seen in my dreams. Palm trees leaned crooked over the shadowed sand; striated azure water lapped against the shore. The sky was cloudless, and the wind, still churning up waves at the other end of the beach, was calm here. We had the entire stretch of sand to ourselves.

After lunch, Katherine and Hayden closed their eyes in the shade and Galen hunted for more sea glass. He'd found far less than he'd hoped for, and I could see him scanning the beach with more intensity than ever. I went to check on him, hoping to talk him into calling off the search. We'd passed plenty of junk shops and souvenir stands, including several that sold bags of rocks and shark-tooth necklaces and leather pouches full of fake pearls. We'd find something for Max. He should relax and enjoy the beach while he could. As I came up beside him, I noticed the sunburned skin flaking away from his neck and shoulders. I'd slathered him in SPF 50 every morning, but he'd burned anyway, the freckles in his skin like sand trapped in amber. I chided myself for not making him wear a T-shirt, though in the peeling skin I also saw the sloughing off of winter and of his self-consciousness. On this beach, at this far end of a remote bay on a remote island in the ocean, we could be as weird as we wanted. Hayden could swear, and Katherine and I could sip vodka cut with pineapple nectar and beer, and Galen could scavenge to his heart's content. It was why so many of our trips led to water, to Lake Michigan and California and now Puerto Rico. It was for this that we'd stayed in our small house, why we'd given up cable, why we continued to lounge on a couch with Hayden's name scribbled on the side. It was also why I swam every morning and took the boys to the pool on Sunday afternoons. In the water, we became elemental: shirtless and shoeless, our barest and truest selves. We could be who we were when no one was looking.

I set my hand on my son's hot shoulder and said, "The funny thing about sea glass is that glass is made from melted sand that's been blown into a particular shape. When you think about it, sea glass is regular glass that's in the process of becoming what it used to be. I read somewhere that a good piece can take years to form. Like, decades."

Galen stopped walking. He stared intently at the indentation in the sand made by his toe. A wave swept in and filled the hole. "Really?" he asked. "That long?"

The question made me unsure of myself. I'd only been talking, but Galen wanted bankable confirmation I was telling him something accurate. "I think so," I said. "I'm pretty sure."

He nodded, and tottered off away from me. I returned to my towel, Katherine and Hayden asleep in the shade.

Obsession is at heart an act of faith. Not of madness so much as hope. If you can bridle every contingency and mitigate every possible disruption, root out every flaw, the system will operate perfectly. The splendid outcome you once imagined and the cranking cogs of the universe will align, and you'll become one, in harmony. The process may be anguished, but the results, when they come, are beautiful.

For the next hour, while his mother and brother slept, Galen gathered up every hunk of broken glass he could find—not sea glass, but ordinary glass, which the beach gave forth in abundance. He carried each fragment to a pile he'd made beneath a palm tree. Once he'd amassed enough, he scooped up the pile and headed for the water, both palms full. He swam with his arms above the surface, his face popping up every few kicks to breathe. He didn't hurry. Thirty yards out, over deep water, he stopped swimming and let the pieces tumble through his fingers and sink to the bottom. Rather than put the glass in the garbage, he wanted to give the ocean a chance to do its work. To worry over the shards and cinders until they were polished smooth and washed ashore for another kid to find.

Get Up the Yard

I couldn't find Hayden anywhere. He'd disappeared while I was scanning our passes at the YMCA, and after twenty minutes of milling around and calling his name like an idiot, he still hadn't turned up. He was cutting into my swimming time, and I was feeling jittery and greasy, which happens when I'm away from the chlorine for too long. The longer I hunted for him, the more I grew annoyed. Then I began to feel guilty because even though Hayden had been coming to the Y since he was two months old and knew the place better than the janitors, he was only eight and easily tempted by candy. With every passing minute, the odds were increasing that he was tied up in the back of a white van headed toward the Canadian border.

The front-desk attendants hadn't seen him. They swore that the front entrance was the only way in or out and that all the back exists had alarms that would sound if the doors were opened. I knew that wasn't entirely true because I often used the door by the Dumpsters as a shortcut to my car. The desk attendants offered to put the facility on lockdown. No one in or out until Hayden was located. That would involve a lot of people running around and the cops coming, so I said, "Let me take one more lap." I retraced my steps, starting with the common area adjacent to the snack bar. I'd come through here at least a dozen times already.

I turned the corner, and there he was, seated alone at the last table closest to the vending machines. He waved when he saw me, as though we'd agreed to meet right here. "Where were you?" I said. "I've looked everywhere. I was getting worried."

"Around," he said.

"You're eight," I said. "You're not allowed to loiter."

"Well, I'm here now."

He sat with his hands clasped together atop the table and his chest pressed tight against the edge. I could tell he was hiding something. I cupped my hand over his shoulder and moved him back. Beneath his thigh, peeking out the hem of his shorts, I caught a flash of red plastic. A candy wrapper. Two, actually: a Reese's Fast Break bar and a bag of Skittles, both emptied of their contents. Hayden's teeth were blue. Leaning closer I could see the faint chocolate shadow rimming his lips.

"We talked about this," I said.

Everywhere we went, people tried to feed the boys sugar. The barbershop, the bank, the dry cleaners—they all had jars of suckers and Jolly Ranchers the proprietors tried to press into the boys' hands with a wink and a glance over their shoulders, like a drug deal was going down. Hayden volunteered to run errands with me on Saturdays because he knew every sugar stash in the city. The old guys who ran the Ace Hardware set out a coffee urn and a package of E.L. Fudge next to the paint display. Hayden could empty the plastic trays of cookies in less time than it took me to buy a light bulb. And that's only the stuff I saw.

School was a whole other problem. Every week at least one kid brought in cupcakes to celebrate a birthday or half-birthday, the school sold Dairy Queen Dilly Bars on Fridays as a fundraiser, and if ever there was a slowdown in the pipeline, the teachers themselves would dole it out. I had a hunch that sending the kids home tweaking on artificial sweeteners was how the teachers paid back parents for dumping our kids with them all week long. I'd seen groups of teachers at the bars a few times, and I'm here to tell you that elementary school teachers can drink. If anyone had steam to blow off, it was them, and after watching a crowd of kindergarten teachers in Christmas tree sweaters pound tequila shots, there wasn't much I was willing to put past them.

In an effort to curb the boys' sugar jones, Katherine and I had emptied the cupboards and freezer of as much junk food as possible. But instead of eating the fruit we left on the counter or snacking on the nuts and raisins we bought to replace the Chewy granola bars, Hayden had turned into a bit of a small-time thief. He'd absconded to the basement with the bowl of Splenda packets we kept beside the coffee maker, emptying them into his mouth one at a time and hiding the evidence behind the washing machine. Once those were gone, he started scrounging for cash. I kept finding the coin tray in my car cleaned out, the change jar on my nightstand reduced to nothing but dirty pennies. We couldn't leave the house without Hayden looking to score.

Before leaving for the YMCA that day, in fact, I'd asked Hayden to empty his pockets. He'd pulled them both inside out, then showed me his hands and shook out his shirt. I even peeked down the back of his undies. His little white buns concealed, from what I could tell, no secret stash of cash.

"Where did you hide the money?" I asked him.

The corners of his stained mouth curled. He was proud of himself for putting one over on the old man. "In my shoe."

"You disobeyed, and you lied to me," I said. "You lied right to my face."

He shrugged. "I wanted some."

I was still angry that evening when I recapped the day's events for Katherine. The longer I droned on, the more her eyebrows screwed closer together. It was the face she made when things weren't adding up. "I don't understand where he got the money in the first place," she said. "He spent all of his last week." I went for my wallet. I'd broken a twenty that morning to buy a cup of coffee. I could clearly remember returning eighteen dollars to my wallet. The ten and the five were still there, but the ones were missing. I stood at the bottom of the stairs counting up all the breaches of father-son trust that had occurred in the last few hours. Not only had Hayden caused me to miss half my allotted swimming time while he gorged himself on 450 nutritionally fatuous calories of partially hydrogenated soybean oil, blue #1, and glucose syrup and then lied about it, but the money used to procure the contraband had been stolen from *my* wallet. When I was a kid, my dad's wallet was like the Ark of the Covenant in *Raiders of the Lost Ark*, a sacred vessel and the source of all blessings and fear. I couldn't recall a moment when I'd touched my dad's wallet without his hand on it, too. It was too powerful to handle on my own. It stung me to realize the boys didn't see my wallet the same way.

I called up for Hayden. It was time for punishment.

But how, exactly, to punish him posed something of a problem. I grew up in an era when punishment took one of two forms: spanking or grounding. Spanking was the preferred method before, say, puberty kicked in, at which point the judicial system switched to grounding. When I was Hayden's age, everyone I knew got spanked. Some friends got spanked in front of company, their parents setting their scotch and sodas on a coaster just long enough to tan some butts before rejoining the adult conversation. Even our school spanked. My elementary and junior high principals both kept wooden paddles wrapped in duct tape behind their desks. If you opted for swats, they'd call your parents to make sure it was okay, and once they got the green light, you'd bend forward, hands on your knees, and think of Christmas. My mom was the MacGyver of spanking. She could make use of whatever she found within arm's reach, whether it was a hairbrush, a spatula, a rolled-up magazine, or, if all else failed, her shoe. Getting grounded, in contrast, was like a teacher making an in-class exam a take-home paper. There was less pain up front, but it lasted much longer.

When it came to my boys, I lacked the paternal instinct for meting out pain. The boys' swearing often made me laugh, and it never seemed fair to chuckle at a perfectly landed "Bite me, asshole," then punish the speaker for saying it. I had a temper that occasionally culminated in thunderclaps of yelling, but the boys had figured out that my bark was much worse than my bite. I'd spanked them a few times, but I hated myself every time I did it, so mostly I yelled until my face turned blue and I ended up hurting myself. I'd stub my toe on the doorjamb, or gesticulate so wildly my hand would knock against the kitchen cupboards, or do any number of stupid things that would make Katherine laugh at my suffering.

To complicate matters, Hayden was a nihilist when it came to facing the music. Having spent much of his life barricaded inside his room at night thanks to the trusty shower curtain rod, the prospect of a time-out struck no fear in his heart. If we quarantined his books and toys, he'd scribble on his walls with a crayon hidden like a shank beneath his mattress. I'd considered strapping him to a chair in nothing but a ribbed tank top and his skivvies—which I was fully prepared to do now if he didn't cop to the theft. The look on my face, and the open wallet in my hand, was enough to convince him to tell the truth. "Am I grounded?" he asked when he came down the stairs.

"Grounded isn't the right word for what's coming," I said.

"What are you going to do to me?" For the first time, he looked actually scared. I considered it a small victory. I tried to think of the worst job I could subject him to that wouldn't prompt the neighbors to call Child Protective Services.

"Get ready to pull some weeds," I said.

Pulling weeds was my father's preferred mode of punishment. If ever I sassed or grew too hyper or slapped my sister, I'd be turned out to the yard with a plastic trash bag and orders to clear the beds along the driveway. Pulling weeds is a fundamentally different activity from gardening. Gardening aims toward sculpting and beautification and can involve the satisfying hum of power equipment or the crisp snip of pruning shears. Pulling weeds is chain gang work, trash picking by another name, Man vs. Nature in the most elemental, back-breaking sense. And in Houston, the weeds, like the cockroaches and pickups and hairdos, were just massive. They'd evolved to grow especially thick in order to withstand the triple-digit heat and sauna-like humidity. Pulling a Texas dandelion out of the ground was like extracting a molar from an elephant's mouth.

I'd tried to make the boys do various jobs over the years, all with disastrous results. After patiently teaching Galen how to use the lawnmower, he'd cut a path through the lawn that looked amazingly similar to the cover of Led Zeppelin's "Crop Circles" box set. After months of empty threats to make Hayden scrub the toilets, I decided to make good and sent him into the john with the caddy of cleansers. He emptied half the can of Ajax into the toilet bowl before pouring the rest onto the living room rug and spraying it with Windex. It formed a tenacious paste that required a putty knife to remove. Pulling weeds, I believed, would prove a simpler, purer task. Just a boy with a trash bag and his thoughts for company.

Early Saturday morning I walked Hayden to the garden beneath the pines at the back of the yard, a stretch of dirt spanning the entire width of the property and long dominated by dandelions and buckwheat. We'd tried once to grow vegetables there but soon realized the grocery store had far better vegetables, grown by farmers who actually knew what they were doing. Galen wanted to grow pumpkins one year, so we tried that, too, and ended up with massive, snarling vines that formed a barbed-wire barricade around the weeds. My last bright idea had been to layer the beds with newspaper to kill everything beneath it, but that only gave the squirrels something to read while they burrowed through it. Bits of shredded newspaper still blew against the house every time the wind picked up.

I handed Hayden his trash bag and the hand spade, the one Katherine used for potting flowers. "Here you go, my friend," I said.

"How many do I have to dig up?" His eyes grew wide as he surveyed the knee-high jungle engulfing his feet.

"Get digging," I said. "I'll let you know when you're done."

I watched him through the back window, the sun on his scalp, his shovel working the soil. Every few seconds Hayden sat back on his knees and squinted at the house—for me or Mom or anyone to rescue him from this purgatory. As punishments went, it seemed to be working, though after an hour of work he'd cleared a section about the size of a dinner plate. "What are you thinking about?" I asked when I went out to check on him.

"I'm thinking I sure have learned my lesson," he said. "Can I be done now?"

It was early May and as fine a day as we'd had all year. I could hear the mourning doves and titmice in the branches. It had been two years since our failed bid to sell our house, two years since we'd decided to remain on this little patch of earth, in our small city in northeast Wisconsin, in our jobs and neighborhood, in communion with our small but delightful circle of friends. We'd kept the possibility of leaving in our back pockets, a last-ditch ejection-seat option in case life here turned out to suck, and we'd come close a few times to pushing the button. But we hadn't, we'd stayed, and for better or worse, the house and the land it sat on were home.

Standing among the weeds with Hayden I recalled how I'd stood in more or less this same spot looking back at the house on the day we decided to buy it. We were fairly certain Hayden was conceived the night our offer was accepted, which meant that Hayden's entire existence was congruent with our possession of the place. I remembered parking the car in the garage on the day we brought him home from the hospital, Katherine and I still shaky with fear after his touch-and-go time in the NICU. He'd learned to walk here, and talk, and in his tiny bedroom beneath the eaves of the roof he'd undoubtedly stared up at the ceiling as the morning light squeezed through the blinds and understood that he was himself, separate from other people, *I* and therefore *not you*. Our house was the only one he'd ever known, and the odds were decent that he'd live nowhere else until he lived on his own. That fact alone gave me reason enough to invest in it. The houses we grow up in have ways of not only containing our childhoods but defining them: They're the stages of our earliest, most primal memories, and from them we each derive our idiosyncratic conceptions of home. What had felt to me like an arbitrary decision eight and a half years ago (we had only a few days to look for a place to live and our budget was tight) would end up playing an outsized role in how the boys thought about themselves, the places they saw in their minds when they considered where they were from. Hayden's DNA was knit with this ratty patch of weeds. I owed it to his future to transform it into something worth remembering.

But when I pushed the spade into the soil, I realized why Hayden had been working so slowly. Last winter's snow had left a crusted scrim over the top layer of dirt. The second and third layers were bone dry from the pine trees along the perimeter. Even with a good shove, the blade barely sank an inch. The earth was as hard as concrete. "See?" Hayden said. "It's impossible."

"Nothing's impossible," I said. "We just need a bigger shovel."

We rented the largest rototiller the hardware store had on hand, an orange Husqvarna with a mouth the size of an oven door and counter-rotating tines ferocious enough to mulch a tree stump. I told Hayden to make sure the dog was inside the house before I yanked the starter cord. A black cloud of exhaust puffed out of the engine, and the entire contraption began to hop and shimmy, itching to gnaw a hole through the center of the planet. Weeds came up whole, stringy roots and all, along with hunks of pumpkin rind, old newspaper, clumps of hardened dog shit, and at least two dinosaur bones. I could have dug a hole for a swimming pool in under an hour had I let the thing go.

Hayden followed behind me, well back from the grinding jaws of dismemberment, gathering up whatever the tiller ejected. He hauled one bucketful at a time, with both hands and plenty of anger, to the compost bin, then came back to gather more. I steered the tiller in uneven zigzags across the garden, then turned and cut even ziggier zigs and zaggier zags in the other direction, Hayden on my tail the entire time. As long as the tiller ran, he kept hauling. Soon the garden was free of weeds, and the cracked, winter-hardened dirt had been churned into a loose, loamy, chocolate-syrup black soil oozing with phosphates and earthworms. Whatever vegetation had been planted here seventy years ago when the house was built had been ground back into its primordial elements.

"Now that we've got the weeds out, what should we plant here?" I asked Hayden.

He lifted his shirt to wipe his face, flashing a bit of his pale stomach. "Money."

"Wouldn't that be nice?"

"Money's printed on paper, right? Paper's made from wood. I'm thinking we find out what kind of wood is used for money paper and plant that. Then we can sell it."

It wasn't the dumbest idea I'd ever heard.

"How about watermelons?" Hayden said. I immediately had visions of vines growing through our windows. "Think of all the picnics we could have!"

"How about we see what the nursery has," I said. I hefted the rototiller into the hatchback and bungeed down the gate. Hayden climbed in up front—tall enough now to ride shotgun—and rolled down his window. He fished my spare sunglasses out of the glove compartment, propped his elbow on the sill, and the two of us headed out.

When I described the garden to the sales associate, noting the five pine trees that shaded the soil, she said bark mulch would probably be my best bet. "You mean, like mulch mulch?" I asked.

She wore dream catcher earrings and had a cat tattoo poking up from the collar of her polo shirt. "Pine trees suck the water from the soil like frat brothers at a keg party," she said. "Not much you can grow under a pine tree. Mulch is no muss, no fuss."

"How about watermelons?" Hayden asked.

"Pumpkins are the better gourd for drier soils," she said. "Or squash."

"I want something green," I asked. "Low maintenance but pretty to look at."

"Well," she said, turning to stare into the canopied section behind her, the kitty stretching into fuller view. "You *could* try pachysandra."

Pachysandra, she told us, was a Japanese plant with waxy leaves "indifferent to drought and cold." I liked the idea of the plants as "indifferent," as if they had better things to do than react to the elements. "Plant them deep and six inches apart and they should be okay," she said. "Water them in real good. Morning and night."

We loaded a flatbed cart with as many as we could fit and rolled the sled toward the register. For a wheeled contraption on concrete it moved oddly like the rototiller. The garden center was busy with shoppers, older women in straw hats and men in white-on-white New Balance sneakers shuffling among the shrubs and trees with their hands behind their backs and futzing over the peonies and the poppies. Steering through them, I felt a pang of worry that I was, without having ever intended it, turning into a middle-aged, middle-class, Midwestern beer-drinking schlub who spent way too much time thinking about his yard when I ought to be planning our next trip overseas or attending Fellini retrospectives. To make matters worse, while I stood in line waiting to pay what amounted to that week's grocery budget on emotionally aloof garden flora, my dad texted me a picture of his bare feet in the sand at the beach. The cobalt wave breaking in the background of the photograph looked glassblown. A bodysurfer slid down the face with his arm extended. "Three to four and building," Dad wrote. "Water temp 65. You should be here."

The road past the nursery led west, first into farmland but eventually, if you kept going, into the mountains and, once you got over those, the Pacific. The gap between where I stood and the picture in my hand was 2,500 miles. For a long moment I thought about it.

Once we were home and on our hands and knees in the garden, turning holes in the tilled soil and lowering the pachysandra plants one at a time, I felt better. Hayden's energy had rebounded, thanks to a burger and a root beer, and he'd stopped asking to go inside and watch TV. We'd stopped talking about the work we were doing as punishment; instead, it was just work. In the same manner that I'd acquired a taste for brussels sprouts and spinach, I'd grown to love work, in particular hard, physical labor. My hands in the dirt, the sun on my back, my knees earth-stained and sore. A full day of teaching and writing could leave me as bedraggled as a ditch digger, even on days when I didn't move more than a hundred feet from my desk. Drudge work offered an unexpected but definitive reprieve. The more my body hurt, the more my mind was at ease. I'd never been especially handy and was all thumbs when it came to machines, but certain tasks I'd hated as a younger man—like helping friends move—I now found oddly enjoyable. There was a Euclidian pleasure to be found in stacking square boxes inside a rectangular truck, all those tidy corners fitting together. At its core, work held the same pleasure as swimming: monotonous and repetitive but also cathartic and meditative. On several occasions, it had even saved me from myself.

I didn't know if my attitudes about grunt labor were anomalous or annoyingly shopworn, and I definitely didn't believe that hard work, whether with body or mind, was a virtue exclusive to men. But I did believe in work as a value worth instilling in the boys. Galen was self-motivated but easily frustrated; Hayden most often sought to complete every job as quickly and as effortlessly as possible. He cleaned his room by shoving his dirty clothes under his bed, and we had to check his math homework at night because left to his own devices he'd answer every word problem with "Just because."

The fact that Hayden had been working for this long seemed a minor miracle. Even Katherine couldn't believe it. She shot me a thumbs-up from the kitchen window. I pulled back the dirt, Hayden lowered the seedling, and together we packed the soil around the base of the stem. "You know," I said, "one day you might have a kid. You'll make him do jobs. Or her, if she's a girl."

"Is that why you had me?" he asked. "So you'd have a slave?"

"Trust me, my young friend," I said. "Having kids is not about saving yourself any work. Or money, for that matter."

"So?" he asked. "Why *did* you decide to have me?"

"Well, we didn't exactly decide. You just happened. Mom and I weren't planning on it."

"I was an accident."

"In a manner of speaking," I said. "So was your brother."

"Were you happy about it at least?"

"Of course I was," I said. "Once I stopped being so scared."

Hayden scooped his hand through the dirt and dropped in a handful of root promoter. He didn't look up. I noticed the scalp beneath his hair turning pink. "You were scared of me?"

"Not of *you*. Just about having you. We didn't have much money when your brother was born, and I didn't know if we could afford to have another baby. I was scared of how my life would change. When you have kids, you're responsible for them. You don't get to do all the things you used to do. Imagine if someone said you couldn't ride your bike anymore. Even if you hadn't ridden it in a while, you'd be kind of freaked out if you suddenly no longer had the option."

"What would you be doing if you didn't have me?" he asked.

The funny thing was, I couldn't think of anywhere else I wanted to be right then. Not even the beach. "Probably this," I said. "Except I'd be alone."

"What would you be doing if you weren't out here with me?" I asked Hayden.

"Watching TV."

"Is this better or worse?"

He sat back on his heels and wiped his hands on his shorts. The pachysandras were spread out in a tidy grid. In a few weeks, they'd blossom with small purple flowers that would turn a deep violet when the sun dropped behind the pines. "A little of both," he said.

The last seedling went into the ground nearly nine hours after Hayden and I had started that morning. I pushed myself to my feet and walked like a humpback to fetch the hose. Katherine came into the yard to admire our work. Hayden stood with his mom while I watered in the plants, the spray from the nozzle throwing rainbows across the garden. Hayden had streaks of dirt on his forehead and shirt and calves, black fingerprints on his cheeks like war paint. I felt the long day in my knees and back and knew I'd feel much worse in the morning.

Katherine said, "Tom Thumb here was telling me all about pachysandra."

"It's from Japan," Hayden said. "That's what the lady at the nursery said. Also that we have to water it good for the next few weeks. Morning *and* night."

"Should we plant more tomorrow?" I asked. "Tackle the weeds behind the garage?"

"No way," Hayden said. "Tomorrow I am definitely watching TV."

I woke up the next morning not to the sound of the TV but of the water running, that unmistakable metallic echo through the walls. I thought I'd shut off the hose sprayer; I had no memory of shutting off the spigot or coiling the hose. If the water had been running all night, the plants would be swamped, the garden flooded, all our hard work washed out. I hobbled to the window and pulled open the curtain, expecting the worst. Hayden stood at the back of the yard in the first morning light, tending to the fruits of his labor.

The Q Word

With two hours to kill before the next game, I suggested we go for a burger. Galen and I had been trapped inside an un-air-conditioned high school gym since seven that morning, and I was dying for fresh air. His basketball team had suffered double-digit blowouts in its first two games, and in case the losses weren't humiliating enough, Galen had missed three out of his four free throws. At home and in practice he was a free-throwing machine, but here the shots wouldn't fall. The fact that the extra points wouldn't have made any difference in the games' outcomes did little to assuage his disappointment. He slumped away from the court with his arms dragging at his sides, a Cro-Magnon tween clad in nylon mesh. I figured a burger and a soda would do him some good.

School had been out for going on three weeks, but basketball season was only now winding down. The Christian school where we'd been sent to play the year's last tournament was in Waupun, Wisconsin, a crossroads town on the highway halfway between our house and Madison. I'd driven past the town a hundred times but never had any reason to stop. It didn't dawn on me until we were driving through Waupun's sleepy downtown that ten in the morning on a Saturday was not only a little early for lunch but for breakfast as well. Plenty of people, including Katherine and Hayden, were still asleep. The town's supper clubs were closed, the neon beer signs reduced to dark shapes in the tavern windows, and though there had to be a diner somewhere, I couldn't spot it. Our choices came down to McDonald's or Culver's, which is sort of like McDonald's only with more butter and ice cream. Culver's had fewer cars in the lot, so I headed there.

Galen and I stood on the front patio while we waited for the front door to unlock. The hydrangeas in the garden beneath the windows were at their zenith, big and pink and open; the only cloud in the sky was a contrail from a plane. There's a kind of Murphy's Law that applied to tournaments: If we were going to be stuck inside all day, the weather would undoubtedly be sublime. Gloomy days, when the rain didn't fall so much as hover in the sky, waited for our weekends off. When our burgers slid down the little aluminum ramp, Galen and I wordlessly agreed to eat outside at a table adjacent to the parking lot. He gathered the napkins and ketchup packets while I carried the tray. I could see the steady flow of cars and trucks heading north on the highway, towing boats or with kayaks and bikes racked on their roofs. I could picture the places they were headed: Northwoods' lakes surrounded by stands of pine, the water clear and deep and teeming with pike and bluegill; the Lake Michigan shoreline dotted with colored umbrellas and blankets. "Man," I said to Galen, "did we miss out or what?"

He shoved half his burger into his mouth. "How long till we have to be back?"

I checked my watch. "We don't play until noon. Plenty of time."

"The team we're playing won their last game fifty-six to nineteen. They're going to cream us."

"You don't know that," I said. Though he did know. I did, too. They were going to get creamed.

He stabbed his fry into his pool of ketchup. "I just want to get it over with."

You and me both, kid, I thought.

We'd spent nearly every weekend since October crisscrossing Wisconsin, eastern Minnesota, and the sprawling burbs north of Chicago for basketball tournaments. Tournaments lasted either all day or all weekend, depending on the size of the trophy. Teams played three qualifying games and then either advanced to the championship round to vie for the hardware or else wound up in what the kids and players somewhat affectionately called the "losers' bracket" to play for places five through eight. If today's first two games were any indication, that's exactly where we were headed. The losers' bracket was billed as an opportunity for the kids to log some extra playing time, but in reality it was a last-ditch chance to save face by squeaking out a win. If your team landed in the losers' bracket, your one and only goal was to get out of the tournament in any place other than dead last.

The prospect of the losers' bracket today seemed a bummer of a way to end the season. Though the boys on Galen's team were only eleven, they took their losses hard. We were a long way from the early days of peewee soccer, when the prizes at the end of the game were orange wedges and grape soda. We were even a long way from Galen's first swim meet, when the bag of cookies had seemed as big a deal as the ribbon. Galen's last year of elementary school unspooled in the car, zooming along the interstate or bumping down two-lane country roads with Google maps open on my phone. If tournaments were close to home, Katherine and Hayden tagged along, but for the most part Galen and I had traveled, just the two of us, through rain and snow and rain turning to snow. We'd smelled the snow coming by the brine in the wind, and months later we'd watched it melt away, the canary grass and clover poking through the gray-brown patches before erupting in a sudden fuzz of greenery. We'd made waffles in Hampton Inns and Embassy Suites in Waukesha and Kenosha and Beaver Dam, bustling metropolises compared with the tiny, downtrodden towns where the gods of basketball most often saw fit to send us.

We'd played in a few slick private sports complexes, but most tournaments were held in junior high and high schools, which in the smaller towns were usually housed in the same building. A table inside the entrance served as a ticket booth (I had to pay between three and six dollars per day for the right to burn my weekend), and once inside I had my choice of one of two places to hang out: the gym, where parents crowded on the bleachers and younger siblings with coloring books and Barbies and gooey Ring Pops saw no reason to respect anyone's personal space, or at one of the folding tables in the cafeteria. The concession stands hawked the usual fare: Skittles and Snickers and M&M's, nachos smothered in Day-Glo slime, paper sleeves of popcorn for a dollar, and slices of Domino's pepperoni for two. Especially enterprising stands also offered hot dogs, and if the stars aligned, you might score a scoop of Crock-Pot-heated Hormel chili ladled inside a bag of Fritos and billed as a "walking taco." Most weekends, I packed a lunch.

In the lulls between games, packs of sweaty boys dribbled their basketballs on the hard floors and huddled around portable video consoles, egging each other on with an intensity rivaling their spirit on the court. The parents sat and visited about the Packers. Would Mike McCarthy pull his head out of his ass and assemble a decent secondary? Could we keep Jordy Nelson healthy long enough to make the playoffs? As though a table full of middle-aged dads and moms trapped inside a cafeteria on a Saturday could somehow affect the tensile durability of a wide receiver's ACL. Now that spring had arrived, there was some talk of the Brewers, though no one expected much out of them. The Milwaukee Bucks, Wisconsin's professional basketball team, were considered too hapless to warrant any discussion.

By midmorning, the trash cans overflowed, the men's room smelled like a chimp pen, and rivulets of Gatorade flowed across the tables and the floor. The stereophonic pinging of the balls against the tiles made it impossible to think, let alone try to read. Instead

I became a wanderer, ambling down the darkened hallways away from the lunchrooms, past the trophy cases and vending machines, stepping around the DO NOT ENTER signs intended to steer me away from the corridors that led into the heart of the school. The signs only made me want to break the rules all the more. I ran my hands along the lockers and admired the student artwork taped to the walls. I cupped my hands around my eyes to peer inside the metal and wood shops, the science labs, the cinder-block classrooms with their orderly rows of desks. A few of the doorknobs I tried opened into storerooms and closets, though one time I was able to get behind the stage in the auditorium where a dismantled plywood set leaned against a brick wall. I felt bad for the kids forced to spend so much time in such dreary places, and I felt bad for myself, for all the hours I spent alone, simply waiting for time to pass. It struck me that being a parent in a high school wasn't all that different from being a student in one: full of frenzy and confusion punctuated by bouts of insoluble loneliness. Whenever I looked out the window at my car in the parking lot and felt the metallic lump of the keys in my pocket, it was hard to resist the urge to make a break for it.

Galen tossed our garbage in the bin, stacked the trays on top, and carried his cup back inside for a refill. I Googled "things to do in Waupun" while I waited for him. The top results were, in order: 1) The Waupun Disc Golf Course; 2) The Waupun Public Library; and 3) The Waupun Dog Park. Numbers one and three were in the same park somewhere near the edge of town and number two was closed.

On the way back to the tournament I decided to detour through the neighborhoods to have a look at where the good people of Waupun lived when they weren't disc golfing or borrowing books or watching their dogs frolic. The houses were Dutch colonials or squat ranches with pickups or minivans in the driveways, mostly older but with neatly trimmed lawns and flowers in the beds. Men in tank tops and blade sunglasses walked behind lawn mowers. Weaving through the streets, I caught sight of a clutch of trees that opened onto what looked like a grassy field, and wondering if I'd stumbled onto the hallowed disc golf/dog park, I steered toward it.

At the intersection, I discovered that what I'd thought was a park was in fact the state prison. The maximum-security prison, though I didn't know that yet. The disjunction between the park I'd been expecting and the lockup I'd stumbled upon was so mesmerizing that I turned into the lot for a closer look. The redbrick visiting center at the front looked remarkably school-like, with an entrance framed by twin flagpoles and green shrubs beneath the tinted windows. A few families moved toward the door from the visitors' parking lot, which was already full of cars.

The yard was encased inside multiple rows of chain-link and spiral barbed wire. I drove as close to it as I could, craning my neck for a look inside. I was gawking and I knew it. Katherine had stood in rooms with women inmates giving birth while shackled to the delivery bed, a pair of male guards posted at the door with front-row seats to the miracle of life in case—what?—the women decided to use the baby as a diversion and mount an escape? More likely the guards and shackles were there so the women wouldn't forget, even in childbirth, that they were prisoners. Moving along the fence of the Waupun prison with Galen beside me, I figured it was better to look than not to look, to take an up-close view of the place while we could so that the next time Katherine told us about the prisoners treated at the hospital or NPR aired a story about criminal sentencing practices, my son and I would better understand the places being discussed. The people inside were human even if—especially if—they weren't always treated that way.

At the end of the chain-link a narrow road looked as though it led away from the prison and back to the street. I could see cars parked on the other side of the grass. I got halfway down the road before I realized it didn't. I was on the perimeter road that cir-

cled the prison. The road wasn't much wider than my car and had
sloped grassy shoulders on either side. If I attempted a three-point
turn, I'd end up in the ditch. I had no choice but to continue to the
corner guard tower, a thermometer-shaped spire with a windowed
observation room up top. As I pulled closer, a guard emerged from
the observation booth and leaned his hands on the railing. He
wore a navy ball cap and was thirty feet up, but I could see his
tightened mouth and the rifle on his shoulder. I flipped a U in the
gravel behind the tower, looked up, and saw that he'd moved to
the back railing to watch me. I waved in a manner meant to say,
Sorry, and he held out his hands in a posture that said, *What the
hell are you doing?*

"We shouldn't be here, Dad," Galen said.

"No kidding." I headed back toward the front, carefully con-
trolling my speed so as not to look like I was trying to flee. At the
far end of the road I could see another vehicle, the chrome grille and
headlights of a pickup, closing the space between us. I pulled as far
as I could onto the shoulder to let him pass. The driver nosed the
truck's grille close to my front fender.

The guard wore the same chambray shirt and navy cap as his fellow officer in the tower. I rolled down the window and held up both
of my hands, not above my head but above the wheel, so the guard
could see them. "I'm sorry," I said. "I thought this road led back to
the street."

"It doesn't." He wore mirrored blade sunglasses and an expres-
sion of unalloyed contempt. "There's a sign back there that says 'Do
Not Enter.'"

"I missed it." I'd been so busy looking through the chain-link
that I'd never seen the sign.

"What are you doing here?" he asked.

"We're in town for a basketball tournament." I pointed to Galen's jersey. "We're killing time between games."

"Well, this isn't a good place to kill it."

"I'm sorry," I said again. This time I added, for good measure, "Yes, sir."

"In the future, pay attention to the signs," he said, stepping back from my window. "So you don't wander down the wrong road."

Back at the tournament, Galen wasted little time ratting me out. He informed his teammates and their parents that his dad had almost been arrested at the prison, thereby obligating me to explain myself to an audience only slightly less skeptical than my first. One of the moms had grown up in Waupun, the daughter of a corrections officer. She echoed what the guard had said. The prison was no place to mess around. As I followed Galen into the gym and took a seat on the bleachers, I found myself thinking about the guard, his icy cop-meets-baseball-coach stare behind his mirrored lenses, and his admonishment to be wary of wandering down the wrong roads. I wondered if he was more right than even he knew.

I'd never quite moved past the ambivalence I'd felt at Galen's first swimming meet—about the time and energy youth sports demanded and the ugliness sports seemed to produce among the parental set. But I also believed in the good stuff: the real benefits of a strong, physically active body, the bonds forged by team camaraderie, the break from technology that sports more or less necessitated, the humility required to win as well as to lose. Though my love for swimming was boundless to the point that I nearly cried when Michael Phelps mounted the medal podium at the Beijing Olympics to receive his eighth gold medal and undisputed title as Greatest Olympian of All Time, I'd long ago promised myself to allow the boys to play the sports they chose for themselves. My past didn't have to become their futures.

When Galen had said he wanted to hang up his goggles and give basketball a try, I'd encouraged him. We'd inherited a hoop above the garage when we bought our house, and Galen had shot on it for as long as he'd been able to hold a ball. By the time he was eight, he could sink the ball through the net from anywhere in the driveway, including a shot that passed through the branches of the maple tree, crocheting the nylon net with twigs and leaves. We signed him up for the boo-boo league at the YMCA where the boys wore cotton T-shirts instead of nylon jerseys. Galen was five inches taller than any other boy on the court; he was also light, agile on his feet, had good hands, and liked the compact dimensions of the court, the hustle and flow of the game. I started sniffing around for club teams and found several in our area, all set up to feed into the high school programs. The boys and girls on the club teams had all been standouts at the YMCA, if they'd bothered to play there at all. Galen was good, but many of the other kids were better. When the club season ended, I arranged for Galen to take private lessons with the captain of the basketball team at the college, a strapping young lad about to graduate summa cum laude, not a single B on his transcript and a good job lined up in Milwaukee. Textbook role model. Galen thought he was the coolest guy on the planet. I was certain I was doing the right thing for my son.

Galen played in a three-on-three league over the summer and returned to the club in the fall. When that season wrapped up, we moved to an Amateur Athletic Union team, a national youth sports organization that, in addition to increasing the level of coaching and competition also expanded our travel radius to a tristate region. The AAU season started the weekend after the club season finished, which I thought was a good thing. Basketball, like every sport, relies on muscle memory. The more he played, the more he'd improve.

After ten months of uninterrupted practice and tournament play, Galen could dribble as well with his left hand as with his right, bounce a pass between an opponent's legs, and run any number of choreographed plays with names like "Nevada!" and "Weed Whacker!" and "Milkshake!" But the more I tried to help him improve, the more there was to do. At every tournament, even the ones way out in the sticks, I passed booths advertising summer basketball camps, shooting clinics, nutritional supplements, professional private coaching. It was all so familiar—such trappings were also hawked to swimmers, as well as to every athlete in every other sport—yet instead of making me nostalgic, they struck me as wrong. Wrong, too, were the team names. In one tournament alone we played against the Gladiators, the Crusaders, the Vanquishers, and my all-time favorite, the Predators. I wondered if their mascot was a guy in a trench coat parked in a Buick LeSabre beside a playground. The Crusaders weren't any less problematic. Run out of a church in a town a few miles south of ours, their website said their mission was to promote spiritual values in service of God's kingdom through basketball. I would have sounded like an elbow-patched prig to suggest the players and coaches read up on how well, and by what method, their namesakes promoted spiritual values, so I held my peace. Our team, thanks to our ferocious winters, was the more doctrinally neutral Blizzard.

I could have dealt with all of it had Galen simply enjoyed himself. But the longer he played, the more the tournaments made him miserable. He'd punish himself for days over missed shots and flubbed passes, even when his team prevailed in the end. Despite his height, he wasn't a starter, and usually didn't land into the game until several minutes in, after the tempo had been established and there were numbers on the scoreboard. He jogged onto the floor nervous about making mistakes, which caused him to play tight and defensive instead of loose and gutsy, which predictably led to mistakes that prompted the coach to sit him back on the bench. He cried the first few times his coach pulled him out, but he'd since hardened himself and showed no emotion whenever he returned to the sidelines. I tried consoling him when we were alone in the car, but the conversations often made him upset. Between games he rarely wanted to talk or play cards or hang around me at all. He sat by himself and disappeared into his iPad. After I finished wandering the school hallways,

I usually wound up sitting alone, too, texting Katherine, reading the news on my phone, and wishing for a meteoroid to crash down upon the school in a gigantic ball of white-hot interstellar fury that would at least break the monotony and put us out of our misery.

For a while I thought I was the problem. I thought I was failing my son by not loving his sport enough for the both of us. Yet when I looked around the cafeterias and the gyms, none of the other parents looked especially pleased to be there, either. As the third game got under way, I made eye contact with another dad at the end of the bleachers. I'd seen him at tournaments for months, but we'd talked only on occasion. He looked as starved for conversation as I was. I scooted over and shook his hand. "Long day," I said.

He wagged his head. "I've been doing this for fifteen years. My oldest is about to graduate from college. She played from the time she was seven." Our team had the ball in the paint, and we paused to watch. His son was as gangly as a baby giraffe but fluid on the court and deadly from beyond the arc. His shot swished the net without grazing the rim. The dad nodded approvingly and continued. "My youngest is seven now and just finished his first season. I figure I've got a decade to go. At least."

"That's a lot of basketball."

He sighed. "I've seen the inside of a lot of gyms, that's all I can say."

"Your older daughter play in college?"

"God, no," he laughed. "By the time she finished high school, she was so burned out she never wanted to see a basketball again. She won't even watch it on TV with her brothers."

"So, was it worth it?" I asked.

"Builds character," he said. I could tell by his half grin he didn't believe it, not all the way. I'd heard that phrase—sports build character—my entire life and I'd begun to wonder whether it was even true. Did youth sports *really* impart discipline and determination in ways that other activities—like learning Greek, say, or long hikes in the backcountry, or painting a fence—could not? I mean, really, how often does a childhood sacrificed on the altar of sports confer advantages in adulthood? With swimming, at least I could believe that if I were to fall off a boat I'd have a good chance of making it to shore. Yet even in that case success would have very little to do with how many races I'd won as a kid.

"Did she have fun at least?" I asked the dad.

"Some of the time, I think," he said. "But it wasn't really about fun."

"What was it about?" I asked. The answer, I realized, mattered a great deal to me.

The buzzer sounded for halftime. We were down by twelve.

He opened his hands and gazed down at his palms. "They're kids. What else are they going to do?"

In the losers' bracket that afternoon, Galen's team faced off against the only other squad that had also managed to lose all three preliminary games. Galen subbed in late in the first half and scored a jumper at the top of the key, then caught the ball under the net for an easy layup in the second half. His team won by six, a tight margin compared with the other matchups, but enough to earn Galen and his fellow ballers seventh place instead of eighth, and a copper medal suspended by an orange ribbon. The team gathered, sweaty and exhausted, before the dais for a final picture. The coach shook the boys' hands on their way out of the gym, thanking them each by name for their dedication and good effort, for playing hard all season and never giving up.

"It was a tough win," I said to Galen as we walked to the car. I bumped his shoulder with my fist. "You should be proud."

He nodded but didn't respond. Merging onto the interstate, I caught him staring down at the medal. I suspected that he saw through the bullshit. A narrow win at the end of a trifecta of blowouts and a two-dollar medal were weak consolation prizes.

I was glad the season was over, glad that with the Fourth of July the following weekend our summer could finally begin. I was glad, too, that Galen had decided not to play in the three-on-three league, though after all these months of practice and playing, eight weeks off didn't feel long enough to remedy his unhappiness.

After a half hour of silence, during which time I tried and failed to say anything that would lift his mood, I blurted out a radical proposal. "Maybe it's time to quit," I said.

I'd been afraid to utter the Q word, even to myself, but our tour of the prison and my heart-to-heart with the other dad had finally pushed it to the surface. Saying it felt like suggesting we rob a bank. "The hell with basketball," I said. "The hell with all of it. It's obvious it doesn't make you happy."

"I like basketball," he said. He peered at the medal lying against his stomach.

"It doesn't seem like you do."

"Well, maybe I don't like it that much. But I don't know what sport to play instead."

"How about *no* sport?" I said. "That's my point. Instead of riding the pine in another awful gym, we could spend our time camping and hiking, skiing in the winter. You know, things we *actually* enjoy."

"You always say stuff like that."

"Like what?"

"Riding the pine. Hit the bricks. Hold the fort. Where do you come up with those?"

"I yam what I yam."

Galen rolled his eyes and crossed his arms over his numbers. I followed his gaze out the window to the rows of corn undulating across the farmlands, the stalks honey-colored and wispy on top, rich and dark green in the furrows. "Every kid at my school plays something," he said.

"Maybe you should be different," I said. "Maybe you should go your own way."

"But then I'll be a nobody."

"Not to me."

He held up his hand. "I know, I know. You love me."

"I'm only trying to consider how our light is spent."

He turned to look at me. "What's that mean?"

"It's John Milton," I said. I'd taught a few of his sonnets the previous spring. "It's about accepting our limits and understanding our purpose in life."

He rolled his eyes again. "Give it a rest, Professor. I just want to go home."

Paroled from basketball, I spent the following Saturday in the yard. I weeded the beds and the pachysandra, trimmed back the maple and dug out the withered roots of a lilac bush that had succumbed to the winter freeze. After lunch I enlisted Galen to help me clean out the garage, shoving the snowblower to the back and bringing forth our bikes and beach chairs. In the process, Galen unearthed my old longboard skateboard, the Sector 9 I'd bought at the end of college.

To call myself a skater at any point in my life would be a tremendous stretch. I was no thrasher, I could neither ollie nor rail slide, and I viewed my various boards far more as toys than as gear. But longboards are made for cruising, and for several years I enjoyed skating along the beach boardwalks in California and down the sloped streets of Salt Lake City. On occasion, I rode with a friend, but I mostly skated alone; it was by and large a private indulgence. I'd put the board away around the time Katherine and I had moved in together, aware that I'd outgrown it but reluctant to part with it forever. The board had somehow survived the move to Wisconsin and had leaned against the back wall of the garage for close to a decade, patiently waiting for my son to find it.

Galen dropped it wheels-first onto the pavement and hopped

aboard with the fluid ease of a natural. Basketball had, if anything, conditioned his balance. He glided down the driveway and into the street, shifting his weight from his heels to his toes and back again, steering the board in long parabolic curves. As he neared the corner, I called after him, "Watch out for cars!" He shot me a thumbs-up without looking back, leaned into his turn, and was gone.

For the rest of the summer, skating was all he wanted to do. He skated to his friends' houses, to the park and pool, up and down the driveway until the light gave out. One evening in late July, he rolled up on me while I was taking out the trash. "Our driveway isn't long enough," he declared.

"It's pretty long when we have to clear away the snow."

"Too bad the driveway can't get longer in the summer and shorter in the winter," he said.

"Can't argue with that," I said. But in his fantasy I found the seed of an idea. I ran inside for my keys and called to Katherine that Galen and I had a quick errand to run. I loaded the longboard into the trunk and drove to the hospital at the edge of our neighborhood. I followed the looping ramps to the top floor of the parking garage. The upper three levels were empty of cars. "Here you go," I said. "One long driveway."

Galen was still buckling his helmet when hospital security busted us. The guard blocked the ramp with his car pointed sideways in the same manner as the guard at the state clink. This guard, though, was younger, his dark hair shiny with gel. "Skating's not allowed in here," he said.

"He's learning," I said. "I was looking for a safe place to let him practice. Can't we try it a few times?"

"No can do," he said. He looked at Galen. "Sorry, buddy."

He waited for us to get back in the car before following us down the ramp and back to the street. He at least had the decency to wave when we turned out of the hospital property.

"I don't know what the big deal was," Galen said. "We weren't hurting anyone."

"Skateboarding is not a crime," I said.

I refused to slink home in defeat. The city maintained several large parking garages downtown. I was smarter the second time. I parked a block away and we entered the garage at the back corner, far from the guard in his glass booth. We climbed the stairs, the board slung under Galen's arm, until we came out on the roof of the building, well above the trees and redbrick buildings lining our main street. The tavern lights had come on, their twisted tubes of neon glowing in the windows, and couples walked together along the sidewalks. A warm wind blew up from the river that ran through the center of the city, pungent with soil and fish and algae. Over the tops of the buildings, our city's modest skyline, the cupola of the college's oldest building shined in the dimming twilight. It was hard for me to fathom that I'd spent a decade in this place, ten winters and ten summers, from the very start of my thirties to the edge of forty, or that the baby I'd once cradled in my arms was now four inches taller than his mom, almost as tall as me.

With babies, a parent's main concern is keeping them safe and healthy, fending off RSV and ear infections and keeping their hands out of the toaster. Their happiness is largely taken for granted. A good meal, a clean set of clothes, and a warm place to sleep—most babies won't ask for much else. I didn't take for granted the boys' good health, their strong bones and immune systems, but lately I'd become far more concerned with their happiness. I'd long ago parted company with the idea that a successful life was a wealthy one; I'd been slower to learn that success wasn't measured in accomplishments, either. All I really wanted was for Galen to look out from a rooftop on a summer night and feel at peace. I couldn't imagine a greater trophy.

I held out my palm to feel the wind and watched it blow Galen's hair away from his forehead. "It's nice up here, isn't it?" I asked.

"Mmmm," he said. "Not bad."

The stairwell door creaked open, and we both turned to look. Three kids stepped through the door, two boys and a girl in their mid-teens, all with stringy, unkempt hair and dressed in baggy cargo pants. Like Galen they carried skateboards, though not one of them had a helmet. They froze when they saw me, and their prolonged assessment gave me a chance to take in the details I may have otherwise missed: the rosacea of acne on the cheeks and neck of one of the boys. The twin rings in the girl's bottom lip, the tattoos on her forearms and wrists. The third boy sucking on a vape pen. A wave of panic passed through me: that by advocating for Galen to quit sports, I was inadvertently pushing him toward the realm of skaters, stoners, and burnouts—a losers' bracket of another sort. I waved away the thought with my hand, as though it were a swarm of river flies, but all the same I could feel its residue prickling my eyes. My son slumped on a worn-out couch in a dirty T-shirt, fashioning bongs from Pringles canisters and garden hose attachments. I was relieved when the skaters dropped their boards to the ground and rolled away.

"Maybe I don't need to wear my helmet," Galen said, once the older kids were gone.

"No way," I said. "No helmet, no skate."

He buckled the chin strap. He pointed the board downhill and let gravity take over. He stood on his toes to carve right, sat on his heels to pull the board back to the left. The wheels clattered softly over the pavement. He turned out of sight, and I moved to the center railing to stare down inside the interior of the structure. The garage levels spiraled down to a small atrium of juniper bushes in a bed of rocks. Galen's wheels echoed in the distance. When he passed by, I heard his voice rising up to me. "Are you okay?" I called down. He didn't answer. His next time around I heard him more clearly and was able to catch the rhythm of the words. He wasn't talking; he was *singing*. His boyish voice was amplified by the cavernous space around him, as well as—there was no denying it—by his joy.

Saturday Night's All Right for Fighting

Pinned to the board above my desk is the picture I took the day we brought Hayden home from the hospital. Because he'd spent his first week and half of life in a Plexiglas box, he'd had to wait until he was eleven days old to meet his brother. Galen caught his first glimpse of Hayden when the nurse helped us strap him into the car, but since Katherine rode home in the middle of the back seat, it's fair to say the boys weren't properly introduced until we'd brought them inside, propped Galen against the arm of our unblemished couch, buttressed him with pillows, and laid Hayden in his arms. Galen's cheeks were red from the early March wind, his hair as orange as a lit match. Hayden's eyes were clamped shut, his lips pursed as if expecting a kiss. Galen looked up and smiled, beatific and protective, and I happened to be standing with the camera at the perfect angle. Most of my photographs come out blurry or with the frame askew, but this one was pure gold. We sent it to our friends and families to announce Hayden's birth. For the rest of that year, I saw it hanging on the refrigerator of almost every house I visited.

What the photograph doesn't show, what Galen's angelic face and

Hayden's kissy face, in fact, obscure, are the events that transpired ten minutes later. I was feeding Hayden a bottle of his foul-smelling, NICU-concocted formula when Galen came galloping across the living room and dove at his brother's face. There was no reason for Galen to do this other than he was two and Hayden had consumed more of his fair share of Mom and Dad's attention in the last weeks. I ducked my head as Galen leapt. He largely rolled across my back and onto the carpet, though not before getting a hand on the bottle and knocking it from Hayden's mouth. Hayden let loose a wail that was as good a sign as any that his lungs were recovering from the illness that had delayed his homecoming for an extra nine days.

Here's the thing: at eleven days old, the idea of an older brother was no more sensible to Hayden than zebra mussels or deep-dish pizza. But as I watched him scream and tried to soothe him, I swore—hand to God—he was milking it.

Nine years later, their dynamic hadn't much changed.

One night Katherine and I were enjoying a glass of wine on our new leather sofa an hour after the boys had gone up to bed when we heard the ceiling creak. We stopped to listen. We heard Galen get out of bed, cross the hallway, release the shower rod, and storm into Hayden's room to beat on his sleeping brother. Once Hayden came to enough to recognize what was happening, he screamed like he was being stabbed in the eyeball with a fork.

"What the hell are you doing?" I called up the stairs.

"I'm bored!" Galen called back.

Hayden whimpered in the darkness behind him. "He's an asshole. Keep him away from me."

It often seemed to Katherine and me that the boys were in a bad marriage. They couldn't get along, but they couldn't leave each other alone. They didn't share a room, but they shared everything else, including underwear and socks and, on most out-of-town trips, a toothbrush. They'd bathed together until Galen swore off baths in favor of showers, and wherever we went, whether across the country or across town, they were stuck together in the back seat. Familiarity breeds contempt, and they were more familiar with each other than any two people on the planet.

If they fought hard enough, we'd send Galen to the basement and Hayden to his room, to put as much space as possible between them. But neither could stand the separation for more than a few minutes. Each was remarkably noiseless when moving through the house in search of the other, and though at first they sounded happy to be reunited, their giggles were a prologue to the inevitable. A non-chalant graze to Galen's elbow while sharing the couch would be answered with a heel driven into Hayden's thigh, who in turn would commence an Apache war scream as he scrambled to the arm of the couch and lunged headfirst for Galen's balls. It happened that fast: elbow graze to groin blow in under thirty seconds. Long before he learned to use the potty or pronounce the letter K, Hayden figured out that a shot to the jewels could fell his enemy more efficiently than an attack on any other body part. He saw no reason to waste time punching elsewhere. Galen's been hit in the baby maker so many times that it'll be a miracle if he's one day able to have children.

Where does this insatiable need to fight come from? Conventional wisdom says it's the Y chromosome—that all young bulls, whether bison, bottlenose dolphins, or boys, are predisposed to lock horns with one other. But in *Testosterone Rex: Myths of Science, Sex, and Society*, psychologist Cordelia Fine argues against the idea that testosterone incites men and boys to fight. "Although we're used to thinking of certain kinds of behavior as 'testosterone fueled,'" Fine writes, "in many cases it would make more sense to instead think of actions and situations as being 'testosterone fueling.' Social context modulates T levels (up or down), which influences behavior (presumably via changes in perception, motivation, and cognition), which influences social outcome, which influences T levels ... and so on." Fine cites a study in which male college students were bumped on the shoulder by a decoy who "added insult to injury" by muttering an offensive word. For the students raised in cultures rooted in male honor and status, the confrontation was correlated with increased aggression and elevated testosterone levels.

Back when Katherine was pregnant with Galen, and especially once we learned we'd be having a boy, we spent a long time talking about how most brands of masculinity hawked to young men celebrated, if not directly encouraged, violence. Video-game soldiers taking aim at enemy combatants, hockey players throwing down their gloves, Aragorn in *The Lord of the Rings* with his Jesus haircut and Excalibur sword chopping off the heads of orcs with every swing of his arm. We deliberately set out to shield the boys from such influences, hoping to raise gentle, peace-loving souls. We asked our families not to send the boys cap guns or plastic swords or slingshots. If such toys arrived, we endured the boys' tears and complaints when we took the weapons away. The same went with video games and movies: *Super Mario Bros.* was okay; *Resident Evil* was not. When the boys pretended to stab and shoot each other with their fingers, Katherine sat them down and told stories from her nights working in the emergency room (in hindsight a bad idea, because soon after, Galen started telling the neighbors that his mom knew a lot of people who'd been stabbed and shot). We even made honest efforts to resist the crude gender divisions that separated the cheap plastic crap sold to boys from the cheap plastic crap sold to girls. When Galen announced he wanted a Cra-Z-Loom for Christmas, we were all for it. Weave away, dude. Hayden was gaga for his Easy-Bake Oven until he figured out the real oven could produce a much greater quantity of brownies in a fraction of the time.

And yet, despite our efforts to fashion ourselves into pacifist-progressive parents, the boys couldn't keep their hands off each other. Friends with daughters were scandalized by Galen's and Hayden's incessant need to drag each other to the ground and slap each other in the face. The fact that Hayden would deign to throw a dart at his brother's leg was seen as inconvertible proof of moral turpitude, and an invitation to make backhanded comments about our parenting. *You must be so patient to put up with all that chaos!* Dads were the worst. I could see them thinking, as their princesses cowered behind their legs, *If those were my boys, I'd rain down discipline like hot lead from a castle wall.* The belief that one could muscle boys into submission stemmed from the same impulse, whether cultural or biological, that made boys want to fight in the first place. Boys fought to establish their places in the world and to protect what was theirs. Or short of that, simply to see who was stronger, badder, nastier.

My boys' penchant for battle may not be fueled by testosterone, but it is undoubtedly biological in another, more specific way. As my sons, they're the descendants of a long line of fighters. Not boxers so much as screamers, shouters, nostril-flarers, gold-medal dish-breakers. My forebears could hurl household objects with an almost artful flourish. My mother had a habit of chucking food down the kitchen hallway when she was upset. Whenever my sister and I heard her ranting in the kitchen, we knew to move carefully around the corner lest we take a jar of peanut butter in the eye. I once arrived at my grandparents' house to find the pendant light hanging over the breakfast table missing one of its glass panels. My grandmother sheepishly confessed that she'd broken it by hurling raw brussels sprouts at my grandfather.

Katherine's a thrower, too, and freely admits it. Her ancestors are Scottish to my Irish and most likely descended from William Wallace and his gang of blue-painted vandals. Her father, uncle, aunts, and grandmother for decades gathered for breakfast on Saturday mornings, an event so predictably pugilistic that my mother-in-law dubbed it the Family Feud. Each week my father-in-law swore he was never going back, but the next Saturday he did, called by the siren of war. I was drawn to Katherine's never-back-down, die-before-surrender spirit that I rightly believed was the hallmark of an uncommon strength, one belied by her small size, her deep laugh, her daily mission to aid the sick and the helpless. In her years as a hospital social worker, she was screamed at, lunged at, swung at, kicked to the ground, and she never once shied away from the job. I found it reassuring that my occasional temper didn't scare her off. She was used to putting up with hotheads, and she didn't take any shit.

Her ferocity could even come in handy. I was once struggling to install a wrought-iron coat hook beside the front door, cranking with all my might to get the screws anchored into the brick wall behind the plaster. After a sweaty and fruitless half an hour, I went to the couch where Katherine was reading and watching me struggle. I insulted her until her face reddened—comments about a woman's figure, I've found, tend to work particularly fast—and when she stood up from the couch I handed her the screwdriver. She had the hook moored tight to the wall in under five minutes. She turned to me, Phillips-head still in her hand, and said, "You're lucky that went your way, Ace." Indeed.

More than any other day of the week, Saturday was our fighting day. When it grew too cold to shoo the boys outside or send them on their bikes to the pool, they turned into a pair of crickets trapped in the same jar. They could slug it out for twelve hours straight with only short breaks to raid the fridge and pee in the snow. The size of our house and the boys' growing heights were undoubtedly mitigating factors. We were essentially four adult-sized bodies competing for space, bumping into one another in the hallways and kitchen. Katherine and I argued more on Saturdays, too. Saturday was the day we waited all week to arrive, our chance to sleep in and catch up on housework, to do everything *and* nothing in the same day. One way or another, Saturday usually ended in frustration and disappointment.

The boys had been going at each other all day, the walls and ceiling rattling like the world's longest freight train was running beneath the house. By the midafternoon, they'd dug into their positions. Galen was in the alcove behind the upstairs half bathroom, Hayden in the built-in shelves hidden beside his bed. From there they'd been launching sorties, storming across the hall, seizing something from the other's room—headphones, baseball cards, petty cash, the last of their candy stashes—before hauling ass back to base. The floor of Hayden's room looked like a table at a flea market, his brother's most cherished possessions laid out for sale. I tried to broker peace, first with appeals to filial loyalty, then with bribes, then, finally, with threats. Having already lost the things they cared most about, neither was in the mood to bargain. The only thing they could agree on was to keep fighting.

By four that afternoon, I'd grown so exasperated that I ordered them into their jackets and gloves and put the dog on her leash. I gave them both plastic grocery sacks and said they were not allowed back in the house until they'd each collected a fresh turd. I wanted to see evidence. Two dumps by our little beagle meant that they'd be out for at least a half an hour.

"Does the poo have to be Allie's?" Hayden asked. I could see the cogs in his mind cranking. Would my son shit in a plastic sack in freezing weather to stick it to the old man? I didn't have a doubt. "If it's anything *but* Allie's poo, you won't see the light of day for weeks." I put my hand on his shoulder. "Walk together, get along. This shouldn't be hard."

"It shouldn't be," Hayden said, a wry smirk curling the side of his mouth. "But it be."

Twenty minutes later, they came down the street, plastic sacks a-swinging. At the edge of our lawn they joined hands and skipped past the window. Their mouths were open and they were laughing, and from a certain angle they looked like each other's closest pals. They knew I was watching. Hayden turned toward the window, and I saw the devilish grin that told me everything I needed to know. They might as well have shot me the middle finger.

I met them at the back door. "Jackets and shoes off and come with me," I said. I pushed the living room chairs against the wall and the big faux-leather ottoman we used in lieu of a coffee table against the window. "If you're eager to fight, then okay," I said. "Let's fight."

I made them take off their shirts. The rules, I said, were simple. No punching in the face or below the waist. I pointed at Hayden, "That means no shots to the ham and eggs." When one said he was finished, the fight was over. First one to quit is the loser. Afterward, everyone got his stuff back. "Clear?" I asked.

"Clear," they parroted. They'd been waiting a long time for this.

"Shake hands, gentlemen." They shook warily, giggling, and then went at each other without bothering to let go. They spun in a circle, hands joined like the knife-wielding thugs in Michael Jackson's "Beat It" video. Galen kicked Hayden in the thigh while Hayden whiffed his knuckles at Galen's shoulder. They jerked away from each other's grip, and Galen leapt up onto the ottoman and commenced an elaborate display of karate chops and high kicks, punching at the air and gritting his teeth. *Hay-yah!* Hayden was so transfixed that he failed to get out of the way, even though Galen didn't attempt to land a blow until the end of his routine. The chop to Hayden's arm sent him reeling backward, his hand at the wound and his bottom lip quivering.

"You can quit anytime," I said. "Just say the word."

Hayden ignored me and trained his gaze on his brother's long alabaster torso. Galen juked and jived, but Hayden had a bead on his target. He powered through the karate barrage and landed a slap to Galen's bare belly so loud it drew Katherine from the other room to investigate. "Ouch," she said.

Galen stared down at his stomach. Before our eyes, the crimson imprint of Hayden's hand came into view, the palm and all five fingers. Galen clutched his stomach, doubled over, and began to cry. Hayden's arm was red, too, and a welt was forming, but in his moment of triumph he'd forgotten the pain. He arched his back and beat his fists against his chest in a full-throated Tarzan yell.

"Are you ready to stop yet?" I asked Galen.

He looked at me like I'd suggested leaving an amusement park after only one ride. "No way," he said. "I'm going to kick his ass."

"Language!" Katherine said.

Hayden swiped the tips of his nostrils with his thumbs. He bounced on his toes. "Come and get some, butt munch."

We've all seen the couple fighting at the gas station, the mall, the moderately fancy restaurant. Instead of concluding with coffee and dessert, dinner ends with a linen napkin tossed over a half-eaten filet and the chair wobbling as the husband or wife stomps away. The abandoned spouse is left staring into his water glass to avoid the stares of the haughty pricks in the dining room while the waiter scurries over with the bill. I've seen it at least a dozen times, and I've shot rooms full of strangers the look a time or two myself. Arguments between couples who've been together a long time have a tendency to rise up out of nowhere like a tsunami; the worst fights come from our deepest submarine trenches, our long histories of past disputes and unrequited good intentions, all the little things that lie dormant ninety-nine percent of the time. There's something cathartic about a good brawl, too, because it clears our closets of its skeletons. I've found that fighting can be a uniquely intimate experience, full of all the heat and ardor of sex, only without the bliss. And therein lies the problem. Allowed to burn unchecked, catharsis can turn caustic.

Even with all the clarity afforded by hindsight, it's difficult to pinpoint the epicenter of the quake between Katherine and me that Saturday last winter. I didn't wreck the car or blow our savings on Internet poker or disappear on a three-day bender. As best I can recall, I was tired. It had been a long week; I'd worked straight through a two-day blizzard to make a magazine deadline while the boys, snowed out of school, had treated their bedrooms and the living room like Keith Richards at the Riot House. The storm had also caused havoc at the hospital, leaving the units Katherine managed short-staffed. She spent most of the morning on the phone, begging nurses to give up their Saturday nights to cover a shift from nine P.M. to three A.M. Not exactly a prime draw. Her phone and pager were ringing nonstop, and she kept closing herself inside the back room to talk, leaving me to run interference with the boys, who were supposed to be cleaning their rooms but were instead hiding with their iPods and bickering. It wasn't fair, I thought, how I got stuck holding the bag of housework and kids while Katherine sat on her phone and fiddled with the spreadsheet on her computer. I swore I saw her looking at blogs about clothes and shoes while she waited for a nurse to call her back. By the time the sun set, the day felt wasted. Katherine was massaging her temples with her index fingers, the boys' rooms were dirtier than ever, and I wanted only to eat dinner and slump on the couch and watch a movie.

Katherine asked me to get a bowl down from a high shelf in the cupboard. As I was fetching it, I bumped her forehead with my elbow. She scowled at me like I'd done it on purpose. "That didn't hurt," I said.

"It hurt some," she said, rubbing her forehead.

"I've been doing chores all day, so maybe you could give me a break."

"Changing the sheets and running the vacuum doesn't help my face feel better," she shot back.

"A little grace would be nice," I said. "You don't have to get so upset."

She dropped the bowl on the counter and marched swiftly away from the kitchen. She tried to lock herself in the bathroom, but I stuck my foot between the door and the jamb before she could slam it shut. I wasn't finished yet. "Stop playing the victim," I shouted. "I was doing you a favor."

"I never said you weren't." She started to cry and turned toward the shower. "Leave me alone."

I didn't want to leave her alone. She was blowing everything out of proportion. It was almost seven o'clock, and I could feel our Saturday night, like the day, on the verge of slipping away. The prospect of a ruined night redoubled my anger to the point that I was yelling at the top of my lungs. I recognized the irony, even at the time, but I couldn't stop myself. William James famously argued that external stimuli led to physiological responses that resulted in emotion, rather than the other way around. Fear or anger were the products of a quickened heart rate, for example. The theory had never been more true than right then. The look on Katherine's face said she was nowhere near backing down. I didn't want her to. I wanted her fury to match my own so that I could continue to holler. After a while, the argument had generated enough hurtful things—accusations launched with such ill-advised phrases as "You always" and "You never"—to keep itself going indefinitely. It was making its own fuel.

I chased my wife from the bathroom to the bedroom to the basement and back again to the kitchen because I hated it when she shut me out and she hated it when I boxed her in. Each room offered new indictments until the original offense, the elbow to the forehead, was burned up like a wad of newspaper between two logs in a bonfire. The argument reached its apogee when Katherine grabbed the car keys and threatened to leave and I punched the bathroom door so hard I felt something crack in my hand. Three weeks later, when I could still barely hold a pen, an X-ray would confirm that I'd broken my fifth metacarpal, an injury known as a boxer's fracture.

The boys had retreated to the living room when the fighting started. They tried to drown us out with the television, but as the argument raged on, they'd had to move farther out of the way until they ended up sitting on the stairs together, the lights turned off as if to hide from us. I'd seen them there as I motored past, but I'd never stopped to reassure them. The clock on the microwave went from seven to eight and then to nine while Katherine and I were howling at each other. I'd fulfilled my own malicious prophecy.

"The boys can hear you," Katherine shouted at one point. We were in the guest room across from the stairs. I cradled my right hand in my left. "They can hear everything you say. Is this how you want them to know their dad?"

"I don't care!" I shouted back. "I don't care if the whole block hears me."

Though of course I cared. I'd cared a great deal. My temper had gotten the better of me. It had flared up against the person I loved most in the world and had made a mockery of everything I'd ever said to the boys about treating other people, especially women (and of all women, especially their mom) with respect. Already I felt ashamed, even if couldn't admit it.

The bedroom door creaked open, and Hayden stepped inside. "I wish you'd stop," he said. In his face, I saw the fear I had discovered when I was about his age. The terror of my own parents fighting and the desperation that accrued with each new argument until I began to grasp that the life I'd always taken for granted as durable was in fact vulnerable to shattering and collapsing. Weeks before my parents told my sister and me that they were separating, I'd sensed it coming. The air in our house had thickened in the same way the sky takes on a dull, flat charge in the hours before a thunderstorm. When they finally brought my sister and me into their bedroom and told us they needed time apart, it felt as though the rain I'd been watching gather had finally come down. There was no surprise in it, only grief. I'd learned the hard way that some arguments were more than passing squalls that rattled the windows in their panes. Some fights could blow down the entire house.

The night before he left Texas, after paying the check at Daddy Did It Fish House, Dad took Devin and me home for the last time. My mother waited in the entryway when we pulled in. Dad usually dropped us off, waving goodbye from behind the wheel as we opened the front door, but that night he shut off the engine and came inside. The papers were signed and filed, the furniture divided, my dad's portion packed on the moving truck that would ferry it to California. After that night, we'd never again stand together, the four of us, in the entryway of the house we'd shared. Devin and I showed Mom our bags of stamped cards and told her about the pictures we'd seen of Dad's new place in California. Dad stood with his back to the door, his hand on Devin's shoulder. My stepmom's maroon Oldsmobile looked foreign sitting in the driveway, a stark reminder that this was happening. He was going. This was the end. My mom said to him, "I'm never going to see you again." This was the first time they'd seen each other without their lawyers present in nearly six months. "Give me a hug," Dad said, and for a long moment they held each other. My mom laid her head on his shoulder. They'd see each other on a few occasions after that night, at our graduations from high school and college, our weddings; over time they'd learn to come together when circumstances required with grace and equanimity approaching an old friendship. But I can't recall them ever touching after this moment.

Looking down at Hayden, I saw in vivid detail every second of that night, the memory so fresh and raw it could have happened that day instead of three decades ago. I touched the back of his head. A jolt of pain shot up my arm from my broken hand. "I'm sorry," I said. I turned to Katherine and said it directly to her, "I'm sorry." Had I said it in the first place, before I'd ever set the bowl on the counter, I could have avoided the entire blowup.

"Me, too," Katherine said, wiping her eyes.

The door widened further, and Galen came in. He put one hand on his mother's shoulder and the other on mine and winched us close. "Kiss and make up," he said. It wasn't a request.

"Not yet," I said, a little too sharply. I was still calming down.

"Are you going to get divorced?" he asked. He grinned like he was joking, but he smiled when he was most afraid.

"No," I said. I put my arms around Katherine. I felt her stiffen and then exhale against me. "Don't worry. Mom and Dad love each other. We were upset."

That seemed to appease the boys for the moment. Enough, in any case, for Galen to let go and step back. One more memory flooded in: the day I sensed the weight of the strife between my parents and asked my mother the same question Galen had asked me. *Are you going to get divorced?* Of course not, she'd said.

Before going to bed that night, I stepped into the frozen night air to let the dog pee and to take out the trash. The tops of my ears turned hard in less time than it took Allie to sniff out a spot to squat, but the cold against my hand felt good. The dome of the night was dense with stars. I let out a long breath and then drew my own steam back inside my lungs, full of regret for the awful things I'd allowed my sons to hear come out of my mouth, the image they now had of their father stomping from room to room. Chances were good they'd never forget it. The night would burrow into their subconscious and wait to be called back up the next time their mom and I argued, or years from now, when they found themselves disagreeing with a person they loved.

The boys had been slugging it out for forty minutes, and there was no end in sight. Their backs and chests and bellies were splotched red. No blood had been drawn, but they'd both absorbed plenty of hard blows. It was time to ring the final bell. A draw was a more than respectable way to end a match. "How about the two of you shake hands, and then I'll get you a snack?" I said.

"Fine," Hayden said, and stuck out his palm. Galen accepted it, his other hand protecting his groin. Given his opponent, it was an understandable posture. "It's over," I said. "Shaking hands means you accept the outcome of the contest. No more punching. Got it?"

"Okay," they said. I pulled the ottoman back to the center of the living room and fished between the sofa cushions until I found the remote. I followed Katherine around the corner to the kitchen. I slid a bag of popcorn into the microwave while she uncorked a bottle of chardonnay. "How long do you think they would have kept going?" she asked.

"Till they dropped," I said. I got a bowl out of the cupboard, this time making sure Katherine was well clear of my elbows. "Hayden fights like you."

"What's that now?"

"He's small, but he fights hard. Dirty, if he has to."

"I fight to win."

"I rest my case, your honor." I emptied the popcorn into a bowl and carried it around the corner. At the edge of the living room I stopped and waited for Katherine to catch up. I wanted her to see. Galen lay on the ottoman on his belly, his chin resting on his hands. Hayden straddled his back. Together they stared at the TV. While Katherine and I looked on, Hayden reached down and raked his fingers through his brother's hair. Galen dropped his head so Hayden could tickle the back of his neck. The boys knew by instinct what I needed to remember: Far worse than losing a fight was the prospect of being apart.

Can You Hear Me Now?

Galen had been dropping hints for months, but that spring he abandoned subtlety for a more direct approach. Every request Katherine and I made of him he took as an opportunity to advance his cause. If I asked him to walk the dog, he'd say, "If I walk her, can I have a phone?"

If I asked him to make his bed: "It's made already. Does that mean I can get a phone?"

If I asked him to hang up his jacket: "Hey, Dad! Did you see that my jacket has a pocket that's the perfect size for a phone?"

"The thing is," I finally said, "I'm not sure you need it. You hardly talk on the phone as it is." I couldn't honestly recall a single occasion when Galen had engaged in a telephone conversation with another person, with inquiries regarding his interlocutor's general state of well-being followed by a discussion of anything constituting a subject. Whenever his friends called, he grunted out a few *what*s and *huh*s before handing the phone to Katherine or me to confer with the other kid's parent. Even when his grandparents called—which they preferred to do via FaceTime so they could see as well as hear the kids—Galen mostly made goofy faces at the screen while my mom or mother-in-law repeated, "Are you there, honey? Can you hear me?"

Hayden, for what it's worth, was an even worse conversationalist. He said neither *hello* nor *goodbye*. If he answered the phone, all you heard was the cessation of ringing followed by the eerie feeling you were no longer alone. When it was time to hang up, he'd simply walk away, leaving you blabbering into the void.

Galen had anticipated my doubts and prepared a rejoinder. "I don't talk on the phone because I don't have a phone," he said. "If I had one, I'd talk more."

"Who are you so desperate to call anyway?" I stared at him sideways for a few moments before the obvious struck me. "Is there a girl you like?"

"Not a girl," he blushed. "My friends." Now that the snow had melted, groups of sixth-grade boys had begun roaming the neighborhood, showing up in packs at one another's houses or gathering in the park to loiter beneath the picnic pavilion. Galen had stumbled across a group one afternoon while riding his bike home from Max's. He asked why he wasn't on the call list and was told, with a shrug, that no one had his number. Because, duh, he didn't *have* a number.

"Please, can I get a phone?" he begged, his hands clasped near his chin.

I was sympathetic to the plight of his social life. Junior high was when organized playdates were shucked off in favor of hanging out, whether at a house or the park or in a parking lot. I could recall the sinking feeling of being left out. Regardless of how it happened, whether your so-called friends had deliberately sought to exclude you or had gone door-to-door trying to track you down, the leaving out was the same. I accepted that the boys would need cell phones eventually. I'd just been reluctant to take the final step.

A recent magazine assignment had given me cause to read several studies tying excessive cell phone use to increased rates of insomnia, depression, anxiety, and weakened cognitive functions, especially among teenagers. Sexting and cyberbullying, both of which occurred among adolescents with alarming frequency, could cause lasting psychological and social damage. A kid texting behind the wheel of a car might as well be drunk. Give a kid a cell phone and you give him a traveling porthole to the electronic jungle. Not only do they walk around with easy access to all the temptations and dangers of cyberspace, but wherever they go online, they leave a trail of digital breadcrumbs that could be stolen or used in some way against them. Our home computer had suffered a nasty virus attack last winter after Hayden had tried to download a game from a dubious website, and it spooked me to think of all the nefarious things Galen might stumble across once he carried the Internet in his pocket. Or of the things that might stumble across him.

The perils of the Net, however, weren't my primary worry. My Tuesday and Thursday classes ran just shy of two hours. For as long as I'd been teaching at the college, I'd maintained a habit of taking a ten-minute break at the halfway point to give the students a chance to stretch their legs and use the restroom, maybe dash to the campus center for a drink and a snack. The year I started, most students had cell phones, but very few had smartphones. They texted, but they didn't text that much, nor did they use every free second to check Facebook and Twitter. As a result, they often spent the breaks talking—to one another but also to me. In this way, I learned about music they were listening to and books they were reading, about their concerns regarding larger, more consequential topics. The environment. The state of American politics. Their hopes and anxieties about the future. Lulled by the informal nature of the chatter and freed from the constraints of the lecture, the students often voiced their opinions in bracingly honest terms. Even the mousey oboist in the forest green turtleneck who assiduously avoided eye contact with me during class for fear of being called on could be coaxed out of her shell. On several occasions, this interstitial conversation became so engrossing that I'd swept my notes aside and let the conversation continue for the duration of the class. But now every student had a smartphone. Flip phones (according to them) were only for construction workers, security guards, and old people. Whenever I gave the class a break, my students' faces immediately plunged to their laps where their phones had been sitting since class began. And those empty ten minutes, once the crucible of so much pleasurable talk, largely passed in silence.

When I'd started at the college, Galen was still in diapers, still drinking from a sippy cup, by all available metrics still a baby. A decade later, he was only a few years younger than my freshmen, many of whom had siblings younger than Hayden. My boys and my students both belonged to a generation that psychologist Jean Twenge has labeled the iGen: a group that has only ever known a constant state of connectivity, who has no memory of a time before the Internet or even the smartphone, a generation for whom "The roller rink, the basketball court, the town pool, the local necking spot [have] all been replaced by virtual spaces accessed through apps and the web." Having witnessed Galen's absorption into video games a few years earlier, which he only ever played offline, I feared that a phone would draw him down a far deeper rabbit hole and sever the last threads that joined us together.

Nevertheless, a phone had become more necessary. We'd dumped our landline several years back, and now that Galen was twelve, he and Hayden both walked home from school several days a week. They'd become, in the parlance of guilty parenting, "latchkey kids." With the boys coming home from two different schools to an empty house lacking a landline, we needed a way for them to reach us. "I'd feel better," Katherine said one afternoon, "knowing I could get ahold of them. I could remind Galen to turn on the lights and unload the dishwasher."

Galen sensed he was on the verge. "Oh, please, oh, please," he said. "I'll turn on every light in the house. I'll unload the dishwasher every day."

I said we could look. I didn't make any promises, even if Katherine had more or less told me it was time to pull the trigger.

The salesman showed us a nice, entry-level device and told me I could set up the plan to exclude data. Galen would be able to surf the Net on Wi-Fi, but away from home or school or Starbucks, the phone would only be good for talk and text. Galen cradled the Samsung like Luke Skywalker wielding a lightsaber for the first time— that is, like a young man on the cusp of his heroic destiny. "I like this one," he said.

I asked the salesman to give us a minute. I pulled Galen aside, into the corner by the Keurig machine. Cars zipped by on the other side of the window and a shaggy-haired teenager in Bozo-red shoes pedaled a bike along the sidewalk, a mere foot from the traffic, his eyes glued to the phone in his palm. I bounced my finger against the glass. "That can never happen," I said, pointing at the texting cyclist.

"It won't," Galen swore.

"We need to agree on a few rules," I said. I used my fingers to count them off. Number one, Mom and Dad got to see all his texts. Nothing would be erased without permission. Number two, no texting during dinner. Number three, the phone stayed in the kitchen at night, not in his bedroom.

"Okay," Galen said.

Since I had some leverage, as well as two more fingers, I decided to add a few sweeteners. "Number four, you'll walk the dog without giving me any grief, and number five, you'll take care of me when I'm an old man. I want a room in your house, my own TV, and three hot meals per day."

Galen pressed his left hand to his heart and stuck out his right for me to shake. When the time comes, I plan to use this book as proof of our arrangement.

•

Within the hour, the phone had been purchased, configured, sheathed in plastic casing, and charged enough for Galen to send out his first text. *whats up max*, he typed.

The text came from a number that had not existed before that afternoon, but somehow Max recognized the sender. Or perhaps Max was as eager to receive a text as Galen was to send one, and didn't care who it was from. Hardly a minute later came the reply: *the ceiling.*

    hey I got a phone

    u suck bunnies

    u suck rabbits

    This is Max's Mom. What kind of texting is this? Enough of this nonsense!

A few days later, we were in the kitchen when Galen's phone began to ring. He'd hardly let go of the phone since he'd come home with it, and so he had it in his hand when it trilled into action. Galen stared down at his upturned palm as though it contained a ticking bomb. His face twitched between bewilderment and dismay. "What do I do?" he asked.

"Go ahead and answer it," I said.

"Uh, hell-lo?" he said, the phone to his ear for the first time. His eyebrows were almost touching.

I could hear the voice on the other end. It was the cell phone company calling to ask if he was satisfied with his service.

"I guess," Galen said, as if he'd never heard a dumber question. Upon hanging up, his thumbs shot to the keyboard. *OMG SO AWK!* he texted.

If these first exchanges were any indication of what Galen's texts and calls would look like, I figured he wouldn't likely get into too much trouble, at least not right away. I did, however, remind him about using appropriate language and being polite on the phone. And I encouraged him to text in complete sentences, with commas and periods and proper capitalization. Many of my students were so accustomed to text speak that "LOL" and "BTW" often showed up in their papers.

"No one texts in complete sentences," Katherine said. "Don't be such a prig."

"Isn't it my job as an English professor to uphold the standards of the language?"

"Yes," she said. "Your *job*. Work and parenting aren't the same." She looked sternly at me, anticipating my argument. "Get over yourself."

Which was, the more I thought about it, the real trick to fatherhood, and to parenthood in general. You have to get over yourself. Parenthood might be characterized as an unending series of interlinked worries, dominoes in an endless spiral. Some of those worries are real, but most are pretty banal and are more about protecting our ideas of our children, the visions of parenthood we conjured before we had actual children to parent. For all the solemn vows we make that our kids will never taste sugar or play violent games or wear clothes made in sweatshops, at some point we have to come to terms with the fact that they, like us, are citizens of a world that's beyond our control, a world far too exciting and glittering and clamorous to keep at bay. If we do our jobs well, our kids will not only grow up, they'll grow out—away from us, into lives defined by the secrets they keep from their parents. Where we stop, they begin. They have to get over us in order to grow.

In April, a conference took me to Los Angeles, and once the festivities wrapped up I caught the Pacific Surfliner down to Irvine, where my dad picked me up. Driving past the manicured eucalyptus-lined office parks; up and over Laguna Canyon, resplendent after a year of good rain; and down toward the ocean, my elbow propped on the open windowsill of the white Toyota truck Dad bought my freshman year of college more than twenty years ago, I had the strange sensation that I'd gone back in time. I was no longer forty, no longer married or a father; I was nineteen, with hair bleached white by sun and chlorine, a kid contemplating the path of his future. Climbing the hill from Main Beach and moving along the coast toward home, my thoughts scurried ahead to a day not long after I'd met Katherine. After a day spent hiking in the Wasatch Mountains, east of Salt Lake City, we sat together on the floor of our friend Matt's apartment, beers in hand and our shins glittered with dust, studying the gigantic map of the United States tacked to the wall. Matt was finishing his degree in geography, and his map, collaged with Post-it notes, was as intricate as it was expansive: six feet by eight, webbed with rivers and highways, dotted with towns too small to appear on most other maps. If I let my eyes go slack, the chaotic tangle of colored lines resembled a Pollock painting. As I moved closer to examine what the lines connected, the map's layers grew so deep and varied they appeared three-dimensional.

Katherine, I remembered, wore khaki shorts and the T-shirt I'd brought her from Hawaii—black with a yellow hibiscus, a shirt she still wears. We'd only been together a few months, but already I felt a momentous hum, an engine running inside my chest, whenever we shared a room. I was at the end of my master's degree and would soon begin work on my doctorate. Utah was supposed to have been a two-year leave of absence from Southern California, after which I'd be returning, posthaste, to a city near, and if at all possible on, the ocean. After two years in the mountains, I still saw the Pacific in my dreams, still heard the waves crashing over the sand and rocks, and so clung to the notion that I was destined—ordained, even—to make my life near it. Now I'd signed on for a much longer haul and was in love to boot, and though I was young and idealistic and naive, I also understood what I was up against. Anyone who's come within sniffing distance of a graduate program in English knows the market for academic positions has been bleak for decades, with hundreds of candidates—all with advanced degrees, publications, and extensive university teaching experience—vying for any available job. Even if I succeeded, I could wind up in a far-flung corner of the country, or worse, the empty middle, a prospect that terrified me.

"Here are the states where I'd consider living," I said. I ran my palm up the Pacific coast: California, Oregon, Washington. "These are the golden three," I said. I moved to the other coast. The states along the Atlantic Ocean north of the Carolinas were also possibilities if I could live in one of the cities, for example New York or Boston. Technically speaking, both cities abutted the ocean. Certain portions of the mountains, like, say, Colorado and Montana, would be okay, maybe. The Southeast was a definite no with the unlikely exception of a school on a beach. The Midwest was its own special kind of no. I stretched out my arms until I hugged the land between Nebraska and Pennsylvania. "This land is *not* my land," I said, laying it on. "This section of the country I hereby declare the Hell No Zone.'"

Matt lay sprawled on the futon, his arm crooked behind his head and a bottle of Corona propped on his chest. He lifted a long finger and pointed at the map. "I grew up in Wisconsin," he said. "It's nice there. Cold as hell, but nice."

I took a step back and appraised the state a second time, for my friend's sake. Equilateral to Michigan, Wisconsin appeared vaguely hand-shaped, though more like a catcher's mitt than a glove. The fact that Lake Michigan formed its eastern border and Lake Superior its northern notched it slightly above the landlocked wastelands below it. At least Wisconsin had some blue around it. As with nearly every state in the Hell No Zone, I had neither visited nor bothered to learn much about Wisconsin; I knew it only by its clichés: dairy farms and polka bands and bearded lumberjacks in flannel. At six foot six, his size-fifteen socks overhanging the end of the futon, Matt was a veritable Paul Bunyan himself. The cliché didn't seem so far-fetched. And compared to the Pacific, Lake Superior was a puddle. I shook my head and swept my arms at my waist, like a football referee calling a dead ball. "Sorry, can't do it. No way. Wisconsin stays in the Hell No."

Katherine laughed and drained the last of her beer. "Good to know."

The words we say to our future spouses often become freighted with importance, even if nothing important was intended when those words were said. As time passes and we trundle past one milestone after another, those early conversations can begin to feel prophetic, as if the universe were giving us a glimpse of the future but not the eyes to see it. I've thought about this day many times over the years, and in my memory I see my declaration before the map as both idle talk on a Saturday afternoon and its opposite: an early glimmer of my destiny. Given my superstitions about the causal links between pride and falls, I see myself laying my hand over the map of Wisconsin and guaranteeing, by virtue of my rejection, that I'd one day end up there.

Yet in spite of my declarations, Wisconsin had become home, far more than I'd ever expected. I missed Wisconsin when I was away from it, a sure sign I belonged to the place. Nestling my chair into the sand at Crescent Bay that afternoon I couldn't escape my longing for the ferns descending the hill from campus toward the river, the way they bobbed in the evening breeze, the desert-stark light when the temperatures plummeted below zero. While Dad peeled an orange with his thumb, I snapped a picture of my bare feet in the sand, the ocean in the background, and texted it to Katherine. *Jealous much?*

Enjoy it while it lasts, she replied. *It's 28 degrees here. I had to chisel the sleet off my windshield.*

Dad broke the orange in two, releasing a burst of citrus. He passed me half. The beach was sparsely populated, and we sat with our ankles crossed, talking like old friends. Thirty years since he left Texas and I'd never stopped wanting his company; I'd never stopped wishing for time to slow when we were together. He told me about his trip to Boise for Christmas, to see Devin and her family. My mom had moved to Idaho a few years earlier, following her divorce, so my dad had spent the holiday with them both. The image of my mother and father seated around the same table was so bygone to me that I could hardly imagine it. "Was it weird?" I asked. "Christmas together?"

"We had a nice time," Dad said. "Everyone got along. She has a cozy house."

"Was it spotless?"

"You could eat off the floor."

He dropped the orange rind into a hole in the sand he'd dug with his heel and used the side of his foot to cover it up. He'd probably buried the skins of a thousand oranges at this beach. I wondered how quickly they decomposed, whether any were still beneath us. He was staring at the ocean, away from me, when he said, "Sometimes it still wakes me up at night."

He didn't say what "it" was, but of course I knew. Certain pronouns are larger than the words they stand in place of.

We'd talked about the divorce a lot in the months and years after he'd left Texas, when the wounds were still fresh and the bandages still needed to be changed. Slowly, though, the topic had fallen out of conversation. For the last fifteen years, we'd hardly mentioned it at all. I'd half thought he'd put the entire episode—as well as his entire past life—out of his mind. Now that Devin and I were grown, with families of our own, the questions of the past had all been laid to rest. But old regrets don't go away, they only burrow deeper down, into our secret chambers, where they wait to ooze up through ever-smaller fissures.

"Do you remember that restaurant we used to go to?" I asked. "Daddy Did It?"

"Great catfish," he said, smiling. "Great hush puppies." He grew quiet again. "That was the worst thing I ever did. Leaving you and your sister."

As a father, it was frequently my job to encourage the boys, to help them make sense of the world. If I had no wisdom to offer, then solace would do. But as a son such opportunities were rare. Dad praised Devin and me, but it wasn't in his nature to seek consolation from anyone, least of all his children. We were alone on the beach and the opportunity was here, so I took it. "I didn't fault you for going," I said. "I was never angry about that. I just missed you. I wanted more time."

"There was never enough time."

"Well," I said, "we had the phone. We talked a lot."

He spit a seed out the side of his mouth. "Wasn't the same."

"It wasn't nothing."

It was so much more than nothing. More important than any wisdom imparted while I stood at the pay phone outside the Safeway or beside the Dr Pepper machine was the simpler, unalloyed fact that he'd answered when I'd called. His voice had come through on the other end of the line; whether we talked for a minute or an hour, he'd been there. Fatherhood, I now understood after years of gnawing on the obligations of the job, was much more about presence than wisdom. Being *there* versus being *right*. The final and most crucial lesson of fatherhood was to keep showing up. To be at the bottom of the stairs in the morning. Or, if you can't, to answer the phone when it rings.

Or, if your kids are like mine and don't know how to talk on the phone, to text. Contrary to my initial unease, the arrival of Galen's phone didn't kill our conversations. Quite the opposite. We talked more than ever. Hayden and I did, too, since his new iPod touch had a Wi-Fi connection and he'd figured out how to use iMessage.

Following Hayden's orthodontist appointment, his mouth now full of stainless steel, we had the following exchange:

Me: *everything okay? how are your teeth?*

Hayden: *They Bert*

Me: *Do they Ernie, too?*

Hayden: *I mean heart*

Me: *you mean hurt*

Hayden: *Dame Otto cerekt*

Every so often, an innocuous string of messages spilled over into actual conversation. The other day, when Galen texted to let me know he was home from school, I thumb-tapped, *How was your day?*

ok

Anything good happen?

no

The response came too fast to be nonchalant, so I ventured one more. *Anything bad?*

friends r jerks

Why?

they said my name sounded gay

Katherine and I had anticipated the possibility of teasing when we settled on the name Galen, and here it was, right on time.

They're idiots, I wrote.

numb nuts

Did you get upset?

yes

That's probably why they keep doing it. Don't let it bother you and they'll stop.

He waited a long time before responding.

ok

I swore I could hear Galen's voice in that long pause, his tendency to minimize whenever he talked about his friends, as though he were embarrassed by the prospect of not fitting in and wanted to hide it from me. I could see myself at a pay phone in Texas, asking my dad for reassurance. Except I was no longer there. I was in my office, and my son was the one calling. I was on the other side of the call.

You're a sensitive boy, I typed. *You always have been. It's your best quality.*

whatever

Have a snack. You'll feel better. There are carrots in the fridge.

ok

I made a point of signing off with *Dad loves you* because I wanted the boys to hear me say it, to know that one thing if nothing else. *Dad loves you.*

ok love you to by

The misspellings threw me off at first. But then it dawned on me, and I realized the only thing a father ever needed to hear had already been said.

Acknowledgments

Thanks to:

Dennis McGlynn, for your wisdom, encouragement, and for always answering when I called. Many of the moments in this book began as stories told over the phone; for years you said, "This should be your next book." It took me a while, but eventually I listened.

Kerry Thompson, Devin McGlynn McBrier, Linda McGlynn, and Paul and Laura Sagers, for your faith, love, and cheerleading.

Men's Health, The New York Times, Parents, Real Simple, O, The Oprah Magazine, This Land, Yale Review, december, Southwest Review, and Wisconsin Public Radio's *Wisconsin Life* for publishing essays from which much of the material for this book is drawn. Among the many editors I worked with, I'm especially grateful to Bill Phillips, Clint Carter, James Ireland Baker, David Sparrow, Holly Wall, Erika Janik, Katie Arnold-Ratliff, Dan Jones, and Roberta Zeff for taking a chance on my work. Also, my dear friend Willard Spiegelman, essayist and editor extraordinaire, for years of walking, swimming, and raconteuring.

Dara Hyde, for Obi-Wan Kenobiing this project from the germ of an idea to a full-fledged proposal and manuscript. Thanks for being the voice of reason and foresight, and for steering the book to

Dan Smetanka, my friend and editor. An hour in your presence, Dan, can cure almost any malady, and I'm beyond fortunate to have you on my side.

Andy Hunter, Megan Fishmann, Alisha Gorder, Sarah Baline, Jennifer Kovitz, Dustin Kurtz, Jordan Koluch, and the entire team at Counterpoint Press, for your good stead and tireless efforts on my behalf. Counterpoint is the undisputed champion of publishers.

My old pal Matt Batt, whose terrific memoir, *Sugarhouse*, helped me to find this book's structure and voice.

Genie Babb, for reading every chapter, essay, and excerpt, and for always keeping my spirits buoyed. Angela Vanden Elzen, for conversation and distraction while I stalked the library. David Lewis, for his whiz-bang tech skills, and the Lewis Crew, for our chance meeting and subsequent far-flung rendezvous. Tom Zoellner, Rachel May, Steve Tuttle, Taylor Larsen, Darin Dobler, Robert Anthony Siegel, and Karen Bender, for your unflagging optimism. Dave Burrows, Tim Spurgin, Gretchen Revie, Jake Frederick, Kate Moody, Peter John Thomas, and Lea Gysan, for coming through when I most needed it. Ben, Max, and Maisie, for being a part of the action.

The morning swimmers, especially Peter Allen, Scott Powley, Jürgen Sidgman, Mike Iacchei, Cindy Maltry, Laura Westfall, and Rob and Alex Bryson, for making sure I kept my head above water. Also, Margaret Allen and Jeanne Powley, for so much delicious food and friendship.

Galen and Hayden: Without you, I'd have nothing to write about, and no reason to write in the first place. Thanks for making me laugh, and I hope this book makes you proud. Please stop bugging each other for a few nights so I can rest. It's also time to walk the dog and unload the dishwasher. Don't make me ask you again.

Katherine: Little did you know when you agreed to go out for Mexican food that your life would end up in a book. Thanks for being a good sport, as well as my light in every dark room. Coming home to you is the best part of every day.

•

Selections from *One Day You'll Thank Me* have appeared in the following publications:

"Sleep or Die" (as "Lowering the Bar"), forthcoming in *Parents*, 2018
"I Not Did It," forthcoming in *Parents*, 2018
"The Q Word" (as "Know When to Quit"), *The New York Times*, 2017
"For Sale by Owner" (as "Small House, Big Life"), *O, The Oprah Magazine*, 2017, and in *O's Little Guide to the Big Questions*, 2018
"Uno Is the Loneliest Number" (as "Uno Every Night"), *Southwest Review*, 2016
"In the Tank," *december*, 2016
"The D Word," *Thin Air*, 2016
"Dead Santa" (as "Santa's Dead"), *Real Simple*, 2015
"The Ride of Angry Galen" (as "Letting Go"), *Parents*, 2015
"Ordinary Time" (as "A Pentecost of Bicycles"), *This Land*, 2014
"Tasks" (as "The Lighted Hallway"), *Kindling Quarterly*, 2014
"Please Forgive My Spotless Home," *The New York Times*, 2014
"The Fourth B" (as "Sex Education at Home"), *AskMen*, 2014
"Sh*t Kids Say" (as "Sh!t Kids Say"), *Men's Health*, 2014
"Heirlooms" (as "My Dad, Bad Santa"), *Men's Health*, 2010

Additionally, "Dead Santa," "The Deep End," and "Heirlooms" were read aloud on the *Wisconsin Life* segment of Wisconsin Public Radio in December 2015, February 2013, and December 2012, respectively.

Author photograph by Liz Boutelle

DAVID McGLYNN is the author of the memoir *A Door in the Ocean* and the story collection *The End of the Straight and Narrow*, winner of the 2008 Utah Book Award for Fiction. Recent work—including excerpts from *One Day You'll Thank Me*—has appeared in *The New York Times*, *Men's Health*, *O, The Oprah Magazine*, *Real Simple*, *Parents*, and elsewhere. Three of his essays have been named Notable Essays in the *Best American Essays* anthology and another, "Rough Water," appeared in *The Best American Sports Writing* in 2009. He teaches at Lawrence University in Wisconsin. Find more at davidmcglynnbooks.com.